Culture and Politics

PUBLISHED UNDER THE AUSPICES OF THE
WILLIAM ANDREWS CLARK MEMORIAL LIBRARY
UNIVERSITY OF CALIFORNIA, LOS ANGELES

Publications from the
CLARK LIBRARY PROFESSORSHIP, UCLA

1.
England in the Restoration and Early Eighteenth
Century: Essays on Culture and Society
Edited by H. T. Swedenberg, Jr.

2.
Illustrious Evidence
Approaches to English Literature of the
Early Seventeenth Century
Edited, with an Introduction, by Earl Miner

3.
The Compleat Plattmaker
Essays on Chart, Map, and Globe Making in England
in the Seventeenth and Eighteenth Centuries
Edited by Norman J. W. Thrower

4.
English Literature in the Age of Disguise
Edited by Maximillian E. Novak

5.
Culture and Politics
From Puritanism to the Enlightenment
Edited by Perez Zagorin

Culture and Politics
From Puritanism to the
Enlightenment

Edited by
PEREZ ZAGORIN

Clark Library Professor, 1975-1976

1980
UNIVERSITY OF CALIFORNIA PRESS
BERKELEY • LOS ANGELES • LONDON

080391

University of California Press
Berkeley and Los Angeles, California

University of California Press, Ltd.
London, England

CONTENTS

PREFACE

One of the most interesting and consequential duties that falls upon the annual incumbent of the Clark Library Professorship is the choice of the general subject of the seminar lectures to be delivered by invited guests under his auspices. Of the occupants of the Clark chair, I was the first historian, the first, that is, whose academic affiliation was with a university history department. All but one of my predecessors had been literary scholars and their seminars were mainly concerned with English literary history. (The exception is Professor Thrower, a distinguished geographer, who devoted his seminar to the history of cartography.) Now, history as an inquiry, since in principle it takes the entire human past for its province, is characterized by its many subject matters and approaches. This is not to say, of course, that it doesn't possess its own distinctive methods and problems. Nevertheless, it has been and remains exceptionally broad in what it encompasses, more so than any of the other humanistic disciplines.

I thought I could best exemplify the historian's contribution by selecting a theme wide enough to subsume related topics of quite different kinds, all of which would be revelatory of important aspects or phases of the history of seventeenth and eighteenth century English culture. I also wanted these topics to possess some degree of coherence. I hope the reader will agree that the present volume achieves these aims. The authors of the papers it contains are specialists in diverse fields. Their subjects are drawn from the history of political, legal, and religious thought, and from litera-

ture, science, and art. They include consideration of great and
lesser individual figures, ensembles of ideas, and various cultural
situations. The result, I think, is a collection of exceptional merit
and interest.

Culture and politics, the terms that keynote the general theme
of the collection, do not lead us toward divided and distinguished
worlds, nor to a simple parallelism, but to intricately connected
domains whose separate boundaries are extraordinarily hard to
demarcate. This is obviously the case in the anthropological conception of culture, which has no normative implications. Here
culture, taken as the determinate patterns and ways of life of any
human community, envelops politics, giving it its assumptions,
values, and ideals. But our engagement in these essays is primarily with culture in its more restrictive normative meaning: if
not necessarily in the perfectionist sense of Matthew Arnold, then
as that, at any rate, which designates the intellectual and imaginative creations of civilization. Perhaps we might then want to
say that politics is the domain of power and of collectivities—of
rulers and ruled, the strong and the weak, of classes, interests,
and parties—while culture is the domain of intellectual, moral,
and aesthetic values in their immediate relation to individual
development and consciousness.

No doubt, this way of putting it seems to get at a valid distinction, which is nevertheless quite plainly inadequate. For how can
we deny that politics too is a realm of values, at least of moral
ones, or that normative culture is also subject to the play of power
and that its shaping role is directed toward collective as well as to
individual consciousness and development? The difficulties we
thus encounter in delimiting culture and politics may perhaps
cause us to conclude that the two are pure abstractions impossible
to disengage from one another. Just as politics bears the stamp of
culture in the values, aspirations, goals, and even the styles of
political actors, so culture responds to relations of power in the
values it projects, the institutions that serve it, and in such of its
forms as high and popular, aristocratic and bourgeois, or elite
and mass culture.

Whatever the complications in defining the respective limits of
culture and politics, no one familiar with the English society that
appears in these essays would be tempted to dissociate the two.
The seventeenth and eighteenth centuries, the age of the Stuart

and Hanoverian monarchies, experienced many changes, but present us throughout with a rich and manifold reciprocity of culture and politics which was visible and acknowledged. While there were of course different modalities of culture in a society so strongly marked by inequality and provincialisms, no cultural activity of the time was carried on as a hermetic pursuit to be reserved from the profane. *L'art pour l'art* (though even this phenomenon is hardly immune from the political) did not exist. Statesmen, ministers, and political men formed a comparatively small elite with many relations to writers great and small, philosophers, and artists, Popular and radical protest movements usually reflected their own distinctive cultural aspirations and identity. The severing of public and private worlds, the one to be abandoned in disgust or despair to the politician, the other to be cultivated as the inviolate realm of the inner life, was unthought of. Poets dealt naturally with public events and political themes. It was not an accident that the two great poems, which are also among the greatest of English political poems, Marvell's *Horatian Ode Upon Cromwell's Return from Ireland* and Dryden's *Absalom and Achitophel,* were both written in the seventeenth century. We may doubt whether any poet of the time, even the most detached — and Marvell in the *Horatian Ode* was extraordinarily detached as he viewed the rise of Cromwell and the fall of the Stuart monarchy — could have consented with moderns like Yeats that the poet "has no gift to set a statesman right" or like Auden that "poetry makes nothing happen." The attention devoted to political satire in both poetry and prose, especially in the later seventeenth and earlier eighteenth centuries, suffices to demonstrate the involvement of writers with political subjects and the latter's accessibility to the demands of art.

Over a large part of this period the interrelations between culture and politics were most obviously affected by the invasive consequences of fierce divisions in religion and public life. The prelude to the eighteenth century "peace of the Augustans" was a century broken in the middle by a revolutionary civil war and overthrow of kingship, and near the end by a threatened civil war, a royal deposition, and change of rulers. The revolution of 1688 was followed, in spite of its finality, by several decades of high political insecurity and unremitting party strife. Only with Walpole and the Whig ascendancy was the governmental system consolidated which made the succeeding era the most inertial and politically conservative in English history. Yet even during these years, as they went on, there emerged the agitation of the movement for parliamentary reform, while at their end came the French revolution with its great divisive impact upon English politics.

Thus English culture invariably stood in mutual connection with explicit political interests, values, aims, and conflicts. This interconnection is noticeable in the following essays and in the termini of the collection as a whole. Each essay explores ideas, beliefs, and cultural situations and responses, which would make little sense out of their relevant political context. Puritanism, a pervasive element in English culture in the early seventeenth century, where these lectures begin, was primarily a religious phenomenon, but its irresistible nonconformity and impulsion to create a godly community led it to be deeply involved in political controversies. The Enlightenment, where the lectures end, carries us away from Puritanism into the deism, free thought, irreligion, and naturalism which gathered head during the eighteenth century and whose contributions to the formation of a liberal political order were immeasurable.

A rapid review of the essays comprising this volume will reveal their scope. The first three papers address subjects set in the span between the closing reign of Queen Elizabeth and the Restoration. In the opening essay, J. H. Hexter presents a reading of Shakespeare's *Richard II* as the basis for a penetrating account of the importance of the idea of property in the English moral and political Weltanschauung. The essay by Charles Gray which follows is one of the most illuminating discussions to be found of the legal mind of Sir Edward Coke, a formidable personality, who as lawyer and judge exerted an influence of the first magnitude on English law and politics. Although not part of his original lectures, I have included Gray's brief appendix on Coke's conception of "artificial reason" as a valuable enlargement to one of its main topics. The third essay by Richard H. Popkin authoritatively recounts the interplay between Christian millenarianism and Jewish messianism at their common high point in the mid-seventeenth century, bringing out inter alia the ironies and misunderstandings implicit in their encounter.

From here we move into the later seventeenth and the eighteenth centuries. J. G. A. Pocock's essay ranges widely in religious and republican thought in its pursuit of the character and sources of the Enlightenment in England which distinguished it from that elsewhere in Europe. The following three papers are all devoted to significant single figures. John M. Wallace's essay offers a discerning interpretation of Dryden's plays which enables us to see their closeness to contemporary preoccupations and demonstrates Dryden's debt to Stoic ethics in his commitment to heroic, noncommercial values. Richard S. Westfall's paper gives a striking portrait of Isaac Newton's career at Cambridge together with an incisive analysis of the conditions that made the university unpropitious to scientific activity. Robert M. Adams's essay on Lord Somers achieves a lively resuscitation of the Whig lawyer, politician, and patron that places him in representative relation to the post-1688 era and incidentally suggests his possible connection with Swift's Tale of a Tub.

The two concluding papers look to the later eighteenth century and beyond. Isaac Kramnick, in his examination of the emerging genre of children's literature, suggests that its themes and content are infused with bourgeois values and the socialization needs of burgeoning industrial capitalism. The final essay by Ronald Paulson deals with both art and literature, with Rowlandson and Blake, as well as Paine, Burke, and Rousseau, and with unconscious as well as conscious motives, in a stimulating exploration of the responses of thinkers and artists to the great French revolution.

This recital should sufficiently indicate the fine variety of the following essays, from which I trust the reader will derive the same instruction and enjoyment as did the audience to which they were first addressed. I recall with pleasure the monthly occasions when the seminar met, all present seated around a long table in the Clark Library's large baroque salon, faculty and graduate students of the University of California and other institutions in attendance, as well as some regular nonacademic guests who joined us. The papers invariably inspired discussion and argument, after which we adjourned for tea and conversation in the library's garden amidst the late afternoon sunshine; and as a sign of nature's benevolence on these occasions, I can testify that during the 1975-1976 academic year I spent in Los Angeles, the sun never failed to shine on the day of a seminar.

I wish to thank the Chancellor of the University of California, Los Angeles and the Clark Library Committee for the honor they accorded me in appointing me as Clark Library Professor and as the first incumbent of this chair to be named from outside the faculty of the University of California. I am especially appreciative, moreover, that my appointment coincided with the Clark Library's fiftieth anniversary year and its attendant festivities.

I am also obliged to the distinguished scholars who accepted my invitation to deliver papers to the Clark Library Seminar and for their consent to the publication of their papers in this volume.

To Robert Vosper, Director of the Clark Library, and to William E. Conway, Librarian, I feel a particular debt of gratitude. Their thoughtfulness and hospitality toward my wife and me, and their unfailing competence and helpfulness, made my stay at the Clark Library most enjoyable and productive. I am extremely appreciative as well to the library staff, which is unexcelled in its courtesy and service.

P. Z.

CONTRIBUTORS

Robert M. Adams, Emeritus Professor of English at the University of California, Los Angeles.

Charles Gray, Senior Research Associate, Yale University Law School.

J. H. Hexter, Charles J. Stille Professor of History, Yale University.

Isaac Kramnick, Professor of Government, Cornell University.

Ronald Paulson, Professor of English, Yale University.

J. G. A. Pocock, Harry C. Black Professor of History, The Johns Hopkins University.

Richard H. Popkin, Professor of Philosophy, Washington University.

John M. Wallace, Professor of English, The University of Chicago.

Richard S. Westfall, Professor of History of Science, Indiana University.

Perez Zagorin, Professor of History, The University of Rochester.

I

PROPERTY, MONOPOLY, AND SHAKESPEARE'S *RICHARD II*

J. H. Hexter

I begin, for reasons that I hope will be intelligible before I end, with William Shakespeare's *The Tragedy of Richard II,* written in 1595 or thereabout. To put you in mind of the bare sequence of events, a thumbnail sketch of the plot would go something like this:

Richard II, son of the Black Prince, eldest of the seven sons of Edward III, reigns in England. Two of his mighty subjects, Thomas Mowbray, duke of Norfolk, and Henry Bolingbroke, duke of Hereford, Richard's own first cousin, are at feud with one another. On the advice of his council Richard sends both Bolingbroke and Norfolk into exile. When Bolingbroke's father and Richard's uncle, John of Gaunt, duke of Lancaster, dies, Richard does not call Bolingbroke back to England to receive his inheritance. Instead he goes to Ireland to put down a rebellion there, leaving his last surviving uncle, Edmund, duke of York, as lord governor of England in his absence. In that absence Bolingbroke returns to England. The people rally to him, nobles and common folk alike. York, finding no support, surrenders to him; and Richard, returning from Ireland, has no choice but to submit to his victorious cousin. He abdicates, and Bolingbroke ascends the throne with the title of Henry IV. Richard is held prisoner in Pontefract Castle, and slain there by Sr. Pierse of Exton, who hopes by his act to win the favor of the new king.

1

Such is the skeleton of *The Tragedy of Richard II,* such more or less was the actual course of events at the end of the fourteenth century, and such certainly was the outline of the story as it appeared in the account Shakespeare knew and approximately followed, Raphael Holinshed's *Chronicles of England, Scotland, and Ireland.*[1]

One peculiar trait of Richard II, the historical person, confronted Shakespeare with a difficulty: for an English monarch he was extraordinarily legitimate. He succeeded without opposition to a throne to which no man challenged his right. In this matter, at least, he was like his distant collateral Charles Stuart, the sole surviving son of James I, king of England. To all men to whom legitimacy of primogenitary descent in the male line from the legitimate kind in accordance with the custom of England constituted sufficient evidence of rightful inheritance of the throne, both Richard and Charles were unchallenged rightful rulers of England. The likeness is worth remark. During the 226 years between the death of the former and the accession of the latter, no ruler had sat on the throne whose title on accession to it was so beyond challenge and doubt as theirs, whose right to reign so few opposed.

One of Shakespeare's tasks was to render it possible for his Elizabethan audience in 1595 to make sense of the conduct of the great men and the masses in coming to the aid of a rebel in 1399. In those dark days Englishmen, highborn and lowborn, had risen against their rightful king and supported and welcomed a usurpation that was to lie as a curse on the English for almost a century. What could lend even a faint color of justification to what Englishmen had done to their king at the end of the fourteenth century? What would make their actions at least intelligible, perhaps plausible, to Englishmen at the end of the sixteenth, to Englishmen who had yearly heard from the pulpit the powerful homily, *Against Disobedience and Willful Rebellion?*

In his quest for such justification, Shakespeare could rely on Holinshed's help in general. In his characterization of Richard, or rather in his catalog of Richard's misdeeds, Holinshed presented Shakespeare with an embarrassment of riches. Holinshed's Richard II was a rotten king and a rotten man. Mostly, Richard appears in Holinshed, no skillful character portraitist, doing ill in action. He gratifies the evil councilors with whom he surrounds himself by issuing blank charters, for example, instruments that allow his corrupt favorites to exact money from his subjects under his seal for their own gain.[2] He even lets the realm to farm to his favorites and ill-councilors; that is, he lets them collect the public revenues for cash advances, to their gain and the realm's loss.[3] Richard breaks faith with many of the great men of the realm.[4] He not only does enemies to death but desecrates their graves.[5] He saddles his people with the high costs of his folly and extravagance by inflicting exorbitant fines,[6] disinheriting rightful heirs,[7] raising forced loans from his subjects, and never repaying them.[8] His family, as well as his people, are his victims. His uncles, York and Gaunt, are among those who suffer from his breach of faith.[9] He wrongfully exiles his first cousin Bolingbroke and confiscates his inheritance.[10] He is guilty of the blood of his uncle, the duke of Gloucester, whose murder he procured.[11] Richard, says Holinshed, in a sentence that seems to have begun in measured judgment and ended in sheer revulsion, Richard ruled "by will more than by reason, threatening death to each that obeyed not his inordinate desires."[12] From there on, the ordinarily flat and factual chronicler buries Richard in floods of vituperation, denouncing his "untrue suggestions,"[13] "pestilent kind of proceedings,"[14] "hard dealing," "willful will," "wrongful purpose," "spite," "envy," "malice."[15]

If Holinshed's Richard is rotten, Shakespeare's is worse. The latter acts out all the nasty traits that Holinshed ascribes to Richard II. The economy of playcrafting does not allow Shakespeare to put on stage all the details of Richard's viciousness which Holinshed offers, but he presents a good many and renders them vivid with a gift for language and drama beyond Holinshed's conception, beyond the gift of any other man who ever lived. Halfway through the play, when he has made it clear that Richard is running headlong toward destruction, Shakespeare has not elicited, has not sought to elicit, a moment of sympathy for him. His Richard II is extravagant and rapacious, pitiless and heartless, envious and spiteful, a weak windy ham, a greedy misruler of monumental incompetence, and monumentally indifferent to the devastation his greed and incompetence cause. Insouciantly, he inflicts suffering on his patient uncles, his cousin, his child wife, his whole people, caring only for his fawning favorites with whom his relations are perhaps queer. By the end of the first scene in Act II, Shakespeare has let us know, by the words he puts in the mouths of others and by the words and deeds of Richard himself, that the king is utterly without redeeming social, political, or moral qualities.

Besides providing Shakespeare with a general representation of Richard as an evil king, whom even good subjects might at least *think* of disobeying, Holinshed afforded the dramatist material for a splendid and powerful scene that makes sense of, if it does not make right, the rebellion Bolingbroke led against Richard. He describes the meeting at Doncaster. Holinshed tells us that even before Bolingbroke, returning illegally from exile, sailed for England,

divers of the nobility, as well prelates as other, and likewise many of the magistrates and rulers of the cities, towns, and commonality here in England, perceiving daily how the realm drew to utter ruin, nor like to be recovered to the former state of wealth whilst King Richard lived and reigned, devised with great deliberation and considerate advice, to send and signify by letters unto Duke Henry, whom they now called (as he was indeed) Duke of Lancaster, requiring him with all convenient speed to convey himself into England, promising him all their aid, power, and assistance, if he, expelling King Richard, as a man not meet for the office he bare, would take upon himself the scepter, rule, and diadem of his native land and region.[16]

Having been moved to action by the sufferings and plaints of his fellow countrymen, Bolingbroke, that "true-born Englishman," sets sail for his native land. Coming ashore at Ravensburgh in Yorkshire, with only a few score men, he makes for Doncaster, still not knowing whether the English, to whom he has come to see justice done them, will join him or crush him. And there in Doncaster the fate of Henry and Richard and England is decided, for there, in full array and with their host of armed followers, are the great northern lords, Westmorland, Northumberland, and his son Henry Hotspur. There they put themselves under Bolingbroke's command. And there, too, according to the chronicler, Bolingbroke

sware... that he would demand no more than the lands that were to him descended by inheritance from his father... [and] undertook to cause the payment of taxes and tallages to be laid down, and to bring the King to good government.[17]

In that great scene at Doncaster, Henry of Bolingbroke undertook to purge and to reform the realm and yet did not threaten to usurp the throne.

Now zealous Shakespeareans may find this account of the meeting at Doncaster a little perplexing. Perhaps they may find it hard to recall, to place, to identify that great scene in Shakespeare's *The Tragedy of Richard II*. Let their worries cease. It is not there; Sheakspeare did not bother to seize on the opportunity Holinshed tossed his way. But why is it not there? Why did Shakespeare not seize the opportunity? At Doncaster, Henry Bolingbroke appears to his supporters as a knight errant seeking on behalf of a people oppressed, to challenge a king turned tyrant. The history we know tells us that John of Gaunt's son and heir was a good deal more than a knight errant and a good deal less; the history that Elizabethans knew, though different from what we know, told them the same thing. The meeting at Doncaster tells us, as it told them, that there Henry showed himself only as a man come to right the wrongs of Richard's subjects, seeking nothing but justice for all. That men so sorely put upon would follow one who so presented himself, particularly when he was by right descent the nearest heir to the throne, surely that is intelligible. However we construe Bolingbroke's behavior at Doncaster, we can understand and sympathize with the actions of many who followed him in rebellion, not intending rebellion or seeing their actions in that lurid light.

Am I second-guessing Shakespeare here? I do not think so, although in view of the recent dismemberments of the Bard by the bold and brilliant spirits that currently infest the theater, one no longer need apologize for second-guessing him. These days we may be grateful for an unexpected mercy if Lear is not portrayed as a hermaphrodite and Shakespeare's lines are spoken, not recited in plain chant or omitted altogether. Still there is no need to second-guess him here. Obviously if the dramatic feasibility of the meeting at Doncaster is evident to me, Shakespeare, searching Holinshed with the world's keenest eye for a dramatic effect, cannot have missed it. If he did not miss it, he must have rejected it, and if he rejected it, he must have believed he had a better alternative.

He did have an alternative, and he used it. Whether it was better is a matter of judgment, a matter that depends in a very particular sense on where one stands. Before we consider making such a judgment, let us examine the alternative. How did Shakespeare actually try to make it possible for his audience to empathize, if not sympathize, with Bolingbroke's followers, even in some measure with Bolingbroke? When and where did he do it, and through what characters?

In the oddly telescoped time scale of the play, Shakespeare makes his move just a few days after Richard has exiled Bolingbroke. John of Gaunt, heartbroken at Bolingbroke's banishment, denounces Richard to his face for his part in the murder of his uncle, Gloucester, Gaunt's brother, and then dies (II, i, 93-115), 124-138). Richard, wholly unmoved, tells his last surviving uncle, Edmund of York, what he has in mind to do, now that Gaunt is dead (II, i, 159-162). Then, abruptly, York denounces Richard no more scathingly, but with a good bit more menace than Gaunt has just done. Says Edmund:

> How long shall I be patient? Ah, how long
> Shall tender duty make me suffer wrong?
> Not Gloucester's death, nor Hereford's banishment
> Not Gaunt's rebukes, nor England's private wrongs . . .
> Have ever made me sour my patient cheek,
> Or bend one wrinkle on my sovereign's face.
> *You prick my tender patience to those thoughts*
> *Which honour and allegiance cannot think.*
> [italics mine; II, i, 163-166, 169-170, 207-208]

When Edmund of York speaks so, when he hints so broadly, Richard cannot miss the point: even his uncle's loyalty may be shaken if the king goes through with his design. He thus gives pause to that feckless monarch. Well may he do so, for his words are those not of a hero, nor of a villain, but of a survivor. Edmund of York is a survivor in two senses. Literally, he is the last of the seven sons of Edward III left in the land of the living. And, second, of those sons, and in a sense of all Englishmen, he is the man who shows himself best aware in word and act of the arts of survival, of what the conditions of safety and security, and of order and sense are in both men and societies, and of the limits that particular circumstances may require a man to accept lest he bring chaos and dissolution to societies, to men—and to himself, especially himself. Later in the play, as lord governor in Richard's absence, Edmund of York will denounce Bolingbroke for returning from exile without the king's permission,

> ...a banished man...come
> Before the expiration of thy time
> In braving arms against they sovereign.
>   [II, iii, 110-112]

But when he sees defeat as the inevitable outcome in the face of Bolingbroke's overwhelming power, York prudently decides to "remain as neuter" (II, iii, 158). He then displays a view of neutrality somewhat compliant to the prospective victor. Immediately after declaring himself neutral he offers Bolingbroke the shelter and hospitality of the castle he is supposed to be keeping for the king. Later, he joins his troops to the triumphant rebel forces, and when Bolingbroke takes the throne as Henry IV, York becomes in turn his most loyal subject. It is this very prudent man who, in Act II, scene i, excoriates Richard after reminding him of the royal malefactions — Bolingbroke's exile, the mistreatment of one uncle, the murder of another, the long roll of civil outrages against his own subjects — that he has hitherto passed over in silence, indeed without so much as a facial twitch to show disapproval. When Richard takes in all this, he is at last willing to attend and hear from York what he has done "to pluck a thousand dangers on his head" and "lose a thousand well disposed hearts," what he has done to prick even York's

> ...tender patience to those thoughts
> Which honour and allegiance cannot think.

He cannot quite make out what he has done to arouse his docile uncle to such an unwonted emotional pitch. Actually, all he has said is that he is off to the Irish wars to show "those rough rugheaded kernes" who is who and what is what, surely nothing wrong with that, and that he is going to use the Lancaster estate, "the plate, coin, revenues and moveables" of John of Gaunt, who died a few minutes ago, to support his effort (II, i, 155-162). So in surprise and perplexity he asks, "Why, uncle, what's the matter?" (II, i, 186). He is ready to listen. So should we be.

Then York tells him what the matter is, what trouble might follow if he were to

wrongfully seize Hereford's rights, call in the letters patents that he hath by his attorneys-general to sue his livery, and deny his offered homage.
                    [II, i, 201-204]

We need to look at that passage and to reflect on it. What we are looking at is blank verse, believe it or not. I have merely omitted the initial capitals of each verse and the line breaks at the end. Here is how it is ordinarily printed:

> . . . wrongfully seize Hereford's rights,
> Call in the letters patents that he hath
> By his attorneys-general to sue
> His livery, and deny his off'red homage.

The first thing we might reasonably think about this exercise of Shakespeare's is that it is not up to much as poetry. One would give long odds against its making a dictionary of quotations, even one rather casual as to standards for admissions. The second thing we might think and wonder at is that it is poetry at all. English law of real property does not immediately strike one as the most promising subject to deal with in iambic pentameter, and only a poet of no imagination at all or one of enormous imagination would consider trying to do it. And the third thing we might think is that given an open option, *this,* instead of the meeting at Doncaster, is what Shakespeare chose to make the very heart of his effort to open the minds of his contemporaries to what made sense of Bolingbroke's illegal incursion into England. According to Shakespeare, not Holinshed, that is, this is what is supposed to have vindicated Bolingbroke's following in their own minds for their rebellion. And what is "this"? It is a brief (but not brief enough) disquisition, in blank verse of all things, on the legal forms of entry of a rightful heir into an estate held by military tenure.

Let there be no mistake, the inheritance of real property is the heart of it. To be certain that his audience does not miss the point, Shakespeare covers the ground again. The second time it is not York predicting dire events if Richard proceeds as he says he intends to; it is Bolingbroke himself at once justifying his own actions and validating York's dire predictions. With his host of followers, he stands in arms against Richard before Berkeley Castle. York, the captain of the castle, comes to parley with him. He upbraids Bolingbroke for his very presence in England. His incursion with "ostentation of despised arms" has put him, York says,

In gross rebellion and detested treason.
Thou art a banished man, and here art come
Before the expiration of thy time
In braving arms against thy sovereign.
                    [II, iii, 108-111]

So Bolingbroke must justify his recent actions, or at least try to.
And try he does.

I am denied to sue my livery here,
And yet my letters patents give me leave.
My father's goods are all distrained and sold,
And these, and all, are all amiss employed.
What would you have me do? I am a subject;
And I challenge law, attorneys are denied me;
And therefore personally I lay my claim
To my inheritance of free descent.
                    [II, iii, 128-135]

And there we are again, a law lecture in blank verse. That this
law lecture of Bolingbroke's is twice as long as the previous one by
his uncle does not make it twice as good. Again confronted with
the dramatic necessity of having Bolingbroke speak as per-
suasively as possible of the grounds and justification of his armed
rebellion, almost incredibly Shakespeare again has him emit a
brief series of technical observations in iambic pentameter on certain elements of the English law of real property and civil procedure. "Sue my livery . . . letters-patent . . . goods distrained and
sold . . . law . . . attorneys . . . claim to my inheritance . . . free
descent."

So again the question, the problem: how could Shakespeare
believe, how could he imagine, that the way to reach his audience
on Bolingbroke's behalf was to dress him out, not as an armed
paladin for justice to all Englishmen, as he had indeed appeared
in history at Doncaster, according to Holinshed, but as a suitor
seeking by force as a last resort to have an infraction of his property rights rectified, and doing so only after every effort to get
what was his through legal process had been frustrated? Again,
note Shakespeare's complete commitment to the second alternative, the one that portrays the returned Bolingbroke as a man
seeking to vindicate his property rights, not as one who comes
heroically to interpose himself between a despot and his suffering

people. To support this view of Shakespeare's presentation of Henry there is more than the argument from silence about the omission of the meeting at Doncaster. Bolingbroke has a good many things to say from the first time we see him after his return to England to the moment when Richard, reduced to despair by his own rhetorical effusion of self-pity, thrusts himself and his authority into his cousin's hand. Only casually and fitfully in his utterances does Bolingbroke take on the role of champion of the oppressed. Thus, after York has capitulated to him, Bolingbroke mentions his pledge to deal with the King's corrupt favorites.

> . . . Bushy, Bagot, and their complices,
> The caterpillars of the commonwealth,
> Which I have sworn to weed and pluck away.
> [II, iii, 165-167]

If Shakespeare had had the least wish to present Bolingbroke as a champion, true or false, of the oppressed, the master of poetic demagoguery who five years later was to produce Marc Anthony's funeral oration for Caesar could surely have done better by his man than that.

A bit later, Bolingbroke, with his usual promptness, deals with two of the favorites, Bushy and Green, by quite illegally "deliver-[ing] them over / To execution and the hand of death." He does, however, "unfold some causes" for his peremptory action. The first and the only faintly public charge is rather vaguely that

> You have misled a prince, a royal king,
> A happy gentleman in blood and lineaments,
> By you unhappied and disfigured clean.
> [III, i, 8-10]

Then follows the accusation, nowhere else referred to, that they have "made a divorce betwixt his queen" and Richard (III, i, 11-15). So much from Bolingbroke on the ill-doing of the favorites: eight lines about the wrongs they wrought on king and queen; nothing at all of the wrongs they wrought on the kingdom. Not, of course, that there was nothing to say which would link the king's favorites with the public wrongs Richard had committed. Some of it had already been said—but not by Bolingbroke—by his uncle's widow, the duchess of Gloucester, by his dead father,

John, late duke of Lancaster, by his uncle Edmund, duke of York,[18] even by the Earl of Northumberland and the other malcontent lords (II, i, 238-255). But not by Bolingbroke. When he has finished his eight-line recitation of the harm Bushy and Green had done the royal pair, Bolingbroke pours out a spate of eloquence twelve lines long on the wrongs they had wrought on Bolingbroke himself: They had brought him into disfavor with the King; they had connived to bring about his exile; and then they had grabbed for the Lancaster lands that were his property (III, i, 16-27). That is the source of Bolingbroke's bitterness all along, his "rights and royalties...given to upstart unthrifts." And whatever his actual intention all along, he protests that he has come back to England only for his own. By inherited right duke of Lancaster, "I am come," he says, "to seek that name in England" (II, iii, 71) or, as he says to the duke of York,

> As I was banished, I was banished Hereford,
> But as I come, I come for Lancaster, . . .
> [II, iii, 112-113]

Finally, there is the time just before those last moments outside Flint Castle in which the defeated Richard effectively surrenders the throne to his cousin by asking whether (or is it "suggesting that"?) they should go together to London. At that next-to-the-last moment, with the cowering king, bereft of support, still shielded by the castle walls, Bolingbroke asserts again, as he has from the beginning, the ground and purpose of all his actions since his landing in England. He will parley with the hopelessly beleaguered king, and these are the terms:

> Even at his feet to lay my arms and power,
> Provided that my banishment repealed,
> And the lands restored again be freely granted.
> [III, iii, 38-40]

At this point we need to look about, because we are in a rather odd position. We seem to have caught William Shakespeare choosing a dramaturgic option that in terms of the choices patently available to him makes bad sense. Why does he have Bolingbroke justify *all* his actions against Richard on the ignoble grounds that he has suffered wrongful loss of property at the

king's hands? Why that alone, when Richard had provided him
with such fertile and noble grounds for acting with disinterested
patriotism? Two possibilities occur. Granted that Shakespeare
was the most successful playwright of his day, granted that to be
so he had to know his audience better than any dramatist of the
age, still if Homer nodded, Shakespeare at times fell sound
asleep. In a long career of writing for the London stage, he
brought forth his quota of "turkeys." Unfortunately for this view,
however, such evidence as we have suggests that *The Tragedy of
Richard II* was not a turkey in the eyes of the audience at the
Globe. It was not caviar to the general, but a dish they gobbled
up. So we may at least give thought to the other possibility. That
other possibility has an obverse and a reverse side. The obverse is
that the playgoers of Elizabethan England may have been a good
deal less sympathetic than we to a man who used a claim that he
was rescuing the people from tyranny as grounds for an uprising
against the government, and less sympathetic than we to those
taken in by such a statement. The reverse is that those playgoers
may have had a more ready empathy than we with a man who expressed his grounds for resisting "the deputy annointed of the
Lord" in speeches containing at the core blank verse statements
on aspects of the law of real property, and whose highest claim
amounted to nothing more exalted than that he wanted his own
property back. Is this possible? Is this the kind of audience that
went to the Globe? And if so, how did it come to be that way?

It may help us to answer that question if we turn from play-
acting and playwriting to a grubby but consequential lawsuit
argued in the Court of Queen's Bench in the last year of Elizabeth
I's reign.[19]

The defendant in the case was one Thomas Allen (or Allyn or
Allin), a citizen and haberdasher of London. By his own admission he had sold a half gross playing cards valued at 13s. 4d. to
John and Francis Freer. In doing so, Allen had inflicted unlawful
damage on Edward Darcy, the plaintiff, so the latter claimed;
and he apparently stood ready to inflict more, since he still had
79½ gross of playing cards on hand to dispose of. The queen,
Darcy proved, had granted him by letters patent "the whole trade
of making and selling of cards in England." Therefore, he
alleged, Allen's sale of a half gross of cards without license from

him was not only a wrong to him but was also in defiance of the intent of the letters patent and, therefore, in contempt of the queen. There was no controversy about the facts, so the issue before the court was whether the letter patent issued to Darcy was lawful. If it was not lawful, Allen had not done damage to Darcy on which the latter could recover, nor had he acted in contempt of the queen; and he could sell of his remaining 79½ gross of cards.

The cast of characters acting as counsel for plaintiff and defendant in the case of *Darcy* v. *Allen* is enough to inform us that much more was at stake than the damage Allen did to Darcy by selling six dozen playing cards. Of the four lawyers retained by Allen, two were themselves shortly to take places on the bench of the High Courts at Westminster.[20] All of Darcy's counsel were to do so, too;[21] one of them, Fleming, was already the queen's solicitor general, a second, Coke, was her attorney general. What brought the queen's counselors learned in the law to the defense of Darcy was the involvement of the royal prerogative in the case.

For several decades the queen had been issuing letters patent conferring on the patentees sole rights to make or import, and sell a considerable number of goods from such monetarily unpromising items as shreds of woolen cloth, horns, anise seed, and the works of Cornelius Tacitus to such highly remunerative ones as sweet wines and salt. As grounds for the grant, the letters patent always cited some benefit that would presumably accrue to the commonwealth from it. It was by the presumption of common benefit that the queen justified her prerogative actions in matters of trade and industry. The prerogative was hers to give her the means of fulfilling her duty to provide for the common good by regulating trade. That the Crown had both this duty and prerogative no one doubted, certainly not counsel for the defendant Allen. That the prerogative was limited by law no one doubted either, certainly not counsel for the plaintiff Darcy, and indirectly for the queen. Indeed, the position on the prerogative taken by Fleming, the queen's solicitor general, represents the late Elizabethan consensus on the political order even more broadly than the decision in Darcy v. Allen does, since it defines a view of the prerogative shared by the lawyers on both sides of the case. Fleming simply conceded that, whatever the pretext, letters patent issued by the Crown which were "contra commune jus," that is, against common right or law, or that "tended to any general charge of the subject [that is, tended to tax him], or to change the law or the course of any man's inheritance were void in law."[22] The common law, the subject's goods, and his inheritance all lay beyond the reach of the royal prerogative. They were not subject to the mere command and will of the ruler, and on this matter, counsel to both parties agreed. Nor, it appears to me, are we to take these itemized restrictions on the prerogative — the common law, the subject's goods, and his inheritance — as referring to discrete entities. In fact, they flow together. A man's goods are the rightful inheritance of his heirs, and the common law is itself the inheritance of every free man, the guarantor against the wrongful taking of anything that is rightfully his by any person, including the Crown. Thus spoke the formidable authority of Edmund Plowden in his report of the case of *Willion* v. *Berkeley*. "By the common law the King has many prerogatives touching his person, his goods, his debts and duties, and other personal things, yet the common law has so admeasured his prerogatives that he shall not take away nor prejudice the inheritance of any."[23]

In the case itself, counsel for Allen was able to show that monopolies like the one granted to Darcy had three inseparable incidents adverse to the public interest: they enhanced prices, debased quality, and diminished employment, and granting them led to no compensating common benefit. Therefore, the allegation that any patent of monopoly save one granted for the invention of a new process or thing was for the common welfare, carries no conviction or weight. More particularly and more to our purpose, Allen's counsel were at pains to show that the patent had deprived the defendant of something that was rightfully his. The queen, one of them argued, "cannot grant a patent that will restrain others from their customary trades and occupations,"[24] and the effect of the Darcy patent was "to deprive" the defendant "of his patrimony,"[25] that is, of his inherited right as a citizen of London and a member of the Haberdashers Company to buy and sell freely anywhere in the realm. A man's right to practice the craft he has acquired is not subject to any person's mere will, not even in the monarch's. That right is his property. It provides the craftsman with the security that due succession to his rightful inheritance provides the landed man.

If any person by his industry had obtained excellent skill in his trade, he might reap the fruits thereof; and that has been thought the surest thing a man could obtain—skill and knowledge—because thieves could not steal it.

A grant of monopoly like Darcy's "take[s] away a man's skill from him."[26] It bars him from his trade; but a "man's trade maintains his life, and therefore he ought not be deprived or dispossed of it no more than of his life."[27]

Looked at from one side, then, a man's occupation is his property by inheritance or lawful acquisition. As Coke pointed out, Roman law was also careful to protect the rights of free men to their labor and its fruits. And Scripture itself had shielded men's property in the instruments of their livelihood. As Deuteronomy said, "You shall not take as a pledge the nether and the upper millstone."[28] And, he might have added, Magna Carta barred amercements that would deprive a plowman of his wain. A man's use of his craft, skill, or trade belongs to him as the estate, rank, and coat of arms of a gentlemen belong to him, if he has inherited them or rightfully acquired them by means that the law sanctions.

In the end, the court held for the defendant. If we are to believe Lord Chancellor Ellesmere, the judge declared the Darcy patent to be against the law, not because of the general harm a monopoly inflicted on the public at large, but "because it sounded in destruction of a trade whereby many subjects get their living."[29] At the heart of the decision was a reaffirmation of the concern of the common law to ensure to each man that which was his own, his property.

No doubt in 1603 tradesmen and craftsmen, particularly in London where there were more of them than anywhere else, were delighted to have the high court certify that their trades and skills were their properties and therefore protected by the law of the land; but it was nothing new. Already in 1575, the brokers and notaries of London had perceived matters as the judges did in 1603. Against the royal grant of a monopoly of registering insurance policies they protested that "the livings of notaries public who do most stand by making of such instruments will be thereby taken away. . . . Every free man," they had added, "ought to be free to occupy his trade in all such things as are for the maintenance of his living by good order."[30] Against a monopoly granted for salt manufacture, the town of Boston in Lincolnshire had complained in 1586 that the patent required that "men should not convert their salt pits, being their inheritance, to their best use. And hitherto the princes of this realm have not extended their prerogatives to the prejudice of the subjects' inheritance in such cases."[31] The men of London and Boston, thus, showed that the language of the law courts and the thought of *Darcy* v. *Allen* were already in the minds of tradesmen and citizens earlier in the sixteenth century. It was, in part, language the high courts had used still earlier about the firm bounds that the rights of the subject to his property placed on the prerogative of the Crown. The brokers and saltmakers had neatly paraphrased *Willion* v. *Berkeley* to their own purpose,[32] and they had already put forth the grounds on which, according to the judges, a prerogative grant of monopoly would be against the law if it deprived men of what the law held to be theirs.

Another circumstance may have further strengthened the sense of many Londoners that the law favored property against mere power, that it supported men's right to hold what custom and their labor made their own. Most tenants of land in England probably held what they held by a tenure called copyhold. What was copyhold land in the sixteenth century had been held in villeinage two centuries earlier. It was only in the latter part of the sixteenth century, so we are told,[33] that the judges offered the full protection of the common law to copyhold tenants, who hitherto had access only to the manor court, that is the court of their landlord, or to Chancery, whose processes in matters of land right were less certain than common law remedies. By the time *Richard II* showed at the Globe, sons of a copyholder, prospective heirs of a copyholder in the London throng, had cause to know that the land their father tilled was more securely his, in the future perhaps more securely theirs, because firm common laws of inheritance insured it to him, perhaps to them. So in the motley populace of London, it was not only the rich who had cause to know that the most secure shelter that existed in England against the willfulness of men of power and of office was provided by the law's protection of what it held to be a man's own, his property, his inheritance.

A while back we asked a question about the audience that saw *Richard II* at the Globe Theatre. Was it the sort of assemblage that would respond sympathetically to Bolingbroke's vindication of his actions by an appeal to property right? Might it even respond more sympathetically to that sort of vindication than to the presentation of Bolingbroke as the champion of the people? In short, what kind of audience was it? Any assertion about the audience at the Globe has a touch of the speculative about it. Nevertheless, it seems likely to have been composed in the main of people who had a strong sense of proprietary right and of the importance of vindicating the law that protected it. Of course, this was true of the courtiers, gentlemen, and lawyers who occupied the threepenny places. But our excursion into their recent historical experience suggests that it may also be true of the citizens and apprentices who took up the rest of the house, those who came to see the play when to the playgoing resident gentlemen of London it was literally déjà vu. Supposing that *Richard II* was performed only half as often as the forty times Elizabeth I in her own moment of poetic license alleged, still if twenty performances on the average filled only half the house, that would bring the total attendance at *Richard II* up to about 30,000. Given a city of not much more than 150,000, and a nation in which the gentlemen probably numbered no more than 30,000, it seems likely that Shakespeare was expecting a large number of plain folk — almost the whole audience, one might think, at the later performances — to share with Bolingbroke his express primary concern for the sanctity of property. And if the audience that attended *Richard II* was indeed largely made up of courtiers, gentlemen, lawyers, and students at the Inns of Court, merchants, tradesmen, and their apprentices, then indeed it takes on the air of an ad hoc and informal Association of Concerned Property Owners. The working men who flocked to the theater in thousands readily recognized those "caterpillars of the commonwealth," Bushy and Green, Richard's favorites, as the likes of the hated monopolists who cared nothing for the property, whether it was the shops tradesmen had inherited or the skills craftsmen had lawfully acquired. Such theatergoing property holders in *esse* or *posse* might well find little to their liking in a man who defied his lawful king on the ground that he has a mandate (God knows who could have given it to him) to seize power for the common good. A man who came to get what was rightfully his own and what had wrongfully been denied him, though he had exhausted every legal remedy, may have been considerably more congenial both to their sense of political propriety and their sense of private property, even though he came in arms.

So we are back to Shakespeare, and perhaps it is intelligible now why I started with him in an inquest into the way Elizabethans above the penury line felt about property. Since a general principle about the use of historical evidence is at stake here, it may be well to be explicit. The principle concerns the use of the writings of literary men as evidence about what these days it is classy to call *mentalité*. The first and obvious point is that there is no general rule, and the second is, be careful. I am now old enough to be encountering reconstructions of the middle class mentalité in the days of my youth, the 1920s, drawn from literary sources. They usually wring from me the protest, "It wasn't that way in Cincinnati." Nevertheless, sometimes a passage from an imaginative genius provides one with an intensity of insight quite unattainable any other way. In the case in point, Shakespeare was able to take the feelings shared by ordinary men and rich men in the 1590s about what belonged to them, feelings they could articulate only clumsily if at all, and express them not as the men themselves would have, but as they wished they could have. This reflects a most common human experience, a reaction that goes, "That is just what I have been thinking, but I could never put it so well." One of Shakespeare's host of gifts was an unmatched ability to put better than anyone ever has, the ways of thinking and feeling which have moved all sorts and conditions of men. In *Richard II,* along with a great many other things, he gave powerful expression to what men feel when others take from them, or show the readiness and power to take from them, everything that they believe to be their own.

Through Bolingbroke, Shakespeare conveys the long bitter anger that goes with helplessness in the face of lawless ouster. When the now victorious prince sends Bushy and Green to a deserved death, he tells them:

> You have fed upon my signories,
> Disparked my parks, and felled my forest woods,
> From my own windows torn my household coat,
> Raz'd out my impresse, leaving me no sign,
> Save men's opinions and my living blood,
> To show the world I am a gentleman.
> [III, i, 22-27]

Here we reach beyond the metric disquisitions on the law of real property to the living substance behind them. The king and the king's favorites have done all that lay in their power to wrench Bolingbroke from his place in the world and to obliterate all the marks that such a place was his—not only his wealth and lands but also the very signs of his station in life, the emblems of his rank, his coat of arms which clearly showed he was duke of Lancaster by rightful descent. "Men's opinions" and his "living blood," indeed, still "show the world" he is "a gentleman," and our modern sensibility, which seeks to separate the true inner man from his place in the world, inclines us to say that that should be enough. Similarly, for a century before Shakespeare's day, humanist discourses on "true nobility" argued that opinion and blood did not make nobility, that only virtue ennobled. That would not do for Bolingbroke, nor, we may suspect, for the groundlings who had paid their pennies to see the show. They knew well enough that men who had their property in the form of their craft taken from then, who could not live as starchmakers or glassmakers or papermakers because a letter patent denied them the right, no longer had the means to be of that craft. And they were likely to think that those only were noble who could live like a noble, those gentle who could live like a gentleman. We may even guess that Shakespeare thought that way too, at least by the time he got around to retiring to Stratford and buying himself a coat of arms. The kind of dissociation of the realm of actuality from the realm of value to which we are accustomed today had small place in the consciousness of Shakespeare's audience or of Shakespeare himself.

Bolingbroke, acutely aware of his own loss, nevertheless knows that Richard's assault on his property right is not just his personal disaster. To unlawfully dispossess the greatest of subjects is to threaten all other subjects. More than that, it is a threat to the dispossessor, to the king himself. Bolingbroke seeks to win Edmund of York to his cause, not merely his forced compliance, but his free support. He says to him, in effect, "see yourself as if you were John of Gaunt, your own brother and my father."

> ...O, then, my father,
> Will you permit that I shall stand condemned,
> A wandering vagabond, my rights and royalties

> Plucked from my arms perforce, and given away
> To upstart unthrifts? Wherefore was I born?
> *If that my cousin king be King in England,*
> *It must be granted I am Duke of Lancaster.*
> [italics mine; II, iii, 117-123]

Or conversely, if I, Gaunt's rightful heir, am not duke of Lancaster, it must be granted that my cousin Richard is not king of England. Thus, from Bolingbroke's mouth, York hears his own prophecy to Richard fulfilled.

Bolingbroke had made the prophecy just after Gaunt died, and Richard had casually announced that he was going to use the Lancaster inheritance to pay for a campaign against the Irish. Before offering a brief synopsis of the multiple breach of property law Richard would have to make in order to lay hands on that inheritance, a synopsis we have already noted, York tried to show his headstrong nephew the shattering implications of such action.

> Is not Gaunt dead? and doth not Hereford live?
> Did not the one deserve to have an heir?
> Is not his heir a well-deserving son?
> Take Hereford's rights away and . . .
> *Be not thyself. For how art thou a king*
> *But by fair sequence and succession?*
> [italics mine; II, i, 191-199]

If the inheritance of John of Gaunt which descended rightfully to Henry Bolingbroke can by mere will be taken from him, is the inheritance of Edward III and its inheritor Richard Plantagenet in any better case?

This is, as we have seen, what Bolingbroke says to York later in inverse form. The law of military tenures that makes him duke of Lancaster by right of inheritance is part of a broader law of property which determines for each person what is his own, determines that a knight shall be a knight by right of due investiture, which is his, that a master of arts may give instruction by *jus docendi*, which is his, and that Richard II is king of England by rightful succession to what is his. All these rights determine a man's property, what is proper to him, rightfully his. For the king to deprive Bolingbroke, or any man, of his property, of what is his, lawlessly shatters the very fabric of law and right by virtue of which he himself is king.

Even more than that. To take Bolingbroke's right, York tells
the king, is to *"be not thyself."* This may strike us as a peculiar
thing to say, although it is implicit in the passages quoted above.
York seems to believe that Richard is what he is by virtue of the
law of property and rightful succession, and that in failing to take
that law into account Richard is at once misunderstanding and
diminishing himself, and putting his kingly office at risk.

This is York's way of looking at things, indeed the way everybody of consequence in *The Tragedy of Richard II* but Richard
himself looks at things. It is alien to what I describe, with considerable misgiving, as our modern sensibility. Somehow that sensibility has divided our selves from what we are and do in the
world. In the world, it is said, we play the roles society assigns us,
and surely this means that the roles we play are not truly us. We
conceal ourselves behind masks to protect ourselves from the
world, so that the world will not seek us out and destroy us.
Indeed, in the end, we hide our real self not only from the world
but from our social self lest, recognizing the danger the real self
poses to the games the social self plays, the social self might turn
on it and seek to annihilate it. This tormented view renders
almost obligatory a peculiar portrayal of the human condition
both in literature and the human sciences. In this view men
always live and act in ways alien to their true selves in a world
from which they are alienated. The social duress under which
modern man lives, the necessity to act in an alien world, creates
in him that shadow-self, his social self, from which he, his real
self, is apart, separate. At least so we are told. So the notion of
alienation provides us with the most convenient of all languages
to justify our less than heroic doings on the ground that they are
the work not of our real selves but of an oppressive society. We
may even claim that the flaccid misdoings of our social selves
inflict more pain on our true but concealed selves than they do on
the world of others. The notions of alienation and role-playing
accordingly provide us, at a cost not easy to assess, with means for
living with what we actually are and do by allocating these latter
to the realm of appearances rather than reality.

What Edmund of York tries to force Richard II to grasp is a
view precisely the opposite of this. In York's view, what Richard
really is is king of England. He holds his crown by absolute right.
The holding of the crown which belongs to him, and all that that

holding has come to entail through the ages, defines Richard, tells him what he really is. For him to act as he does, like a vain juvenile delinquent with thespian aspirations, is false to what he really is, a king. Thus when, his courage buckling under earned misfortune, Richard has surrendered to despair, ordering "all souls that will be safe" to "fly from my side," his faithful ally, the duke of Aumerle, speaks to him,

> My liege, remember who you are.
> [III, ii, 82]

And for a moment, but not for long, Richard indeed calls to mind who he really is.

> I had forgot myself. Am I not a king?
> [III, ii, 83]

For once, Richard has got it right. What a man really is in this world he knows by the place that belongs to him in the world by right, whether by right of inheritance or of lawful acquisition. Entitlements may come in a variety of lawful ways, but if I am entitled, they belong to me. My house, my goods, my skill, my profession, my rights and my duties, are mine, my property by a right as firm and unshakable as the right by which a legitimate ruler's titles, honors, powers, rights, and duties belong to him — and of course vice versa. The indefeasible *property* of the subject, the his-ness of what is his, is not only the obverse, it is also the condition of the absolute prerogative of the king, the his-ness of what is His Majesty's.

One other word on the iniquity of depriving Bolingbroke of his inheritance deserves our attention. If you would take his rights away, York tells the King, then

> ...take from time
> His charters and his customary rights,
> Let not tomorrow then ensue today.
> [II, i, 195-197]

If I read this correctly, York is saying that in the world of man the succession of men to that to which by law they are entitled is as deeply rooted in due order, is as inherent and as necessary as that in the natural order night follows day and day night. That in the political order men should not succeed to what is theirs by law is as ill-omened as if in the order of nature the very cosmic movements that determine the sequence of things in time were to fall into disarray. One might reasonably regard such a view of things as, in fact, a bit toplofty, a bit of Shakespearean bombast. But then one might be wrong. Some thirty years later, a Parliament met whose members had suffered for two years the wrongful taking of their property and that of their constituents by King Charles I. They were determined that it should happen no more. As they moved to deal with the matter, Sir Nathaniel Rich, an unbombastic member of Commons of much experience and habitual self-restraint, spoke to the issue. "If there be no propriety of goods there's a confusion. What needs justice to distribute *meum et tuum?* And if no propriety there will be no industry, and then nothing will follow but beggary, and if no propriety there will follow no valor. What shall be fought for? It destroys the kingdom and justice." In this there is something of *Darcy* v. *Allen,* something of the plaint of the London brokers, something of Bolingbroke's insistence that he be given what was his due.

When we try then to understand how the notion of propriety or property moved men in the fifty years on either side of 1600, we do well to remember the resonance it had in Shakespeare's *Richard II,* to remember that to his audience and to the many Englishmen circumstanced like his audience, property meant goods, but it also meant more than goods and more than estates. Men had a property in them, indeed, but they also had a property in their liberties and held the law itself as a due inheritance.

NOTES

1. The passages in Holinshed's chronicles which parallel passages in Shakespeare's *Richard II* are conveniently printed with references to the relevant act and scene of the play in the Signet Classic edition of *The Tragedy of Richard the Second,* ed. Kenneth Muir (New York: New American Library, 1963), pp. 157-190.

2. Raphael Holinshed, *Chronicles of England, Scotland and Ireland,* 3 vols. (London, 1587), 3, 496.

3. Ibid.

4. Ibid., pp. 490, 492.

5. The earl of Arundel, for instance; ibid., p. 492.

6. Ibid., p. 496.

7. Ibid., p. 493.

8. Ibid., p. 496.

9. Ibid., p. 490.

10. Ibid., p. 496.

11. Ibid., p. 489.

12. Ibid., p. 493.

13. Ibid., p. 495.

14. Ibid., p. 497.

15. All ibid., p. 496.

16. Ibid., p. 497.

17. Ibid., p. 498.

18. The Complaint of the duchess is against Mowbray, her husband's slayer (I, ii, 45-53). For Lancaster, II, i, 57-60, 97-115; York, II, i, 17-30.

19. There are three law reports of *Darcy* v. *Allen:* Coke's 11 Co Rep 846 (*English Reports Reprints,* King's Bench 6.1260, hereafter cited *E.R.,* K.B.); Moore's, Moore 671 (*E.R.,* K.B., 1, 830); and Noy's, Noy 173 (*E.R.,* K.B., 3. 1130).

20. Croke and Tanfield.

21. Dodderidge, Fleming and Coke.

22. Noy 175 (*E.R.,* K.B., 3. 1135).

23. *Willion* v. *Berkeley,* 1 Plowden 236. (*E.R.,* K.B., 4. 359).

24. Moore 672 (*E.R.,* K.B., 1. 830).

25. Ibid., 673 (*E.R.,* K.B., 1. 831).

26. Noy, 179 (*E.R.,* K.B., 3. 1137).

27. 11 Co. Rep. 87a (*E.R.,* K.B., 6. 1263).

28. Ibid., Coke's scriptural quotation is from Deut. 24:6.

29. Lord Ellesmere's Observations, p. 7, quoted at *E.R.,* K.B. 6. 1265, note G.

30. *Tudor Economic Documents,* ed. R. H. Tawney and E. Power, 3 vols. (London: Longmans Green, 1924), 2:247.

31. Ibid., p. 259.

32. See above, p. 16 and n. 23.

33. By Charles Gray among others. See his *Copyhold, Equity and the Common-law* (Cambridge, Mass.: Harvard University Press, 1963), pp. 58-66. For a discussion of the divergent views on the dating of the extension of common law practition to copyhold by a historian who argues for an earlier date than Gray does, see Eric Kerridge, *Agrarian Problems in the Sixteenth Century and After* (London: Allen and Unwin, 1969), pp. 65-77.

II

REASON, AUTHORITY, AND IMAGINATION: THE JURISPRUDENCE OF SIR EDWARD COKE

Charles Gray

It is hard to introduce Sir Edward Coke without one eye on the mythological figure of that name, for it was Coke's fate to be mythologized even before his life was spent. But let me try, for the purpose of putting him on stage, to keep my eye on the literal ball. For twenty-eight years (1578-1606), Coke was a successful barrister, which is to say, a practicing advocate mainly in the Court of King's Bench. For the latter half of that time, he doubled as a government lawyer in the successive offices of solicitor general and attorney general—"doubled" because his public capacities were compatible with a thriving private practice. Lawyers do not have much chance of living on in general historical memory, but in the darker purlieus of technical legal history, Coke would probably have a claim on survival if he had done nothing but practice law. Law formation in the late-Elizabethan and early-Jacobean King's Bench has scarcely been explored across its many departments; were it to be, I suspect that Coke would deserve the glory to which an advocate can aspire, not merely the brief gratification of winning cases and making money, but the durable accomplishment of influencing the judges' perception of the law. In his government roles, the "early

Coke"—fifty-four years of a life that turned out to cover eighty-one—merits a historical footnote, for example as "vicious prosecutor" in a few causes célèbres, or as an ambitious politician of the second rank on whom some reflected light falls from a rival of the same description with more grandiose ambition outside the law, Francis Bacon.

Coke's career as a practitioner overlaps with a second one as a law teacher, which, in its fruition, would have sufficed to guarantee his fame. In the first instance, his assuming a teaching role was routine for a lawyer of his eminence: Coke "read"—that is, gave courses of lectures—at Lyons Inn and the Inner Temple. Like many practitioners before and after him, Coke displayed his erudition to students and his peers on a couple of difficult property-law subjects. However, his lectures do not make an unusual contribution to legal literature. It was Coke's conscious decision to teach by publishing which made him an extraordinary "professor of law." The decision was creative in a lawyers sense: based on precedent, it extended the precedents to meet a new need. Coke's first publishing venture took the form of reports of recent cases, the first volume of which appeared in 1600, to be followed by ten more between 1600 and 1615. (Volume 12 and 13 of *Coke's Reports* are posthumous.) On the precedential side, reporting the colloquies of bench and bar for the instruction of students and practicing lawyers was almost as old as the common law. In the sixteenth century, the orderly medieval mode of doing that—preserved to us as the Year Books—fell off, but in the latter part of the century, reporting came strongly into fashion. From those efforts, a large repository of manuscript reports survives. Coke's idea of printing some of the reports he had compiled was precedented, most notably by his immediate model, Edmund Plowden. (It is a sign of Coke's mentality that as a longer-run model he claimed the "first reporter," Moses.)[1] From Coke's example followed a flood of printed reports, giving us a body of material which the good luck of being printed has metamorphosed into the authentic record of what the courts decided, and further changes in thinking have transformed into the law.[2] Coke intended, in the case of his own books, that print should do magic. He was innovative in designing his reports as a teaching instrument. They were not to be unselective accounts of what he had heard in court, but syntheses that, without loss of accuracy, would bear the editor's impress and show the way, through the chaos of a litigious age, to a correct grasp of the law. Hostile contemporaries were aware, and legal historians cannot help becoming so, that accuracy was sometimes the loser; Coke's power to shape the law under color of reporting it was to exceed his expectations.[3]

Aside from the effect of his reports, Coke's professorial importance depends largely on the four treatises he called, imitating Justinian, his "Institutes." Only the first volume was published in his lifetime. They are successively about real property ("Coke on Littleton," for that part is in the form of a commentary on a fifteenth-century textbook on the same subject), the medieval statutes, criminal law, and the court system.

Coke's literary career began when he was a practitioner and continued through and beyond the time he was a judge. During ten years, he was successively chief justice of the Common Pleas and chief justice of the King's Bench. He is known to general history for the controversies that rendered his judicial service brief compared with most other great judges. (Contrast, for example, Lord Mansfield's thirty-two years, Holt's twenty-one, Hale's eighteen.) Coke was dismissed by the king in 1616, whereas his natural lease on what was usually, though not legally, a life office extended to 1633. Technical legal history is as yet unprepared to give a full account of the use Coke made of his tenure, though we have fragmentary knowledge of his day-to-day contributions to the law to put alongside our clearer picture of his leadership on behalf of the rule of law. By removing Coke from the bench, King James made possible the last of his four careers. The practitioner, teacher, and judge became, in the final act of his life, a parliamentarian. In that role, he is famous as a weighty addition to the "opposition" of the 1620s. He was also an instrument of constructive legislation that does not reduce to opposition's occasional success. As a legislator, Coke was useful to the law in ways a judge cannot be.[4]

My subject is Coke's jurisprudence. Having introduced the man, I need to define the activity I am attributing to him. *Jurisprudence* sometimes means no more than ordinary law stated in a certain way, with a special completeness and taxonomic elegance. I have already implied that I could not speak about Coke's jurisprudence in that sense even if I wanted to. Too much about his approach to substantive legal questions remains to be worked out.

As a treatise writer, Coke was essentially a commentator — an ad hoc mind, alien by temperament and principle from the impulse to restate the law in a systematic and abstract form.[5] The other usual meaning of jurisprudence is "legal philosophy." To the perennial questions of legal philosophy Coke hardly responds in terms. A sketch of his career is enough to suggest that he breathed the atmosphere of law and legal politics, an air thick with particulars, not the thinner element of philosophy. He was an insider of the common law; the bent of his mind and the preoccupations of his life made it impossible for him to survey the whole domain of law and its appurtenances from a speculative peak. Yet it is Coke's jurisprudence, in a sense close to "legal philosophy," which I propose to discuss. That would be to apply Procrustean torture were there not a way in which the characterization I have given him needs to be qualified. He did not think philosophically; philosophic questions cannot be pitched too high if they are to harmonize with Cokean answers. Even so, Coke was aware that there are problems about law transcending the substantive issues of English law. He did not take on such problems so much with the front of his mind as in the back of it, as he moved from one context to another of "mere legal" concern. But in his attitudes, the outlines of a jurisprudence are discernible. Coke was distinguished in his generation, not only for seeing more deeply than most others into the mysteries of the common law, but also for looking farther beyond them. He was an "insider" to be sure, but not a prisoner of his professional art — or if a prisoner, one by choice and for reasons.[6]

From these generalities, let me go at once to an unmistakably jurisprudential question to which Coke gave a distinct answer: the problem of the "case of first impression." What is a court supposed to do when a new case comes along, one for which the positive legal sources — statutes, precedents, maxims common to the profession, and the pronouncements of its sages — suggest no solution? Coke did not discuss this question in the abstract, but in one context he faced it directly as a judge. The setting was Calvin's Case, or the case of the *Post Nati* (1608),[7] where the issue was whether a person born in Scotland after James I's accession to the English throne could maintain a real action at common law and a parallel equitable suit to acquire possession of deeds relating to an English freehold. In effect, the question is whether such a

Scottish-born person could own land in England, as aliens could not; therefore the issue was whether a Scottish *post natus* was an alien. The last thing Coke was ready to admit about this case was what offhand seems most obvious: that it was unprecedented. The king of another country had never inherited England before, and so, it would seem, whether children born later in such a king's other realm are aliens in England was a problem that had never before arisen. Not at all, Coke said. Of course the literal situation was new, but so in a trivial sense are most controverted cases; a case is not legally new when with a little research one can find precedents and accepted principles evidently in point; such material may not be mechanically applicable, but when one has it in hand one is not floating in a sourceless void; normal lawyerly argument about the accuracy with which relevant established law fits the present situation can go forward. In Calvin's Case, Coke thought not only that there was plenty of material in point, but also that it left no serious doubt as to what the decision should be — that the infant plaintiff born in Scotland was not an alien. (Two judges dissented, but a large majority agreed.) The most straightforward side of Coke's successful contention was the argument from precedent: cases from the time when England owned Gascony were held to be indistinguishable from the instant case and to establish the governing principle that those born into allegiance to the *person* who is king of England at the time of their birth are not aliens in England, even though they are not born within the *legal entity* called England.[8]

In his long and literary opinion, Coke generalized from his approach to the case. How marvelously "copious" is the common law![9] Here is a situation that to the superficial observer looks new and baffling, but actually, the law's horn of plenty supplies abundant material to work with. Indeed, the case was all but solved some two hundred years ago. The common law is like an infinitely experienced man, who has been everywhere, seen everything, heard it all before. A solution to the problem of the "case of first impression" is implicit in this picture: it does not exist, in England. However, Coke did not stand quite pat on this conclusion. Pushed too far, it offends common sense, strongly though the present case may remind us that what looks new in an ancient legal system often is not. Calvin's Case seemed novel enough, if only to the superficial, to stimulate reflection on what the courts should do with the unprecedented. One point of view Coke was especially eager to put down: when there are no ordinary legal sources to draw a solution from, the solution must be legislative, and legislation is Parliament's job. This position must be stated carefully, because there is, of course, a sense in which the courts cannot throw up their hands once a dispute is before them. What they can do, in some cases, is acknowledge a class of "political questions" which courts ought not to take on without clear guidance from their sources; they can decide such questions conservatively, pending legislative determination on a course of change.[10] There was considerable political impetus behind just such a view of Calvin's Case: recognize its novelty and the public stake in the outcome; hold Calvin an alien because the proposition that all natives of independent realms are aliens is at least not clearly rebuttable; let Parliament decide whether the national security and the country's economic interest would be well served by naturalizing all the king's Scottish subjects born since 1603.[11] Parliament's reluctance to legislate such naturalization had driven the government to seek the same result by adjudication; Coke was driven to defend the courts' title to decide.

If we grant that there is no objection to their deciding and, for the sake of argument, that a solution from ordinary legal sources is not forthcoming, where are the courts to look? To "reason," the answer suggested in Calvin's Case? Even in the most ancient and copious legal system, every case was new once. Then, in the absence of a relevant statute, it must surely have been decided by "recurring to reason." Coke went out of his way to resist conceding this obvious answer in its obvious sense, namely, that when courts recur to reason they resort to the faculty that all sane people possess in more or less perfection, the ordinary capacity to think straight and make correct moral judgments. Instead, he maintained that reason has a place in English adjudication only if one means something called "artificial reason."[12] That conception is perhaps Coke's main gift to legal theory. By insisting that reason in English law means artificial rather than "natural" reason, he was provocative. That his point did not appear to contemporaries to be an empty or harmless one is evident from a lengthy concurring opinion in Calvin's Case by the chancellor, Lord Ellesmere, who, rather than Bacon, was Coke's greatest critic on hard-core professional matters.[13] His opinion concurs with Coke both on the result and the grounds for it; the dissenting element comes at the level of theory, for Ellesmere goes out of *his* way to insist that reason in law is the same as reason elsewhere. Amid a chorus of agreement, Coke and Ellesmere took conscious issue on mere reason versus artificial reason; the theoretical dispute was plainly important to them.[14]

Coke used the term *artificial reason* a few times apart from Calvin's Case, most celebratedly when he congratulated King James on his excellent endowment of natural reason but denied his competence to pass on a legal question for want of the artificial variety.[15] What did he mean?

The expression artificial reason suggests a *substitute* for reason —an artifice that does a job better than the natural faculty. In some contexts, this sense predominates. The artifice is simply the law: there are cases for which a lawyer can draw a solution from positive legal sources. Such a legal solution will be better than the solution an ideally wise person would reach with only natural reason to depend on. That is true because the law is a collective product, a repository of many wise men's thinking about related problems over a long stretch of time.[16] The value of a correct legal solution will sometimes not be evident to a critic whose cognitive and moral acuity, however distinguished, are only his. It is permissible to toy a bit with language here and say that what seems reasonable to one person, or one age, will not typically be as rational as the law, whose rationality is not fully visible in any single perspective. When one has laid hold of this truth and presumed in favor of the law's rationality, one will of course begin to see it.[17] But the seeing requires detailed familiarity, and the presuming, perhaps, demands commitment.[18] Only a lawyer who knows the law is quite in a position to believe, and then to understand, that it is good.

A second sense of artificial reason makes it, not an artifice superior to reason, but the natural faculty improved by cultivation. To the degree that courts must recur to reason, Coke thought it important to emphasize that the deciders are *lawyers* of deep training and experience. For them to base a decision on reason —which we now grant to be different from producing a positive legal solution —is not the same as for any intelligent man to do so. Naked reason, even when nature has given it to someone in superabundance and the best general education and exercise have strengthened nature's gift, is not the same, or as good for particular purposes, as natural capacity shaped by training in a particular art. The craftsman's judgment in his craft, the mathematician's in mathematics, and the lawyer's in law will not always correspond with the amateur's and will have advantages over it. The expert's advantage is not purely in acquired knowledge, but in the ability to solve problems for which mere knowledge is inadequate, new problems that one can "know how to solve" without "knowing the solution," such as cases of first impression in law.

Up to a point this idea is truistic, but it may be tempting to take it as a more obvious truth than it is in application to legal problems. It is helpful to remember that Lord Ellesmere thought it worth resisting, as if, carried beyond the sense in which it is a platitude, it had important, and to Ellesmere dangerous, implications.[19] It is hard to quarrel with certain common-sense grounds for supposing that an experienced lawyer sitting as a judge will respond to a novel case differently, and probably better, than a gifted amateur. His mere knowledge will permit him to tell whether the case is really new—an improbability by Coke's doctrine of "copiousness." Assuming it is, the decision will be directive for future cases—judicial legislation in that sense, though the terms should not imply "made-up" or "willed," as opposed to "drawn from a higher 'law.'" A lawyer will have had experience with legislation, judicial and Parliamentary, and will have learned the inevitable lesson: statutes are often well-meant, decisions often fair in the immediate situation in which they are made, but statutes and decisions have consequences, and those often turn out to be unanticipated and undesirable. A lawyer making new law will be likely to look ahead to more remote ways in which his decision may make a difference; an amateur will be too likely to favor his judgment of what is just or socially beneficial without counting the hidden costs.[20]

Can we, however—and did Coke—go beyond these advantages of the lawyer-judge (and the still more obvious advantages of mere familiarity with a vocabulary and with the areas of human affairs from which legal disputes arise, of mere practice in dialectic)? Unless we can, we can hardly do more than recommend making lawyers judges—when in doubt, when one is not pretty sure of an amateur candidate—for the situations in which legal rules need to be made, or imported into positive law from moral law, are only situations of everyday life. They may be unintelligible to some laymen because they come out of specialized areas of business, but laymen can be experienced in business. It is unfair to imagine the ideal lay judge as a moral philosopher or divine lacking in practicality, or the practical layman as morally dim-sighted compared with a don.[21] In this way, it seems misleading to assimilate legal problems to those of shoemaking, mathematics, or music. Law belongs to Everyman; it is about right and wrong and sensible rules for orderly social living. The pitfall I have mentioned — the hidden costs of "good" decisions — may be something lawyers are attuned to, but it does not seem mysterious in principle. "If others seek to imitate or obey you, are they likely to do so in inappropriate circumstances and so to do what you would not approve?" seems an obvious question for any thoughtful person in authority to ask, and one we ask in ordinary life when we tell people what to do or expect them to be influenced by our example.

I believe that artificial reason can be pushed deeper in two, ultimately converging, directions. The first is copiousness extended. Calvin's Case as Coke saw it — and Ellesmere too — showed straightforwardly how rich the common law is. It was striking that a case so new in appearance could be so well covered, but it was, the argument goes, simply covered. There is another type of case, however, whose novelty is harder to dispel. Such a case will be seen as covered by existing law only through a refined sense of relevance, whereby things that, in a sense, really *are* unlike reveal their relationship, and remote analogies become perceptible. One could solve Calvin's Case — the argument goes — by knowing the Gascon cases and taking some fairly obvious ratiocinative steps; for other legal problems, one must of course know the law in all its branches to be furnished with material, but to make use of the material takes what I suggest calling "imagination."

Coke's claims for artificial reason are in one aspect claims for the "legal imagination." I mean by that an analogue of the artistic and scientific imaginations, like them, as they are like each other, though each of the three is also *sui generis*. In all departments, imagination must be distinguished from its subordinate Coleridgean faculty "fancy," the knack for linking things that cannot be sensibly connected, however amusingly they can be confused. Imagination seems to be an indispensable supplement to the more prosaic ratiocinative process, a way of discovering relationships by leaps and in places where one would not automatically look for them. What it finds cannot escape a certain tenuousness—the theory that waits on disverification; the metaphor that taste may debate or fancy reclaim from imagination; the pattern whose cogency lawyers will inevitably argue down on one side and up on the other, for law is about disputes. Imagination is always somewhat at odds with necessity; what must be seen by sheer force of reason need not be imagined; in moral and legal discourse, what is "naturally" right stands off from what is "artificially" persuasive. *In specie*, the legal imagination looks into the legal system as an ordered organic whole, looks for ways in which a rule or ruling on one point fits with the given state of the law in other respects. Its attunement is to harmonies, and distant ones count, as they do in an artistic composition. "Ear," aesthetic feel, is required to find and grasp the concords and discords of a rich system, and that, in one respect, is what the lawyer gains from deep initiation in his art. As poetic and scientific imaginations depend on studying and writing poetry or on practising a particular science, so does legal imagination develop from mere knowing and from experience with the easier, more imitative modes of elaborating a tradition.

To bring the categories of art into law is not, from the Cokean point of view, to trivialize the work of the legal imagination or to make the aesthetic satisfaction of lawyers an end. Its serious task is to see that the complex legal system *does* cohere, that a decision here, which may be plausible in itself, does not jar with rules or concepts used by the system for some other purpose, perhaps one remote from the context the judge is in at the time. It is important to avoid disharmony because sooner or later the authority or power of the law to convince will be weakened by it. Pieces will seem to make no sense as bricks in the same fabric; what remains functional here may in consequence be torn away to accord with what has been carelessly intruded there; at any rate, the law will have the disquieting feel of "just happening to be," this way on this subject, that way on another, without—well—reason.[22]

Against this Cokean point of view it is allowable to protest. Does it avoid putting the aesthetics of the lawyer ahead of the

plain uses of law? Is the harmony of the legal system all that valuable, or all that noticeable to those whom the system serves and
whom it can only hope to guide by large-lettered signs? When the
courts must deal with novel situations, is not their first duty to
give the parties a right solution by standards accessible to them—
so far as possible, a "natural" and "necessary" one by the common light of day? What is more dangerous to the legal system's
credit than that its results should appeal too exclusively to the initiate's feel for its coherence? Would it not be well to celebrate the
law's copiousness insofar as it relieves the judge of deciding hard
issues with the limited insight of one mind or one age, but to
admit that he can try too hard to take himself off the hook? For
Coke, solutions somehow implicit in existing law were superior to
imported ones. Ellesmere may have been concerned lest the
trained ear listen for such distant harmonies that the voice of justice be inaudible in the theater of the world.

The second way to enrich the sense of artificial reason is to say
that almost all important moral deciding is artificial. If we encounter a situation that is not simply covered by law and guaranteed morally by the law's testedness, then—let us grant—the task
is to find a right solution somewhere outside the law. But where?
Suppose I were to deny that there is any universally valid solution,
or at least to assert that any *semper et ubique* solution must give
way to a more localized alternative. My ground for so holding
would be that there is no moral standard dispersed throughout
the world, or if there is—such that judgment between nations or
the subjects of different ones is possible—that, at any rate, judgment within a nation ought not to be governed by it. Rather,
each nation has its own morality. Insofar as the courts' highest
imperative in new cases is to convince the parties that justice has
been done as it must be done, the appeal is to this native standard. A more universal one, conceding its possibility, will not
necessarily conflict, but it may, and then, to look past the indigenous to the universal is to miss the relevant source of "rightness."
It is of course misleading to call this immediate, operative standard artificial if the word suggests the contrived, that which goes
against the natural grain of people's thinking and feeling. It is
entirely natural for Englishmen to have English moral judgments. But the word remains appropriate insofar as it means
"man-made," as opposed to given in the way nature and human

nature are constituted, or "acquired," as opposed to evident without conditioning in a particular social and historical community. National societies in the process of their history—and long ago in a long history, if not at the "original institution"—have made certain moral choices. Granting that universal ethics compel some distinctions between right and wrong, they leave others open. Choices within the indeterminate area are those which, because they are not axiomatic, tend to be relevant in disputed cases, moral or legal. Paradoxically, because in an abstract sense which way is right cannot be totally disengaged from arguability, a choice must be made to foreclose argument. For example: is telling the truth to another's damage worse than the stifling of truth that is a cost of charity? If I have been robbed and the thief has sold the loot to someone who did not and could not know he was buying stolen goods, am I on solid ground in demanding them back? Is establishing the truth of an accusation worth pressing the accusee to betray his own guilt? Is the continuity of families from generation to generation a value to which individual members of the family should be willing to sacrifice their interests? I state these questions as moral ones to show that they can be—that they are questions that could arise and be resolved in people's prejudices before coming up in litigation. Affirmative answers to all of them do, of course, issue in familiar rules of English law: truth is a defense to common law defamation; the owner generally prevails over the bona fide purchaser in an action for converting chattels; the "privilege against self-incrimination"; primogeniture.

If the right moral standard is an indigenous, historically chosen one, how is it to be discovered? A populist answer is possible: ask the jury, let ordinary people decide, those in whom the native standard is most genuinely "second nature" because it is not in conscious conflict with any other. The claims of an especially intelligent or educated judge are not, as such, very strong: he is too likely to be aware that English rightness is not rightness everywhere and too apt to be ambitious to fetch an airtight solution out of his superior sensibility. But the populist answer can be opposed by the claims of the *legally* learned. Here we double back and reinforce the view that a positive law solution is worth straining after and will be convincing in the long run even though the legal imagination, to find it, must reach beyond that obviously relevant law to which the layman can easily look for guidance, for the law is the surest depository of more than law—of native morality and national character. The populist answer makes too little of the common man's passions and confusion about his own values; it is the age-old law that is the most objective and reliable source for the considered commitments of *this* society. Most of them are embedded in such indisputable rules that it is easy to miss how invaluably "mere law" testifies to character. It is when mere law fails that legal imagination takes on its gravest task—to discover native morality, which we would risk violating in an unfamiliar situation if we were to assume in haste that none was to be found within the horn of plenty.

I believe I have stated a point of view that Coke had in mind, though it is hard to pin down directly.[23] He was not alienated from the natural law tradition in the radical, romantic manner. He certainly believed in universal ethical standards. He was often concerned, not to make out the uniqueness of English law and its enveloping morality, but to show their consonance with those of other nations, especially with Biblical law.[24] The narrower formulation of the "antiuniversal" position is the cogent one in the abstract and the one that is seriously attributable to Coke: Natural law exists; it provides an answer to some problems that can arise in the real world and a basis for arguing about others; it is often embodied in rules of English law; but it does not solve all questions, least of all those likeliest to arise in novel cases, where reaching beyond the law is in one way required, though that turns out to mean looking more deeply within it.[25]

Writers more disposed than Coke to embrace natural law unreservedly, often had trouble showing the purpose and justification of man-made law. The going was relatively easy when the human role amounted only to taking natural things, in themselves indifferent, out of the realm of indifference for the sake of such benefits as the advancement of national prosperity via trade restrictions, or when that role functioned only to attach specific penalties to natural crimes. Sin could be blamed for keeping us from observing the natural law and thus generating a need for human legislation, which would declare our natural duties and back them up by sanctions, and which, in return for that service, was entitled to carve further duties out of the zone of indifference. Thenceforward, the going gets tougher and theories hazier:

human law is in some way a "revelation" of a hidden higher law, on the analogy of divine positive law; it is a "probable" deduction from a natural law that is too abstract to make its implications entirely clear; natural law is an ideal that must be fitted to the material it has to work with in a particular nation; human law is the basis for property, which may be a mixed, if unavoidable, blessing and therefore require more human law to keep the institution within moral bounds.[26] Another approach is to isolate the central problem of natural law as its indeterminateness on questions where choice is necessary and where the choice is ineluctably moral—as between truth and neighborly benevolence, or two such innocents as the victim of theft and the bona fide purchaser. The choice is moral because without one there can no more be a community functioning by opinion and social sanctions than there can be a legal system, and because it is not satisfying (though a little tempting) to think that the choice must be made by coin tossing—or by appointing a sovereign and letting him choose in accord with his predilections as an individual. About such choices there remains a penumbra of arguability, room to doubt and to hope that one's society has chosen right, and better ground for tolerating others than the supposition that their coins have turned up tails. When I suggest that Coke came closer than his predecessors—and for that matter his successors—to putting his finger on the place of human law in a universe from which natural law had not been exiled, I am admittedly translating into the language of theory what he never said in those terms. Central among my arguments is his sheer resistance to natural reason as an adjudicative tool of last resort. Ellesmere would probably have explained that resistance as Hobbes did in his strong attack on Coke half a century and more later: to exclude natural reason is to exclude criticism of the common law judges when, under the color of artificial, they make up law in unsettled areas to suit themselves.[27] An answer to the charge is that artificial reason, though perhaps pervertible into judicial arrogation of sovereignty, expresses a valid objection to the natural law jurisprudence which, in Ellesmere's hands, was ultimately the basis for claiming a role for the king in shaping the law. That claim should not be regarded as an extremist or unreasonable one; in a manner of speaking, it was the "progressive Tory" line in the early seventeenth century. But it does involve some faith, on the part of a basic conservative such as Ellesmere, that the natural law game can be played without gradually detaching the law from the ancestral choices that make England England. In the end, the contest is between two brands of creative adjudication—when there is no option except to create. Either look away from the law to the solution that is best in the abstract, or into the law for its indirect testimony to values that, for better or worse, define the national identity. The risk of judicial encroachment on legislative territory, Coke would surely have said, is much greater if the former course is taken. The legal imagination stretches beyond mere law and everyday legal reasoning, but it proceeds in judicial form, and where business as usual leaves off and creativity begins is inherently vague.

Against what I called the populist version of Coke's basic approach, I think he can be seen arguing—again, not expressly, but through the intent of some of his detailed positions. If anything is manifest in Coke's writings, as in his performances at the bar and on the bench, it is that he relished the subtlety of the common law and its many distinctions. That proclivity is offset by a contrapuntal theme of his thought—the belief that the virtue of the English system lay in its fundamental simplicity, whence it periodically degenerated and to which it yearned to be restored.[28] But some legal rules—and the moral choices behind them—were subtly qualified. The populist fallacy would be to come close but to miss the exact point, to see the main societal decision between conflicting goods, but to overstate it. For example, free alienability of land was a major English choice—a facet of choice for a commercial and mobile society. One embodiment of that choice was a rule against conveying land in fee simple on condition that it not be alienated.[29] However, it was acceptable to convey one piece of land on condition that the feoffee not alienate another piece owned by him. Popular judgment might find the second rule inconsistent with the societal choice expressed in the first one and known to common consciousness as the English way. The truth is that the choice was not *simply* for free trade and circulating property, but for that in complex conjunction with other values. My point here can also be expressed by saying that one advantage of judicial discernment of societal choices by artificial reason is that it avoids jumping to utilitarian conclusions. Coke was wary, not only of judging by naked reason, but also of assessing the choices behind rules with too exclusive a view to their superficially apparent purpose. The ban on conditions against alienation seems to exist because England favors free exchange and disfavors the dead hand—and so it does, and for that reason, in part, the rule exists. But it is not the only reason, and the rest of the reason (which accounts for the consistency of the apparently anomalous parallel rule) does not reduce to a purpose which the practical lay mind can so easily imagine as being legislatively chosen. Ultimately, the choice is in every aspect a purposeful election among goods, but it is not simply the choice between free circulation and freedom to tie up your own. When we go about, in a correct Cokean spirit, to discover the ideas implied in the rules, in order to bring these ideas to bear on new situations and avoid falling back on universal reason, we must avoid selecting those "policies of the law" which our time-bound individual minds can get a ready grasp on and which appeal to our rough, if patriotic, prejudices. If we are not careful about that, we will only repeat the fallacies of natural law jurisprudence, only drift away from the judgments *really* rooted in our history.

This discussion of new cases and artificial reason may perhaps serve as a way into other aspects of Coke's relation to higher law theory. It is implicit in the points above that conflict between natural law and established common law was not a practical problem for Coke. I do not believe that it can be ruled out theoretically, nor that custom as such is guaranteed to conform with natural law. Local custom had the same virtue of being time tested as the common law, yet the courts must approve its reasonableness before giving it legal force. I am not convinced that natural law or universal standards can be excluded from the criteria by which the reasonableness of local customs was judged, though it was not the sole criterion.[30] That the common law, in contrast to local customs, was a *judicial* product is important for its virtual immunity from natural law criticism. In addition to enjoying the presumption in its favor raised by time itself, common law was the result of a constant process of internal adjustment, new problems being solved, and the solutions being incorporated into settled law by reference to principles that typically represented choices within the range of natural indeterminateness. The "penumbra of arguability" about even those choices cannot be escaped, but for practical purposes there was no tension in the Cokean universe between natural reason and settled common law.[31]

Coke's response to whether parliamentary legislation is subject to any test for validity by the courts is a theme to which historians have given much attention. In my opinion, Coke at most flirted with an affirmative answer.[32] His characteristic position was the standard one: the validity of a statute is beyond challenge, once its verbal meaning and its purpose can be specified. But what statutory words seem to mandate and what they really mean are often problematic. Like other human utterances, statutes sometimes fail to communicate directions that the auditor can plausibly take as something the speaker intends him to do. In other cases, what is said may be an inept—or just a nonliteral—expression of what is meant, but the intention may be pretty confidently inferred and acted on. By modern lights, the courts in Coke's day were uninhibited about construing the legislature's intention against the literal sense of its language; the difference between modern lights—which include an element of obfuscation—and traditional common law practice in dealing with statutes depends on numerous historical changes. In one context—rather in reflecting on Dr. Bonham's Case than in deciding it—Coke may be seen as asking himself, typically, one more question than most other lawyers would have raised to consciousness: is there a significant line between interpreting statutes within permissible bounds and passing on their validity? If sometimes the courts may overlook a statute as unintelligible and sometimes strain the language to get at a believable meaning, are they implicitly embracing the idea that there are limits beyond which the legislature can by no contrivance go—criteria of validity in effect? Coke's suggestion that the answer might be yes was perhaps not ultimately convincing to himself; it had some influence, but not much future in the law.[33]

That the common law could be changed by statute was obvious to all experience, and no one was so conservative as to explain that reality away entirely by interpreting every apparent change as a restoration of the common law to its original condition, or to conformity with its "spirit," or conformity with the communal choices that ought to shape particular decisions and rules, but which can sometimes be neglected or misunderstood. Coke was given to saying that statutes that change the common law in fun-

damentals do not last, that is, their folly is sooner or later seen
and they are repealed, as the judges' occasional folly is corrected
by the kind of legislation that does "restore the common law."[34]
So to say is to acknowledge that mischievous statutes can happen,
that they are perfectly valid, and that they cannot always be
evaded by interpretation. Doubt may be raised in the limiting
case, where a statute appears to encroach on such an important
and unmistakable principle that one cannot believe that it means
what it seems to — at which point, it is sensible to wonder whether
getting around it is construction or invalidation. For the identification of such cases, intolerable disharmony with the rest of the
legal system, rather than conflict with a substantive law of
nature, should probably be thought of as the test. If a case is that
extreme, it may not make much difference which criterion is
chosen, but the courts' title to control statutes — or, if one is willing to cross the linguistic equator, to invalidate them — rests most
securely on their rights to say, "We cannot run a legal system *that*
incoherent — and it is we who have to run it day by day. A consistently wicked system would at least be manageable."

The principle involved in Bonham's Case — no man should be
judge in his own cause — can illustrate this point. It sounds like a
self-evident moral truth, and indeed Coke thought it one.[35] Yet
whether it is can be questioned, too, for to make some men judges
in matters affecting them is only to trust some men to be fair
where most would have trouble being so. If, however, we look to
English law, it is unmistakable that the national commitment is
against reposing such trust, however justifiable it might be in a
particular instance. Not even the king, who can do no wrong, is
in practice his own judge. There is a sense in which to allow Parliament to make an exception to that commitment would be to
introduce confusion as to whether the commitment itself still
stood and made sense. As the law was, the king by a grant of jurisdiction could not make the grantee judge in his own cause. If the
king with Parliament's consent may do so — may say that A is so
trustworthy that he may be excepted out of the policy of the law
— is it altogether clear that the king should not be able to make
the same judgment out of Parliament? Is parliamentary collaboration all that significant for the purpose of identifying persons of
extraordinary trustworthiness? Of course, in a sense, it *is* altogether clear that the king has no extraparliamentary power to

make people their own judges; I would not *really* be worried about the next case on a royal grant if the statute were upheld. But it is legitimate to worry about confusion, about argumentativeness where formerly there was no room for argument, and about subversion of the authority of the law by making a man's un-English and morally questionable power to be judge in his own cause depend on whether he has been lucky enough to get someone to push a bill through Parliament or has only persuaded the king of his saintly objectivity. Ascend a high enough imaginary mountain, and perhaps it is best to admit — as Coke might well — that Parliament could repeal the whole policy against auto-judges. It could repeal Magna Carta too. Here in the real world, it is perhaps best to say that keeping Parliament from messing up the law for nothing that any sane person could consider important — for the mere advantage of one favored individual (or, in Bonham's Case, corporation) — is a matter of interpretation. What it is called, when the real end is preserving the coherence of the legal system where legislated and nonlegislated law will inevitably interact, is not of the essence.

There is another, less familiar, context in which Coke's attitude toward the common law itself as a form of higher law can be inspected. The courts in England which did not administer the common law, but rather ecclesiastical, Admiralty, and equity law, were procedurally under the control of the major common law courts. That is, they could be prohibited from proceeding, by a judicial writ called a Prohibition, when the King's Bench or Common Pleas saw fit. The elementary use of the writ was to keep such courts from exceeding their subject-matter or local jurisdiction, but the question often arose whether what they did in a case within their jurisdiction was controllable. From responses to that question in various situations, a general doctrine can be constructed along the following lines: clearly, church courts, say, do not have to model themselves on the common law in detail. They are by definition outside the common law system, have their own traditions, and deal with matters the common law does not handle. If a church court does something utterly unreasonable and unjust, it is not the common law courts' business to interfere. The ecclesiastical courts are as beholden to the law of nature as the rest of the world; if it has been violated, the victim should appeal within the generous appellate system the church provided. There is, however, a point beyond which disconformity with the common law on the part of ecclesiastical courts goes too far. The point must be defined in the terms we have been discussing—when church law ceases to be reasonably analogous to fundamental articles of the common law, or to English communal undertakings that both shape and transcend the law. A basic concord or unidirectionality must exist among all courts in England, and it is the common law courts' responsibility to see that it does.

The position I describe is an idealization, but some judges were close enough to it, while others disapproved of interfering at all with the extra-common law courts so long as they stayed within their jurisdictions. Coke was rather a moderate. That may come as a surprise, because he was not only accused by his enemies of seeking to aggrandize the common law courts, dethroning both Parliament and Reason in the process; in addition, he is associated historically with strong use of the Prohibition to curb extra-common law tribunals. The association is perfectly correct to some intents. It is also true and celebrated that Coke took the heat of a political attack on the courts by the extra-common law jurisdictions that considered themselves unduly curtailed. In defending the artificial reason of the law against that attack, he was defending the right and duty of the judges to decide Prohibition cases as they saw them, without being called to account out of court and told to change their ways in accord with the king's "inartificial" opinion of what the law should be. His defense was not the only cause of his fall, but one among others closely related causes. On our immediate question, however, Coke's position was restrained. For example: church courts required some facts to be established by two witnesses. It was often argued that the practice was harsh and discordant with the common law, which did not put similar obstacles in the way of parties trying to prove similar facts. Coke persuaded his courts to reverse some contrary precedents and refuse interference with the ecclesiastical courts' normal procedure. The same point holds essentially for a more famous example. Coke is sometimes considered a hero in the history of the privilege against self-incrimination. *Nemo tenetur seipsum prodere* has a claim to be a natural maxim, and it certainly represents a deeply ingrained commitment of the common law. Sometimes Coke, as well as other judges, prohibited ecclesiastical courts from using the inquisitorial procedure that their tradition permitted. On close inspection, however, that does not turn out to be a good example of law held to be so fundamental that it must be observed throughout England. Coke contributed significantly to defining, but did not really go beyond, what I believe can be called the law on the subject: ecclesiastical courts may not hail someone in and swear him to answer any questions he is asked, because if that and only that is what they appear to have done, there is no showing that the examination is about something in ecclesiastical jurisdiction. Neither may they make a man confess facts that could be used against him in common law proceedings. But if the examination is shown to be infrajurisdictional, and it is on a subject where there is no danger that the examinee will be worse off in the common law sphere for anything he might confess, there is no basis for interference. In my earlier colloquialism, the ecclesiastical courts were not allowed to mess up the law of England by practices that jarred with it; though his position over the whole relevant range was more complex than these examples suggest, Coke was not much disposed, compared with some other judges, to erect parts of the common law into a kind of constitutional law binding even on the extra-common law jurisdictions.[36]

There speaks his feeling for distinctions. Everything in its place, each channel in the complicated legal-political waterworks flowing within its proper banks, was a central Cokean theme — the king's prerogative upheld, the subject's liberty protected; matters of state not confused with matters of law; the High Court of Parliament and the ordinary courts of justice, different yet partners in the guardianship of the law. At a lower level, jurisdictions such as the church's, which had been adopted into the English system for special purposes, should be allowed to be themselves and disallowed from touching with alien hands the network of relations defined by native law. In that instance, the polarity of spiritual and temporal is to be kept polar, as, in a sense, is the antithesis of national and international law in the case of the Admiralty, or natural and human when the legitimate scope of equitable remedies is in question. About the location of all those boundaries there were many disputes, especially in the early seventeenth century. Coke's specific positions were often displeasing to royalist politicians and to the representatives, not only of the interests of the common law's jurisdictional competitors, but also of an alternative vision of harmony in the mixed legal system.[37] But there were judges more inclined than Coke to let the "spirit of the common law" spill over boundaries once drawn. For Coke, the choices informing English law were always refined. Among them was a complex series of "federalistic," balancing decisions — to have many courts and kinds of law contributing to the totality of justice in England, as well as an intricate division of the larger labor of governance, and to mesh the numerous parts by precise differentiating rules. Commitment to the common law's place in the system was as important as commitment to the rules and values of the common law. Its place must be at the center for the ideas of which it is the depository to count as commitments; in most of their relationships, for England to be England, people must live and be judged under the ancestral choices the law holds in memory. But even this riverlike truth was qualified and enriched by lesser tributaries. Nothing under the historical moon is as simple as naked nature — not even second nature.[38]

In talking about Coke's thinking in the jurisprudential register, I hope I have suggested affinities with general cultural history more successfully than I could state them outright. Along with others whose interests and motivations were primarily legal, Coke is important for the discovery of history and the historical discovery of England at the end of the sixteenth century. His nativism and his very readiness to find political wisdom in the crabbed sentences of "Gothic" law put him in the drift of "counter-Renaissance" — granting always, in legal thought as elsewhere, that if we can feel such a drift we must feel the undertows too. The concepts of Nature, Reason, and Art were alive in their endless ambiguity for Coke as for Shakespeare, though not so terrifyingly alive. If it is not too artificial to relate the lawyer and the poet, I should say that there is a great deal more resolution in Coke. The chronicle of wasted time yielded more to work with and hope for — the invaluable sense of continuity with our ancestors and ourselves, standards that can be lost and yet recovered. Coke's Art was not false and painted, not so at odds with Nature, readier to do duty for her without the painful costs. Natural reason unclothed by custom and civil experience was threatening for Coke as for Shakespeare, and in some ways they shared the gift for seeing beyond the threat to assurance — to a conviction that the evil face of rationalism is not rationality. But for Coke it was easier. In his life as in his thought, he was a confident man. Yet in the network of general ideas, spun around the extroverted consciousness of an active lawyer, there are tensions, complexities, and poetry enough to place Coke among the great late-Elizabethan intellectuals.[39]

NOTES

1. In Calvin's Case (n. 7 below), 629; Preface, 6 Rep.; 1 Inst., 394b, where Moses is "the first writer of law." (Rep. and Inst. stand for Coke's *Reports* and *Institutes*).

2. To say, "the law . . . is composed of the rules which the courts lay down for the determination of legal rights and duties" (John Chipman Gray, *The Nature and Sources of Law* — 1909 — , p. 84) takes a larger step away from the mentality of Coke and his age than may be immediately apparent. Gray thought that difficulties about identifying the law with what the courts lay down came from confusing the law with its sources. Coke and his contemporaries would probably have found it puzzling to speak of the determinants of judicial decisions as any less "the law" than the decisions themselves (or the rules implicit in the decisions, as those rules are explicated by canons designed for getting the rule out of the decision. The idea that there such methods for extracting the rule reflects a legal "inductivism" that grew up in the later seventeenth century and beyond. By "inductivism" I mean the concept of law as that which can be constructed from the cases, as general statements about nature are constructed from particular facts). Without at all denying the authority of judicial precedents, Coke was critical of painful and prolix citation — as if lawyers could not discuss legal issues without standing on a pile of inductive evidence: (Preface, 10 Rep.; 1 Inst., 16b).

3. The best evidence of Coke's ideal of reporting is his practice, especially in contrast with other, less synthetic reporters. In various passages he reflects consciously on his standards and purposes, sometimes modestly, sometimes warning the reader against putting quite as much stock in reports as came to be put in his own (Prefaces to 3, 6, 7, 10 Rep.; 1 Inst., 370a; 4 Inst., 17). Note also Coke's modesty about his claims as a treatise writer at 1 Inst., 395a. He often reminded the student of the importance of going to the sources, of not trusting too much in books. For an example of how Coke's reporting could slip away from mere rendering of what was said in court, see C. Gray, "Bonham's Case Reviewed," *Transactions of the American Philosophical Society* (1972). The story of the influence of Coke's *Reports* in, but especially beyond, his lifetime has still to be worked out. Coke's *Reports* represent a good-sized proportion of all reports printed in the late-sixteenth and early-seventeenth centuries; their detail, clarity, and didactic confidence, and the author's reputation, both professional and patriotic, gave his

Reports an influence *out* of proportion to their share as a source of information.

4. See the Ph. D. dissertation of Stephen D. White, "Sir Edward Coke in the Parliaments of 1621 and 1624: Parliament, the Law, and The Economy," Harvard University, 1972.

5. Coke thought that attempts to restate the law in digestible form would only succeed in abridging it in the same way as the existing, much-used abridgments of the Year Books (Fitzherbert, Brooke, et al.). Such works were useful tools, but they were all too likely to teach an impoverished version of the law compared with the rich and accurate one to be gained from full reading of the sources (Preface, 10 Rep.; 1 Inst., 395a). Bacon's restating quasi-codifying impulses in law (cf. n. 13 below) would have met with skepticism from Coke, but I am not sure that that skepticism was so very alien from Bacon's own cautioning against a premature "methodizing" urge in all fields of learning (*Advancement of Learning,* Everyman ed., p. 32). Coke's own use of the term, *jurisprudence,* makes it a mere synonym for the study of, or learning in, law (1 Inst., 395a).

6. In loose connection with this point, it is worth noting that a generous humanistic culture was part of Coke's store and, to his own sensibility, relevant in "doing law." He should not be parodied as a crabbed lawyer, ravished only by the fine distinctions of real property and most at home with his nose in a Plea Roll. Apart from more serious matters touched on below, such as the comparativistic consciousness in law that kept him from being an entirely provincial common lawyer, one should observe in his works, both judicial and literary, his relish for the classics and the Bible, the supply of nonlegal allusions he could call on when something in his legal life suggested an association, his familiarity with general historians (even though he considered them dangerous to the uninitiated as sources for legal history — Prefaces, 3 and 8 Rep.), even his humor and anecdotage. Most lawyers stick to business more soberly. A nice illustration of Coke's literary and good-humored side is 4 Inst., 289, in taking up the forest laws: "seeing we are to treat of game and hunting let us recreate ourselves with the excellent description of *Didoes* Doe (then quoted from Vergil)." 1 Inst., 235b: Coke's recommendation of university training in the liberal arts for future lawyers. For some sheer flights of "fancy" (see text below): 4 Inst., 106; 1 Inst. 155a.

7. 7 Rep., 1, for Coke's opinion. See Preface, 7 Rep., for Coke's estimation of the singular importance of Calvin's Case and his explanation of how he came to write up his opinion for publication in more elaborate and polished form than that in whch it was originally reduced to writing, much less delivered in court as an oral argument. Coke's opinion is reproduced, along with Ellesmere's (below) and other documents on the case, in 2 State Trials, 559 ff. Hereafter, page references in Calvin's Case are to the State Trials.

8. For the Gascon cases and Coke's most direct insistence that the case was "overruled" by judicial precedents: Calvin's Case, 640 ff.; 623-624

for another precedent claimed as decisive by Coke. That these cases *actually* decide the present one is a most arguable proposition. They may be better examples of how it is legitimate (or, some would say, not) to make inferences from rather exiguous and distantly connected material. The point, however, is that Coke claimed not to see them that way. That he wanted not to takes nothing away from his view of the frame of the case, in whatever degree *that* was willed.

9. Calvin's Case, 612. The copiousness of the law is of course a consequence of its age, as great an age as could be attributed to any legal system outside the Bible. Though Coke was skeptical of the Brutus legend, which has the effect of making the English and Roman systems twin offspring of Troy, he did not need the legend to get the same virtual result (Prefaces, 3 Rep. especially, also 6, 8, and 9 Rep.). It is important that Coke really believed that the English legal system was functioning in remotest antiquity with some recognizable — though not simplemindedly literal — resemblance to its present self. For the distinction between "really believing" that and merely believing that historical evidence was not available to rebut the presumption that some long-established legal institutions were even older, see C. Gray, Introduction to Sir Matthew Hale, *The History of the Common Law of England* (Chicago, 1971), especially xxvi-xxvii. It is significant that Hale, who in many ways can be taken to represent the Cokean frame of mind in a later, more careful and disillusioned, generation, both tended to substitute skepticism for the belief that English law was alive and well in more or less the days of Aeneas *and* admitted more willingly than Coke that sometimes there are cases that have no positive solution and must be approached with mere reason. The admission, I should say, has a touch of discomfort about it — something which a realist must, alas, confess (ibid., p. 46).

10. Isolating the "political question" is of course not the only way to make out that one decision is a kind of nondecision, or act of deferring to the legislature. "Plaintiff's burden" is the formalistic way: if one in the plaintiff's position has not only never been held entitled to recover on legal argument, but also has never recovered de facto (defendant not contesting, or taking issue only on the facts or technicalities), then judgment should go for defendant. This approach is applicable enough to *Calvin:* plaintiff born outside England and not legislatively naturalized has never recovered in an assize (the form of action in question). However, insistence on plaintiff's burden is more clearly justifiable when there is a significant public stake in whether the scope of remedies should be expanded; otherwise, the unprecedented claim, or use of a writ, should arguably be allowed when the plaintiff seems more like than unlike those who have been permitted to recover before — as a Scottish post natus can be considered more like a native Englishman than, say, a Scottish ante natus (whom no one thought capable of maintaining a real action in England). The precedents relied on in *Calvin,* however useful in their way, do not directly countenance attempts by a plaintiff in Calvin's position to maintain an action.

11. The principal formal objection to naturalizing the post nati, and hence to the result in *Calvin,* was that Scots infiltrating England and gaining property and exportable wealth there would be a security threat in the event that the Scottish and English thrones should ever devolve on different people. This "policy argument" is answered by Coke at Calvin's Case, 656, and related practical arguments on the adjoining pages; see also p. 640. Worry about mere economic competition from Scots was added to simple xenophobia in the political atmosphere.

12. Coke was led into discussing the place of reason in adjudication by citation of the alleged civil law maxim, "si cessit lex scripta, id custodiri opertat, quod moribus et consuetudine inductum est; et si qua in hoc defecerit, recurrendum est ad rationem." Lord Ellesmere (Calvin's Case, 674) clearly accepts the maxim in effect, though instead of stating it in exactly the terms above, he says that "when there is no direct lawe, nor precise example, we must "recurrere ad rationem, et ad responsa prudentum.'" Coke's first point about the maxim (Calvin's Case, 641) is that it was being miscited (the words after "in re hoc defecerit" should be "tunc id quod proximum et consequens ei est; et si id non appareat, tunc jus quo, urbs Romana utitur, servari oportet" — nothing about reason). But then Coke relents, with the decisive passage (ibid.): "Secondly, if the said imaginative rule be rightly and legally understood it may stand for truth: for if you intend *ratio* for the legal and profound reason of such as by diligent study and long experience and observation are so learned in the laws of this realm, as out of the reason of the same they can rule the case in question, in that sense the said rule is true: but if it be intended of the reason of the wisest man that professeth not the laws of England, then (I say) the rule is absurd and dangerous; for "cuilibet in sua arte perito est credendum, et quod quisque norit in hoc se exerceat. Et omnes prudentes illa admittere solent, quae probantur iis, qui in sua arte bene versati sunt.'"

13. Ellesmere was chancellor throughout Coke's judicial career, and in the legal disputes of tha time — mostly over the jurisdiction of courts (see below) — he occupied as natural a leadership position on one side as Coke did on the other. He wrote a number of tracts and "briefs" expressly against Cokean positions. However, Bacon may have been a greater intellectual critic of Coke, at a less bread-and-butter level. Whether he was, I am not prepared to judge. Paul H. Kocher in "Francis Bacon on the Science of Jurisprudence," *Journal of the History of Ideas* (Jan. 1957), reprinted in Brian Vickers, ed., *Essential Articles for the Study of Francis Bacon* (Hamden, Conn., 1968) makes a useful contribution toward making sense of Bacon as a legal thinker, but the subject requires more technical and contextual investigation. Bacon was on Ellesmere's side at the legal-political level. His Olympian posture as a general intellectual was at odds with Coke's professionalism. Bacon was as critical of the overreaching of all professions as Coke was ready — some would say, including Bacon — to overreach for his own. When, however, one looks hard at Bacon when he was being most serious about

law—as Kocher does—it is not evident to me that he was on a track fundamentally at odds with Coke. How deep the kind of difference mentioned at note 5, above, goes is hard to say. That there is very much of Bacon in Hobbes's important attack on Coke is not clear to me. (See Joseph Cropsey, Introduction to Thomas Hobbes, *A Dialogue between a Philosopher and a Student of the Common Laws of England* [Chicago, 1971].) Bacon, like Ellesmere, was a defender of the equity courts on a relatively narrow front of contemporary controversy; it took Hobbes's radical powers to propose that the equity system swallow up the common law. Strict respect for the jurisdictional division of labor was a Cokean theme and also a Baconian one—see Bacon's speech upon assuming the chancellorship (*Life and Letters,* ed. Spedding, VI, 182).

14. Calvin's Case, 659 ff., for Ellesmere's opinion. The most important jurisprudential passages are between 669 and 677, but the opinion as a whole must be read alongside Coke's as a whole to catch the full flavor of Ellesmere's concurrence cum dissent. There are many undertones of criticism of Coke, touching petty mannerisms and prejudices as well as matters of the highest importance, beneath a surface on which most of Coke's substantive arguments are repeated.

15. 1 Inst., 97b; 12 Rep., 63, the encounter with the king. Doubt exists as to whether Coke said to the king what he claimed to have said, but he wrote, at any rate, that he had reminded him of his want of "artificial reason"; see Roland G. Usher, "James I and Sir Edward Coke," *English Historical Review* XVIII (1903). These passages, like that quoted from *Calvin* (n. 12 above), do not use artificial reason in one or the other of the senses discriminated in the text below. They combine the two main senses. This may signify their inseparability in Coke's mind; it does not, I think, indicate confusion, properly speaking, for though Coke lets himself slide from one sense to the other, the two stand out as distinct from each other clearly enough. I try to show below that they ought to be thought of simultaneously, as two sides of a single truth, and so Coke implies by eliding them.

16. To speak of the law as a collective and time-tested product understates its claim compared to insisting, with full literal force, on its *prescriptive* title—its historical and presumptive claim to immemorialness, to never having "started," to not being a product of historical change. The prescriptive claim for the common law, in all its abstract and concrete ahistoricalness, is classically discussed in J. G. A. Pocock, *The Ancient Constitution and the Feudal Law* (Cambridge, 1957), Chaps. II and III—with, I think, a bit too little favor toward the "common law mind's" capacity to cope with change and with historical evidence; (see Martha A. Ziskind, "John Selden: Criticism and Affirmation of the Common Law Tradition," *American Journal of Legal History* [Jan. 1975]). There is a sense in which prescriptive title is more title than one needs to claim great advantages as artificial reason for a law elaborated over a long time, and in large measure by the "refining" process (Calvin's Case, 612) of judicial response to specific problems. Advancing his-

torical knowledge, with its presumable faith-shaking powers, may be most liberating for those who are already prepared to believe that the conservation of common error and vested interests originally secured by force is the major product of time and the particularized judicial mode of hanging on to the established by modulating it peripherally.

17. It matters whether that which may not seem reasonable is finally *rational*. There is a convenience in using two different words for the "seeming" and the "being," but it is toying indeed if one evades the question whether rational is the right word for what the law finally is. Its value, or acceptability, or claim on allegiance, does not have to consist in *rationality*. (So in the theological parallel lurking in my language, when, on the foundation of faith, one *understands*, does one see that what one believes "makes sense," or that it does not need to—that its acceptability as "the way things are" is not receivability into *my* categories of conceiving and judging? Is this the difference between rationalist or nomist theologians, such as Hooker, and the voluntarists?) For Coke, I think rational is right. This is a function of the point (below) that he does not reject natural law. Someone who *could* see what is right in human affairs by an ultimate, universal standard *would* see that the historical product English law—with allowance for circumstances and an element of indeterminacy in the ultimate requirements—is justified in judging as it judges. So the lawyer believes, and *that* is what he comes to understand. I am inclined to see the threat of the opposite solution lowering in Sir Matthew Hale's sensibility: the historical human law is not really amenable to being *right*. It's the way things are; they must, after all, be some way; fundamentally, law is a voluntaristic creation. Right is not just something we have no way of being as individuals or momentary collectivities; it is something human institutional contrivances have no theoretical title to. If that sad truth is hard to live with, one had better let mythos supply the place that logos cannot fill. By all means let the people believe that gods and heroes gave the law, that if its source is not intelligible it is at least admirable. My points about Hale depend mainly on his *Considerations touching the Amendment or Alteration of Lawes* (Hargrave Law Tracts, 249) and his *Reflections on Mr. Hobbes his Dialogue* (printed in W. S. Holdsworth, *History of English Law*, Vol. V, Appendix III). I do not pretend that one must see the tendencies in Hale which I ascribe to him; his language is guarded; one cannot point to particular passages and show that a radical meaning is unmistakably there. But from the preoccupations and contextures of these tracts, as well as his *History of the Common Law*, one can, I believe, project drastic ideas from a cautious and moderate surface.

18. Perhaps. Distrust of reason in comparison with tradition—and that with some consciousness *of* reason (because many heads, much time, and the process of facing particular problems go into making tradition)—is certainly accessible as a popular attitude. My suspicion would be that Coke was rather inclined to identify the legal "priesthood" —and his own kind of passionate intimacy with the law—with real and

reliable capacity for the *credere* and hence the *intellegere;* see below —
Coke on "populist" consciousness of fundamental societal choices. In
Hale, by contrast, one can see awareness of the possibilities of alliance
between the lawyer's antirationalism and the man in the street's; see
works cited in note 17 above. The common law's strength in the face of
a revolution and much expressly rationalistic attack may have assisted
that awareness, for popular conservatism certainly contributed to its
strength. There is no better example (from, of course, the ranks of
exceptional laymen) than Commissary General Ireton's counterattack
on "naked reason" in the Putney Debates.

19. An important feature of Ellesmere's defense of natural reason in
Calvin is his leaning over backward to clear his point of populist implications. He is at pains to say that holding a legal problem properly
soluble by mere reason does not imply that anyone adult and sane could
solve it, or would produce the same solution as an intelligent and educated person (Calvin's Case, 686). Hobbes made the same point — Dialogue (n. 13 above), 99-100 — by suggesting, tongue in cheek, that bishops would make the best judges. Holding, infinitely more radically than
Ellesmere, that all civil cases not governed by statute should be decided
by "mere reason," Hobbes too thought it important to emphasize that
intelligence and training, especially aptitude for moral thinking, were
required for good performance. It is hard to say how much Ellesmere
would concede to one *kind* of intelligence and training over others. He
was a common lawyer, not a bishop or a moral philosopher. In *Calvin,*
he develops a theory of relevant sources for deciding new cases *before*
one is driven back to reason alone. The king should have a role; attention should be paid to extrajudicial opinions of the judges; expressions
of opinion in Parliament, short of legislation, could count; historically,
the Chancery clerks had had a role in developing law for new situations;
comparative law is relevant when English gives out (Calvin's Case,
mainly 664-672). In short, Ellesmere was in no hurry to "recur to reason" in all its nakedness. Part of recurring to reason should consist in
consultation among those who have a particular expertise in governmental and legal affairs. What it does *not* have to be is an exclusive
operation of the judges sitting judicially and owing no duty to take
account of what anyone else thinks. While he escapes populism without
asserting any special virtue in lawyers, he may concede about all that
common sense demands.

20. Hale (works cited) developed this argument for lawyers especially
strongly — very much in the context of asserting that the reason of lawyers is distinctive, as the best reason for particular purposes is always the
trained reason of a special craft or profession. The interesting question
about Hale is whether he was willing to push the claims of lawyers
beyond the common sense arguments: "hidden costs"; a certain attunement of the legal mind to popular prejudice and popular good sense;
the practical man's immunity against the perfectionism of Hobbesian
"bishops," his gift for brushing under the rug questions that are not

likely to arise in practice. Perhaps he was, up to a point, but I think this residual difference exists: Coke was his own kind of perfectionist, a believer in the power of the law and the lawyer, as decision-maker, to be right, while Hale was inclined to be content with the lawyer's capacity to avoid being terribly wrong. For Hale, all law, even the common law, was imperfect; it was desirable that it not be made worse in the hope of making it better, and fortunate that popular prejudice gave it a little more credit than it deserved; it would, however be less fortunate if lawyers participated too completely in the same prejudice and therefore resisted all change; part of their special calling was to keep change responsible. (For the last point, see especially *Amendment*, Chap. III — against a too passionate attachment to the common law, perhaps one can say an anti-Cokean passage at heart.)

21. Hale (especially in *Reflections*) may be accused of weighting the case for the lawyer by making his competitor the moral philosopher (whom he visualizes as a follower of one of the ancient schools, an eternal disputant about the nature of the Good, with little notion of how to go about containing the Bad in this life) — not an obviously unfair move when the object of his critique was Hobbes.

22. "Without reason": it would be hard to imagine one supreme and comprehensive lawmaker designing a system with these discrepant features. He would find it hard to "say why," to give a reason for doing *a* this way and *b* that way, to convince you that he was "considerate," that he *meant* to make such clashing judgments, so clashing for *one* person to make in different contexts. There is of course no *logical* incompatibility between the discordant features. Compare the Hookerian "rationalist" conception that even God's work is in a sense law governed. It is heresy as well as error to suppose that there is some standard prior to God, constraining Him insofar as He wills to avoid lawlessness. He does, however — authority tells us — proceed from counsel or judgment. Things do not "just happen to be" as they are, one by one, because God wills it so. From down within the cosmos looking up, we find it impossible to doubt that God could say why, though we shall never know what He would say, never enter *into* His counsels. Such is the experience of living within what seems to be a discoverable cosmos, a concatenated order. (Richard Hooker, *Laws of Ecclesiastical Polity*, Bk. I, especially Sect. II.)

23. I am conscious of having advanced my most important point about Coke's meaning without offering evidence. (Artificial reason is in one dimension conceived as a kind of imagination and is legitimated and cleared of objections by being seen as the tool for discovering supralegal societal commitments in the most reliable depository.) Space forbids me to undertake what I regard as the most satisfactory demonstration from Coke's literary works, which is to take his list of the "fountains or places" which are the source of "proofes and arguments" in the law (1 Inst., 11a-b) and the citations given to illustrate them and show by what various and subtle routes he thought legal reasoning could and should

journey to its conclusions. However, for a sample of that reasoning, based on just a couple of entries on the lengthy list of "fountains," see Appendix below. Such analysis seems to me to show how much of an exercise of imagination — how informed by a kind of aesthetic and the "long reach" for significant relationships, how far from the simple paradigm of legal ratiocination — the exercise of reason can be conceived to be. I think it can also be shown that what imagination leads to is typically something like national moral character. Unfortunately, working this out takes a lot of words and has to traverse technical grounds — the kind of ground that Coke was almost always on. What follows is a more extraneous attempt to make my hypothesis colorable: Coke *was* stubbornly opposed to letting naked reason intrude where artificial reason was the proper tool. His artificial reason as I have interpreted it can be seen as an unarticulated answer to a rather persistent problem of English jurisprudence, which typically combines natural law premises with great respect for native law and has trouble linking the two. For a couple of simpler demonstrations of artificial reason at work: Coke's argument, in connection with the Petition of Right, that the "reason of the law" gathered from quite diverse and remote sources supported the proposition that the king may not imprison without showing cause (3 State Trials, 126 ff.); his insistence that the legislated antienclosure laws made a coherent pattern with the common law of waste (1 Inst., 53b, 85b); 4 Inst., 37-38 — condemning a man by bill of attainder without a hearing is *valid,* but it is legitimate and advantageous to say it is against English law (as it were, a matter of repealing Magna Carta), as opposed to saying, though truly, that it is simply wrong or against divine law; 1 Inst. 91b — England's character as a commercial and maritime country is revealed in even so trivial a detail of law as that an exotic product may be reserved as rent; 1 Inst., 190a — one does not really need a special theory about the king to reach the rule that there cannot be a joint tenant of Crown property with the king, because that rule is necessary to preserve coherence with the rule that a spiritual corporation and a layman cannot be joint tenants.

24. There is no stronger demonstration of Coke's allegiance to the natural law tradition than in *Calvin,* where, ironically enough, he makes an explicit reinforcing argument from natural law (in effect reduplicated by Ellesmere). Briefly, personal allegiance to a king under natural law is temporally and logically prior to positive law, ergo being born into personal allegiance, rather than into a civil state, determines "nationality" — a political theory much closer to Filmer than to Locke, *quod nota* (Calvin's Case, 629 ff., 692-693). In another passage in *Calvin,* Coke argues for the express proposition that the law of nature is part of the common law — a somewhat problematic passage, because the sense of the law of nature implied in the evidence for the proposition is closer to the necessities of physical nature, including "family feeling," than to the natural moral law in general (Calvin's Case, 630-631). Other passages testifying to acceptance of natural law: 1 Inst., 11b — *lex natu-*

rae is one of the "diverse laws within the realme of England"; 116b; 373a—the effect of a collateral warranty to bar an entail depends on the common law's incorporation of natural standards, here deference to nature in the sense of "family feeling"; 30a—a common law rule given the interpretation that accords with natural reason; 235b—the importance of lawyers' being trained in academic logic, with the apparent implication that logic without positive legal knowledge can lead to "probable" construction of what the law is. Passages testifying to Coke's belief in the correspondence of English law with Biblical law, foreign law, and the principles of other "arts": 1 Inst. 9a, 49a, 80a-b, 116b, 168a, 317b, 339a; 3 Inst., 25, 63, 90, 181.

25. My phrase "reaching beyond the law . . . turns out to mean looking more deeply within it" suggests a modern jurisprudence that, in fact, acknowledges Coke and seventeenth-century legal thought generally as a source: Lon L. Fuller, *The Morality of the Law* (New Haven, 1964). Formally, Professor Fuller's position qua interpretation of Coke corresponds to mine: substantive natural law is avoided, but the internal morality of the law—which may be thought of as something beyond mere law yet discoverable by "looking more deeply within it"—operates as a control on what can be accepted as law. Professor Fuller's "internal morality" is rather the properties that all law must aspire to in order to count as law than the commitments of a particular community deposited in its law. I think that Professor Fuller may disengage seventeenth-century "fundamental law" too much from its insularity—its claim to tell us who we are, rather than law what it is. However, the effect may not be so different. What we discover about ourselves is partly that we have *these* moral commitments, but also that we have *moral* commitments—not just rules, but ideas the rules express, and those profoundly engraved in our identities. When the tests come which, in Professor Fuller's view, legal positivism must fail—when the question is how awful law can be and still remain law—the incoherence of calling *that* law and still pretending to be yourself may be almost as much of a stumbling block as the more abstract incoherence of finding yourself with a shattered conception of law as such. One of Professor Fuller's standards for identifying law is consistency. The legal imagination I attribute to Coke is a way of pushing consistency hard, or worrying about whether the law in one article is consistent with the law in another. Why can it not be pushed into conflict with the "rules of recognition" which positivism tends to treat as *the* way of identifying law, and as permitting *any* substantive content to pass? How is it that we are more committed to those rules (essentially the constitutional underpinnings of the legal system) than to others? (Hale may be close to saying they are more fundamental, therein departing from Coke. C. Gray, Introduction to Hale, pp. xxvi-xxix.)

26. The points in the preceding sentences are too complex to document intelligibly without a separate essay. In general, I consider Sir John Fortescue, especially in the *De Laudibus Legum Angliae,* and

Christopher St. German in *Doctor and Student* the most important jurisprudential predecessors of Coke in something like an immediate tradition. He knew both works well, and Fortescue was one of his chief heroes. Fortescue manifestly, and St. German on correct analysis, I believe, were great "patriots" of English law, in Coke's spirit. Both make much clearer obeisance to natural law than Coke does. Both, I think, were troubled by the problem of fitting human law into a natural law universe. Hooker is a more surprising case, since his reputation is very much as a natural lawyer and since he was not a common lawyer, but I believe that in some ways — as the superior thinker — he was more acutely aware of the tendency of human law to preempt the place of natural law in the real life of particular countries, and perhaps more aware of his inability to account for just how this would happen (*Ecclesiastical Polity*, Bk. I, Sect. X). For the persistence of the problem, see Introduction, section 2, of Blackstone's *Commentaries*. Blackstone was a true enough heir of the Cokean tradition and the natural law tradition as well, and he fails where many fail — on the "fit" of natural and human law. The not-very-successful efforts of these authors to describe the fit are reflected in the text — solutions of a sort.

27. Hobbes, *Dialogue*, 55. Though that is very much Hobbes's analysis of the motive of Cokean jurisprudence, his own theory does not, in my opinion, resemble a Benthamite one: save the legislative function for the legislature by extensively codifying the law; let the inevitable choices be made by "appointing a sovereign and letting him choose." Rather, with some exceptions (crucially, criminal law), Hobbes thought the way to keep the judges judicial was to liberate them to be natural law judges. "Detaching the law from ancestral choices" was what Hobbes least feared; in a manner, he was the one seventeenth-century advocate of a strong and progressive judiciary, boldly remodeling the law as needs and values changed.

28. For this theme, C. Gray, Introduction to Hale, pp. xxiii-xxv.

29. I take this example from one of the "fountains" in 1 Inst., 11a-b (n. 23 above) — the argument *ab utile*. The "rest of the reason" lies in the law's limitations on the kind of conveyancing language which it will treat as intelligibly expressing an intention (a kind of "artificialization" of language). That ultimately has to do with a very important English commitment, more important than mere free alienability, though on its side in the long run: keeping the interests in real property simple — not an entirely successful project historically, but that, as Coke thought, was just the trouble. For further discussion of these points, see Appendix.

30. Cf. the conflicting opinion on the reasonableness standard for local custom in C. K. Allen, *Law in the Making* (Oxford, 1927), Chap. II. "Not the sole criterion": the other main one was the "fundamental" common law. By definition customs differ from the common law, but some decisions holding customs unreasonable may be interpreted as expressing the qualification "yet not too much." In my opinion, such decisions are also quite often explicable by a kind of contrast thinking:

customs by which someone is better off in one aspect than he would be at common law are unreasonable if there is no trade off, no conceivable gain, to whoever, in a reciprocal position, is worse off. I think I would take that as a "natural" standard for the claim of private arrangements — contractual or local-customary — to the force of law. Coke (1 Inst. 110b) speaks of custom as one "triangle" of the law, together with the common law and statutes. That is conventional enough, but the picture of an equilateral triangle it evokes may serve as a warning against over-identifying the judicially elaborated law with custom. In the same passage, Coke says that an unreasonable custom would be better called a "usurpation" than a custom. That can be taken as reticence to speak of an "unreasonable custom," as if it were a contradiction in terms to say that a product of prescription is unreasonable. However, I think the word *usurpation* may point to what I call the contractual theory of custom: a one-sided arrangement has managed to last, someone with undue "bargaining power" has usurped an advantageous position and held onto it. Law under constant judicial scrutiny cannot conceivably have that fault. Coke's judicial decisions on the reasonableness of customs would make a worthwhile study.

31. The exception to this "virtual immunity" which is implied in the existence of equity should be noted. Coke was pretty quiet about the place of equity in the English system. He does recognize its legitimacy, however (4 Inst., 79), and he was not as a judge unfailingly restrictive toward courts of equity (for this I rely on my own unpublished work on prohibitions — n. 36 below). What he was notoriously *not* quiet about was one much-controverted issue: may a court of equity enjoin execution of a common law judgment (as opposed to enjoining the party with equities against him from pursuing a judgment)? Coke not only said no but also, in what was perhaps his most overextended position in legal politics, maintained that to seek an injunction after judgment is criminal under the Praemunire acts. There are good practical reasons for the substance of that position, but further symbolic reasons seem to me to fit exactly with what I say in the text: the common law qua judicial product must not be called in question by a higher-law standard; the presumption that it cannot be is sacrosanct. It is another matter, to this way of thinking — a perverse one in the eyes, above all, of Lord Ellesmere — merely to enjoin a party from taking inequitable advantage of his legal rights, before the judiciary has actually said in his case that they are his rights.

32. C. Gray, "Bonham's Case" (n. 3 above) for the basis of the essential position expressed here. Other literature is cited there.

33. The closest I can find Coke coming to a statement that a statute of a certain sort would be absolutely invalid (for Bonham's Case furnishes only a most oblique suggestion to that effect) is 1 Inst., 129a; naturalization (ordinarily by private bill, quod nota) may not be for life, in tail, or on condition — contra for denization. But does this point really transcend the assumptions about language and its imperfections that

explain most old-fashioned instances of freedom in dealing with statutes? I.e., a statute that *says* "We naturalize you in tail" will be disregarded on the ground that one who makes that statement cannot know
what "naturalize" means. But what about a statute that spells out the
privileges of a natural subject and confers them in tail? The answer
might be that there is nothing wrong with such a statute, except that the
privileges cannot be spelled out exhaustively, wherefore the statute will
at some margin fail of its intention.

34. E.g., 3 Inst., 6, 14, 204; 4 Inst., 31, 39-41, 42-43. 3 Inst., 76, is a
good example of evading a bad statute by construction. See 4 Inst., 77,
for Coke's estimate of the importance of reform *by* legislation — in this
case, a parliamentary contribution for which he himself deserves much
of the credit.

35. Inst., 157; also, 1 Inst., 141a. See D. E. C. Yale, *"Iudex in Pro-
pria Causa;* An Historical Excursus," *Cambridge Law Journal* XXXIII
(1974).

36. The statements in the above paragraphs are based on my own
extended and as yet unpublished study of Prohibition cases and other
modes of common law control over the extra-common law courts.
Proper documentation would require lengthy explanation of contexts.
The general point to be emphasized is that whether Coke or anyone else
was a "prohibiting judge" is a complex question utterly dependent *on*
context. There are fields of jurisdictional law in which Coke was cen-
trally responsible for breakthroughs to positions unfavorable to the prohibited courts, others where — as in any area of . the law — even the
strongest judge is hemmed in by precedent and other constraints. It is
only to correct unbalanced assumptions about Coke that I emphasize his
occasional conservative role. There are other instances than those mentioned in the text. On the spectrum of issues about the High Commis-
sion, for example, his courts tended to take less restrictive positions than
some precedents would have supported. As one might predict from his
general jurisprudence, Coke was not averse from "narrow grounds"
decisions. His tendency as a reporter and writer to lay down the law
more broadly than the courts had actually done can be misleading as a
symptom of his judicial behavior. As for his prejudices relevant for jurisdictional law, he was an ardent Erastian (see 5 Rep., 1 — Cawdrey's Case
and the accompanying "treatise" on the Royal Supremacy), with a thoroughly anglican respect for the privileges of the church and little use for
Puritans.

On the matters treated specifically in the text: The leading case on
the two-witness rule, which Coke disapproved of and refused to follow,
is *Bagnall* v. *Stokes* — Cro. Eliz., 89; Moore, 907 (but better reported in
manuscript). The arguments on self-incrimination are more complex.
Such extrajudicial formulations of the rules as 12 Rep., 26, work against
my case, but little support in decisions can be found for some of those
laid down there. The well-known case of Burrowes et al. (reported in
print, under various names, at 3 Bulstrode, 49; 1 Rolle, 220, 337, 410;

Cro. Jac., 388; Moore, 840) is a good example of restraint in cracking down on inquisitorial investigations: long delay in releasing prisoners whose claim to escape inquisition was largely based on the most open-and-shut grounds (collateral exposure to common law detriment). For a contrary view of that case and the question generally, see Leonard W. levy, *Origins of the Fifth Amendment* (New York, 1968), especially chap. viii.

37. The alternative vision in brief: The Reformation purged England of a foreign church that *did* have to be kept in its place. Now all courts were essentially parts of one system under the king. Jurisdiction was less than urgently important, and practical considerations should govern the division of labor, rather than rigid rules and elaborate theories. Much more faith and credit were due from one branch of the system to the others than the common law courts were ready to accord to the extra-common law. Since the branches were peers, with the king and Parliament equally above them, all were equally competent to interpret the statutes, and the king had some right to supervise their relations personally. The modernism and practicality of this line could be applied to the benefit of the Admiralty as well as the ecclesiastical courts—let a specialized court for maritime and mercantile business handle a fairly generous share of it. That this view was anathema to Coke should not be allowed to imply too much about his opinions on the actual locus of jurisdictional lines, which depend on different variables in many different situations.

38. For Coke's general acceptance of the complexity of the legal system—the absence of any visible wish on his part that the common law were all in all—it is perhaps enough to cite 4 Inst., passim. Note the (unpaginated) epilogue: "our desired end is that all these high and honorable Tribunals . . . may prosper and flourish in the distribution of justice." Such passages as 1 Inst., 11b ("Divers laws"), reflect no distress at diversity; the common law is fourth on a list of fifteen. Coke may be forgiven for believing that courts that exercised coercive power over people should have a warrant for doing so; a certain charity toward the status quo is reflected in his proposal that a couple of courts with weak warrants be set right by post facto enabling statutes (4 Inst., 98, 246). His insistence that laymen stay out of the territory of the common law *peritus* has its counterpart in a certain reticence about discussing ecclesiastical law—the territory of the civilians, another set of experts (4 Inst., 321).

39. The connections in this paragraph are too much "imagination" to document, but, I would argue, not "fancy." In my general book, *Renaissance and Reformation England* (New York, 1973), pp. 102-113, I give a brief impression of the ways in which I think some of the intellectual figures of the late-Elizabethan generation, including Shakespeare and Coke, have to do with each other. I think there is a lot of pessimism in Shakespeare's history cycle about the recoverability of the past and the redemptiveness of redemptive processes. Coke had his share of contempt for "these costermonger's times" (*Henry IV*, Pt. 2, I, ii)—

swarming with attorneys, excessive litigation (4 Inst., 76; 2 Inst., 249), prolix pleading, and overcomplication of the ancient common law — but his faith in the law's power of recovery was abundant. Edmund in *King Lear* (I, ii) is of course *the* example of natural reason exposed. An excellent passage to put alongside the great speech is Fortescue's demonstration (*De Laudibus,* Chaps. XXXIX-XLI) that "nature's children" are by nature evil — part of his vindication of the common law's hard line on bastardy, which was particularly to its credit because the church itself failed to see so deeply into the nature of nature.

APPENDIX

FURTHER REFLECTIONS ON "ARTIFICIAL REASONS"

One property gained by intense training in English law (besides sharpening of common intellectual faculties and stored-up knowledge of rules, cases, research methods, etc.) is an "aesthetic" feel for the system that operates as a control on stock responses. An initiate possessed of this property will sometimes be disposed to resolve first-impression cases in a different way than an exemplary lay reasoner (whether a better way is perhaps a hard question). Here the ordinary modern use of "art" may be a guide: A lawyer is an "artist," not only in the sense that he has a *techne* or skill, and not only in the sense that he deals primarily with man-made or "artificial" law that cannot be known by deduction from universal truths, but also in the sense that long acquaintance with a certain type of artifact has given him a refined sense of "what fits," of what response is correct on an unexpected occasion. Analogously, I daresay if you asked me to choose among a number of alternative bars of music to follow some I had just heard, I would not make the same choice — within a limited range of subtlety — as a jury of symphony players. I would probably avoid crude errors, such as choosing a snatch of Sousa to continue a Beethoven quartet. But offered several plausible answers, I daresay I would not be able to tell the difference, and in effect would decide by tossing a coin, or else I would pick something too obvious — not necessarily something disastrously cacaphonous, but not what the experts would agree is most truly consonant with what went before.

Let us look at just one of Coke's examples. There was a rule that if A disseises B and dies, and A's heir enters, B may not re-enter on A's heir, but is driven to his writ of entry — i.e., must sue to recover the land, or assume the plaintiff's role in a trial of the title. An exception to this rule held that B does not lose his right of reentry if he makes continual claim — i.e., does enough (whatever exactly counts) to avoid the appearance of acquiescing in the disseisin. A further exception held that B does not lose his right of reentry if he is abroad in the king's service when he is disseised, even though he has not made continual claim. The idea, obviously, is that somebody overseas does not have a fair chance to know that he has been disseised and thus to exercise the option of continual claim. His being abroad, moreover, is not of his own choice, but pursuant to duty. Therefore it cannot be objected that in going abroad he undertakes the risk of being damaged while he is away. In addition, the law ought to show a certain bias in favor of good soldiers off fighting the king's wars. As between two innocent parties — an heir who has entered on his ancestor's apparent property and an old soldier disseised by the other party's ancestor — it is fair enough to tip the balance toward the old soldier.

Now comes the case of someone disseised when he is abroad on his own business. The right answer is that this man is to be treated like the old soldier: he may reenter on the disseisor's heir even though he has not made continual claim. Obviously he is somewhat in the same case as the old soldier and somewhat not. He cannot have made continual claim as easily as someone at home. However, he can be said to have incurred the risk by going abroad voluntarily. He will not suffer a terrible loss if we hold against him. He will only suffer the necessity of bringing suit to recover his own, if it is his own. There is no policy reason, analogous to "veteran's benefit," to favor him.

This is the kind of situation in which I suspect Coke of thinking that the layman is likely to jump the wrong way, not from lack of intelligence or of a clear enough appreciation for the *basic* equities, but from a lack of refined sense for what "feels right" in the whole setting of English law. The layman may be too inclined to "toss a coin" or to see the choice as "tragic" or trivial, a matter of throwing a certain inconvenience onto one or the other of two parties, neither of whom is morally blameworthy. Or the layman may be too inclined to the "gross" solution of favoring the main-line rule: on the whole, the law makes people bring suit when they wait around until their disseisors die. It makes some exceptions, but the best policy is usually not to make exceptions if it can be helped. It can be helped here on *cessante ratione* grounds. Since the special considerations applying to old soldiers don't apply here, it is better not to analogize the cases.

Now, perhaps the lay solution is less than a disaster. If the law went that way it would probably not quarrel with the law of nature or lose its right to hold up its head in foreign company. The solution is not disastrous, just a little inartistic. Why? Well, the "sensitive" approach is to emphasize the way in which the old soldier's case and the foreign traveler's *are* alike—neither can easily make continual claim. But isn't that just an arbitrary choice of which aspect to emphasize?

Here we reach the interesting touches in Coke's analysis. He classifies the sensitive argument in this case as the argument *ab impossibile,* and considers it related to more obvious instances, as where the law does not enforce self-imposed duties impossible of performance: The foreign traveler *can't* make continual claim, so don't hold it against him when he doesn't. Part of the point depends on a relationship with more obvious instances: isn't it a little jarring to hold that people need not perform promises that turn out to be impossible for reasons beyond their control, and at the same time to hit a man who might have helped himself by making continual claim but couldn't? Is it coherent to throw the risk on the foreign traveler in our case and yet not to make prom-isors insurers against acts of God? The spirit of the approach begins to emerge: The "artist" will look beyond the immediate context, to coherence with more remote areas of the legal system. The right answer must harmonize with chords the lay judge will not hear.

Another step increases the subtlety. Coke recognizes that "impossibility" is slippery. Sometimes when we talk about the impossible in law, we refer, not to what is literally impossible, but to what it is unfair to expect, including what it is unfair to expect people to anticipate when they make contracts or go on vacations in Paris. With this in mind, the foreign traveler's side in our case will seem to weaken. It is not literally impossible in every case for a disseisee visiting in France to find out about the disseisin and hurry home in time to make continual claim. People in England may have equally good hardluck stories — as if I am disseised in Yorkshire while lying sick at Brighton — but we don't excuse them on grounds of impossibility. In most cases, if foreign travelers left their affairs at home in reliable hands they would find out about disseisins in reasonable time. The law might stretch a point as to what counts as continual claim; for instance, if a man asks his friends to inform him of disseisins and, being informed, takes steps as quickly as possible, we'll say he has done as much as need be to make continual claim. But why be sorry for someone who has tarried abroad for ten years and wanders home to find his affairs in a mess? Why treat him like old soldiers, who, though they may find out about disseisins, really can't take steps to protect themselves, at least not without unthinkable violation of duty? So the pendulum seems to be swinging back to the "vulgar" solution.

But then the artist thinks of something more remote. It so happens that English law holds it impossible for juries to find events alleged to have taken place abroad. Plainly, this is legal impossibility, not realistic impossibility. Juries proceeding on evidence obviously can make reasonable judgments about whether something happened in France. But by presumption of law they "cannot" — a presumption reflecting the ancient theory of the jury. It would be incoherent for the law to presume that juries are as incapable of determining foreign facts as blind men of seeing, and yet for it to take note of the realistic possibility that visitors to France are not hopelessly incapable of keeping informed about their interests in England and getting home fast when they are in danger. If English law is blind to France in one respect, so — for the sake of artistic coherence — must it be in others. If juries cannot conclude from the testimony of twelve bishops that a contract was made in France, the law must say that for all it knows there are no post offices in France, and all sojourners in that country are stuck in insuperable mud.

Needless to say, one man's art is another man's silliness. I think, however, that the example is of the type of several others in Coke. If one wants to use general everyday language about the example, one might say that a spirit of "generosity" can be picked up from the study of a lot of English legal rules and situations — a tendency not to insist on formalisms, on various kinds of "strictness," on rules that disable from doing what comes naturally, at least when people haven't a sporting chance to avoid them. Such a tendency might reflect the same contingent "national character" that Sir Thomas Smith, for example (in his *De Republica Anglorum*), invoked to account for various features of English law: The English are a rustic, active race, and a "generous" one. (This includes shadows of older senses of generous, not just "liberal"/ "lenient," but "magnanimous," "possessed by a kind of carelessness that is both aristocratical and rural.") Folks that get disseised are inclined to go out and take it back. There are good reasons for restraining them if they wait too long and propose to dispossess someone who personally did them no offence, but strict insistence on that hasn't worked out. Exceptions have been made in a generous spirit, the national character has been yielded to. Yielding to that is not unlike yielding to *pudor*, giving way to notions of decency or becomingness which, as a rude but chaste people, we are sensitive to. (Compare the argument *ab inconvenienti* in Coke: A woman doing homage shall not say "I become your woman." The onlookers would blush, hearing a lady say that to a man not her husband.) Nor are these cases unlike giving way to Nature, as in the examples in Calvin's Case. The law has better taste than to fight Nature. Knowing when Art should make way for Nature is itself Art, perhaps the highest kind.

A somewhat different sort of case is illustrated under Coke's argument ab utile. (Note the heading, but watch that "utile," for the main point may be that while the law respects utilitarian considerations in their place, it avoids the vulgar temptation to focus on them too narrowly.) Take the undisputed rule that I cannot convey Blackacre in fee with a condition of reentry if the feoffee alienates Blackacre. The natural man will tend to suppose that this is simply a rule favoring trade and limiting the dead hand. In truth, it has those purposes even primarily, but they are not *all* it involves. Suppose the case comes along where A conveys Blackacre to B in fee on condition that B not alienate Whiteacre. A lay judge will probably latch onto the social policy behind the first, undisputed rule and hold that the condition in the new case is void. It seems essentially the same sort of thing—an attempt by use of conditions to tie up land and prevent people from trading freely with their own. But the lay judge will be wrong. The prohibition on attaching a condition against alienating Blackacre to a conveyance of Blackacre in fee involves an elusive nonutilitarian idea that does not apply to the Whiteacre case. The idea is hard to express. It is not clearly a moral idea, though it is allied with a certain order of moral ideas (those that try to locate the wrongness of some acts—such as not keeping promises—in an affinity with self-contradictoriness). Roughly, it is "repugnant" (i.e., self-contradictory) to use your freedom to divest yourself of all interest in a tenement and *in the same breath* to try to prevent someone else from doing the same *with respect to the same tenement.* That has an affinity with saying "I give you a fee but I don't" = "I, having an alienable interest, propose to put you in my place, retaining no reversionary interest to myself, yet I do not propose to put you fully in my place, because I do not mean for you to have an alienable estate." Talking that way is represented as a mixture of unintelligible speech and wickedness, though to natural reason it is not especially unintelligible, and if it is wicked it is only because a free-alienation policy is useful, and that as much for Whiteacre as for Blackacre.

I do not suggest that this is defensible thinking, and I daresay that it was sometimes imposed on Coke by the need to save the phenomena. My only suggestion is that he found it convincing. Generalizing, he believed that it is too easy for the layman to suppose that practical or policy reasons explain rules that are actually explicable in part by what I can only call "funny sensibilities"— nearly incommunicable feelings that *are* rather like trained-instinctive canons of suitability in the fine arts. "It just won't do"— which isn't to say for a moment that policy reasons aren't at least 90 percent of why it won't. But the other 10 percent... Perhaps long study, not of law, but of common law real property would instill in any normal person a kind of aesthetic, an aptitude for funny sensibilities—precisely the sense that understanding the practical purposes of the rules and the everyday moral judgments behind them is, by and large, the way to right results, and yet that there is a residue where the only explanation is the poetry of the system. For that residue, the justification for "in tune" decisions is not so much their intrinsic virtue as a presumptive interest in not untuning the system as a whole and starting a process like cosmic decay. Remember that real property was the heart of legal learning in Coke's day, and that it was Littleton's elementary introduction to that subject which he considered "the most perfect and absolute work that was ever written in any humane science."

III
JEWISH MESSIANISM AND CHRISTIAN MILLENARIANISM*

Richard H. Popkin

Jewish prayers and services are replete with hopes and expectations of the coming of the messianic age. Almost every page of the services prays for some of the following: for the coming of the promised Messiah, for the rebuilding of the Temple of Jerusalem and of the Holy Land, for the reestablishment of the Sanhedrin, for the reunion with the Lost Tribes, and for the marvels of the messianic age. The prayers from ancient times (presumably post-biblical and after the Fall of the Temple) are all put in the form of the hope that God will act so that the Messiah will arrive, the Temple be rebuilt, and so on.[1] There is no hint at all that people can accomplish any of these desired ends, or that any human action will help bring about these goals.[2] Not only are people incapable of influencing the messianic course of events in traditional Judaism but also they are not supposed to speculate about when these wonderful things will happen, since it is up to God to decide in His own good time when to transform human history.[3]

Jewish messianism has been one of the strongest forces in main-

*Some of the research for this study has been made possible through the help of NEH Grant No. RO 22932-75-596, and a Fellowship from the Memorial Foundation for Jewish Studies. I should like to thank both organizations for their generous support.

taining the Jewish community in the face of the dismal history of the Jews from Roman times onward. It has provided a hope that temporal misfortunes will be overcome and that all suffering will be rewarded by the messianic promises. To some extent there has been a close relationship between the immediacy of the messianic expectations and the adversities in the world; catastrophes usually bring about serious expectations of relief very soon. The prevailing view of the rabbis has been that one should *not* try to calculate when the Messiah will come, but this has not stopped all sorts of famous Jewish scholars from offering predictive dates.[4]

Jewish messianism[5] has always influenced Christian millenarianism,[6] first in the obvious sense that the Christian expectation is built on the Jewish ones, and is offered in the Revelation as the fulfillment of the Jewish hopes. Second, features of the Jewish expectation are signs for the Christian of the millennium, such as the return of the Jews to Palestine, the rebuilding of Jerusalem, the return of the Lost Tribes. Third, prophecies in Daniel play a role in both the Jewish and Christian expectations. Of course, one critical differences, which will loom large in this paper, is that for the Christian millenarian the conversion of the Jews to Christianity is central,[7] while for the Jews it is their redemption as Jews that is crucial.

Without surveying the background in detail, a little should be said about the situation of messianism and millenarianism in the sixteenth century. From the Jewish side, one of the greatest catastrophes in Jewish history, the expulsion of the Jews from Spain, occurred in 1492. The Spanish Jewish community was the most highly developed, successful community in Europe, and had a glorious cultural past. Its destruction through expulsion, through forced conversion of hundreds of thousands, through Inquisitional persecution, sent shock waves throughout the Jewish world. The day of the expulsion was symbolically the same day on the Jewish calendar as that of the Fall of the First and the Second Temples, and it is still celebrated as a joint fast day for these three coequal disasters. Refugee survivors of the Iberian tragedy (since the expulsion was repeated in worse form in Portugal in 1497) appeared all over the Jewish world and spawned hosts of messianic movements.[8] From the time of the expulsion, various rabbis expected divine intervention to save the day. After the expulsion, movements developed which expected immediate deliverance through messianic activities. The strange appearance of David Reubeni (apparently an Ethiopian Jew) in Italy in the 1520s, proclaiming he was Elijah announcing the messianic age, and his prophet, the court secretary of Portugal, Solomon Molko, preaching the message across Europe, are part of this ferment.[9] The magnificent work of Samuel Usque, *Consolations for the Tribulations of Israel* (155?), is an attempt to place all of Jewish history up to the expulsion in the perspective that all will be rewarded by the coming messianic age.[10] Lastly, the cabalistic theory of Isaac Luria and his disciples made the expulsion a cosmic prelude to the Redemption. It was part of the inner working of God, and the days of salvation were at hand. Thus, from the Jewish side, the overwhelming force of the events in Spain and Portugal had produced fervent expectations of messianic redemption.[11]

Jewish-Christian contact was never nonexistent, and it increased in many parts of Europe during the Renaissance and Reformation. Both the humanistic and theological desire to learn Hebrew and to study the Jewish sources brought about a fair amount of contact between the two religions at a high intellectual level. The Reformation and Counter-Reformation pressed pretty heavily on the theme of converting the Jews (the Jesuits were officially founded to convert Jews and to save fallen women). Hence, there must have been a fair amount of polemical interaction. It was unsafe for Jews to give their views about Christianity, but at least the writings of Queen Marie de Medici's doctor, Elijah Montalto, show that Jewish answers were made to Christian messianic claims that the Messiah, attended by the prophesied events, had already come in the person of Jesus of Nazareth.[12] The writings of the Christian cabalists from Reuchlin and Agrippa van Nettesheim onward show a great Christian desire to learn Jewish secrets, including the secret interpretations of the prophecies. Many Christians developed their predictions of the date of the great events to come from Jewish sources. And when the new cabalist interpretations of Luria and his school were carried from Palestine to Europe, they were quickly incorporated into the basic source material for Christian millennialism. So, by the end of the sixteenth century, a fair amount of interaction was going on.[13] Jewish rabbis were being consulted on biblical matters. Converted Jews were often the Hebrew teachers at European universities. Jewish sources were being used by Christian theologians. As many have pointed out, this concern with Jewish themes, with Old Testament mores, and the like, probably was greater in England than elsewhere in Europe by the early seventeenth century. Some of the dissident Protestant movements became more and more interested in the Jewish roots of Christianity, and people were arrested and condemned for adopting actual Jewish practices.[14] There are indications that Jewish messianic reports, chiefly about the reappearance of the Lost Tribes, found their way into print in England. The most significant publication early in the century was Sir Henry Finch's *The World's Great Restauration, Or The Calling of The Jewes and with Them of All The Nations and Kingdoms of The Earth, to the Faith of Christ,* 1621.[15] The work foresaw the imminent emergence of the Jews as the dominant force in the world as they became Christians. The book is millenarian and conversionist, but it held that Jewish power was about to take over the world. Finch was arrested, since the king saw a seditious threat in his doctrines, and he was forced to recant. There is evidence that a whole school of English (and Dutch) millenarians, like Joseph Mede and his disciples, held a view like Finch's, namely that God would soon restore the Jews to temporal power, make them Christians, and then the Antichrist would be defeated and the millennium would be underway.[16] But how did such a view relate to the actual situation in England or Holland? Holland had a functioning Jewish community, but England officially allowed no Jews as residents, though several hundred, especially Spanish and Portuguese refugees, had moved in. The English theory of the restoration of the Jews seems at first to have been speculative and apart from the local situation. By mid-century, however, as Puritan views developed, the role of Jews in the English millennial picture grew more important. If the Puritan Revolution were ushering in the millennium, then the Jewish role had to be brought about through English events. Some solved this by declaring *themselves* the true Jews and the biological Jews a decayed remnant. The true Jews would fulfill the scenario of the milennium in England by establishing the Sanhedrin as Parliament, and so forth, while the biological Jews could rot in the ghettos of central and eastern Europe.[17] This view, that the saved English were the pure or true Jews in contrast with the decrepit remnant of the biological descendents of ancient Palestine, developed into both a theory and movement, a theory that Britain derived its civilization from King David, and a movement, the British Israelites, based on the belief that the millennium would come about through the fulfillment of the millennial events in Great Britain by the actions of the British people.[18]

There were, however, those who took the Jewish role in bringing about the millennium more literally and saw that it had to happen through genuine Jewish events. A spate of philosemitic tracts appeared, centering on the need to convert the Jews and to restore them to their central role in divine history. This became one of the main reasons offered for readmission of the Jews to England, and for tolerating their subversive anti-Christian views.[19]

In this context the major contact between the English millenarian thinkers and any Jewish messianic leader was with the Dutch rabbi, Menasseh ben Israel. The interaction between Menasseh's views and those of English millenarians will form the main theme of this paper, that these views affected each other, but that a basic misunderstanding was always present. Christian millenarians probably could not take Jewish messianism at face value, since its basic claim that the fulfillment of Jewish messianic expectations was imminent was a denial that the Christian Messiah had come.

Menasseh ben Israel played a bizarre and intriguing role in seventeenth-century thought whether which has not, I believe, been fully understood, since his efforts are either seen in a purely Jewish context, where he was a misfit, or in his effect on English events, where the millenarian and political interpretation of what he was doing became the focus.[20] Menasseh was first and foremost a victim of the Iberian tragedy. He was born in Madeira in 1604 of parents who were forced converts to Christianity. His family fled to La Rochelle in France and then to Holland, where the only free Jewish world in western Europe existed. Menasseh became a teacher in one of the Jewish schools there at the age of eighteen. He was also a printer, and soon became a well-known author and preacher. He wrote in Spanish, Latin, and Hebrew on theological and philosphical subjects. His work is not highly regarded among Jewish authorities, since he did not contribute seriously to the mainstream of Jewish writings in any of the major areas of traditional Jewish interest. The only work that gets reprinted, *The Hope of Israel,* is probably regarded more as a curiosity than a serious theological or religious work. In Christian circles, however, Menasseh soon became well known and was considered *the* Jewish philosopher. He wrote in accessible languages. He was erudite in Jewish and non-Jewish sources. He explained many Jewish views for the general audience. He was steeped in the messianic views of Don Isaac Abarbanel, and of Luria and his disciples, and made them known to the world of letters. By the 1640s Menasseh was in contact with many of the leading intellectuals throughout Europe—Grotius, Mersenne, Bochart, Vossius, various English millenarians, and many others. Menasseh was probably unique in the European world as a Jew who was considered a leading figure in the republic of letters.[21]

In his writings Menasseh was developing a general messianic view, seeing the tragedy of Iberian Jewry, subjected to forced conversion or driven into exile, as the prelude to the messianic Redemption. The Marranos were like the Lost Tribes who would be brought back at the turning point in history. The imminence of the messianic events was probably reinforced for Menasseh by the next great Jewish catastrophe, the vast pogroms in eastern Europe in 1648-1649.[22] Many Jewish cabalistic calculators had predicted the messianic age would begin in 1648. Instead, the worst catastrophe of death and destruction prior to Hitler took place across eastern Europe. (A graphic picture of what happened appears in I. B. Singer's *The Slave*).[23] Eastern European Jewry was in terrible disarray.

Just at this point of utter dismay at the plight of the Jews, Menasseh received news that made it seem possible that hope was at hand. A Portuguese explorer, Antonio de Montezinos, had come to Amsterdam from South America and reported to Menasseh that he had stumbled on to a tribe of Indians in the Andes Mountains who were practicing Judaism. Menasseh had Montezinos repeat his account before a notary and then began informing his friends of this wonderful news.[24] As we shall see, Menasseh held a minimal interpretation of Montezinos's discovery, namely that a part of a Lost Tribe had been discovered. Before he had worked out the theological implications of this news from America, English millenarians were making a gigantic case out of the story. The best-known work is Thomas Thorowgood, *Jewes in America, or Probabilities that the Americans are of that Race.*

Thorowgood based his claim on two letters that his friend, John Dury, received from Menasseh telling Dury of Montezinos's discoveries. Thorowgood argued that the Jews are dispersed everywhere and so must be in America. And all of this showed that "The Jewes before the end of the world shall be converted to Christianity; this truth is to be found in the Old and New Testament, and hath bin the constant beliefe of the faithfull in every age."[25] So the millenarian conversionist interpretation was immediately offered. A dispute ensued in England over whether the Indians were Jews.[26] Soon Menasseh offered his version in his best-known book, *The Hope of Israel* (1650). This work was written in Latin and published in Spanish, Latin, Hebrew, and English, and hence was intended for a Jewish and non-Jewish audience.[27] It became the most important text for the Jewish Indian theory, and out of all the literature on the subject is still the work most frequently cited. However, the work is much more than a recital of evidence that the Indians are Jews. It is a strongly messianic tract living up to its title, *The Hope of Israel*. It begins with a dedication to the revolutionary government in England, whose appearance on the scene Menasseh saw as a portent of the messianic world. There is a gentle suggestion that this new government, divinely ordained, wants to help the Jews.[28] Menasseh was not quite ready to press his point about England's role in bringing about the messianic age, namely readmitting the Jews. Instead, he recounted how the discovery of Jewish Indians, of other possible Lost Tribes, of Jewish survival from disasters, of Jewish total dispersion, of the suffering of the enemies of the Jews like the kings of Spain and Portugal, all presaged the coming of the promised Messiah of the House of David. The book is a mixture of explorer literature, Jewish history, anthropological speculation about human dispersions, and prophetic interpretation of human history. Although Menasseh does not claim to know when the Messiah will come, he indicated it was pretty soon, referring to it as "The shortnesse of time (when we believe our redemption shall appear)."[29] Throughout the work (which is only ninety pages in length) Menasseh indicated that he was working on a continuation of Josephus's *History of the Jews,* which would show the progress of prophetic history toward its imminent culmination.

Menasseh's *Hope of Israel* was an immediate success in England, being published in 1650, in 1651, and in 1652 was translated by the millenarian, Moses Wall. Although the book is a straightforward presentation of world events seen through the eyes of a thoroughgoing Jewish messianist indicating all the signs that Jewish messianic expectations are about to be fulfilled, Wall appended to the work, "Considerations upon the point of the Conversion of the Jews."[30] Wall believed that the conversion would come by 1655 with the gathering of the Tribes from the four corners of the world and their restoration in Palestine.[31] In the 1652 edition, he printed a letter from a certain E. S. attacking Menasseh's book as Jewish nonsense and propaganda. Wall defended himself first by saying that he thought one should see how the present day Jewish heart and mind operates, and then stressing that what he, Wall, was trying to accomplish was to convert the Jews. Another letter, presumably from the same critic, then appeared, applauding the hopes of the conversion and recall of the Jewish nation but doubting that Menasseh ben Israel would ever be converted.[32] As we shall see, each step Menassah took toward helping to bring about the Jewish messianic expectations was seized upon by the millenarians as evidence that the prophecies were about to be fulfilled, that the Jews would be converted, and that the millennium was about to begin.[33]

Menasseh's work played a part in the rising discussion about readmitting the Jews into England. He was officially contacted by English leaders,[34] and was written to by millenarians.[35] The question of Jewish readmission has been treated in terms of its political and economic consequences. Here, I just want to deal with the eschatological aspects. From the millenarians' side, the issue of Jewish conversion was central. For them, or some of them, the possibility of bringing about the conversion required the presence of Jews. And if the English saints were the true Christians, they were the ones best suited to bring about this marvel. So some millenarians were pressing for readmission for the purpose of conversion. A second point that seems to have arisen out of Menessah's correspondence with millenarians is that the end of the world cannot come about until the *total* dispersion of the Jews takes place. The discovery of Jews in America shows that it is almost total; but the legal absence of Jews in England is holding up the complete dispersion. Menasseh wrote Cromwell that "the opinion of many Christians and mine concurre herein, that we both believe that the restoring time of our Nation into their Native Countrey, is very near at hand."[36] This restoration requires the fulfillment of the prophecy in Daniel 12:7 of complete dispersion. The only place Jews are missing is "this considerable and mighty Island [England]. And therefore this remains only in my judgment, before the MESSIA come and restore our Nation, that first we must have our seat here likewise."[37] So Menasseh clearly stated his Messianic interpretation of what was at issue. The stages of the negotiations have been studied by British and Jewish historians, but the theological background has been mostly overlooked. In the period 1653-1655 when Menasseh was waiting to go to England, he became quite involved with English millenarians like Henry Jessey and Nathaniel Holmes.[38] They fed each other's hopes, though the English were, of course, conversionists. In 1654, Menasseh went to see Queen Christina of Sweden, right after her abdication. He probably met the French millenarian-messianist, Isaac LaPeyrère there, or at least read his book *Du Rappel des Juifs,* which talked of the imminent coming of the Jewish Messiah, of the Jews becoming Christians, and of a millennium run by Jewish Christians (Marranos).[39] On returning to Amsterdam, Menasseh met the strange Czech millenarian, Paul Felgenhauer, who was so excited by Menasseh's view of the imminent coming of the Jewish Messiah that he pressed him for an exact date. Felgenhauer wrote a work right away, *Bonum Nunciam Israeli quod offertur Populo Israel & Judae in hisce temporibus novissimus de Messiah* (1655). This good news for the Jews is dedicated "Ad Virum Clarissimum, Philosophum atque Theologum Hebraeum Manasse Ben Israel." Felgenhauer reveled in the great news that the Messiah was coming but also saw this as the basis for the conversion of the Jews.[40] The book contains Menasseh's answer, dated 1 February 1655, giving no signs of the coming of the Messiah and citing five people who also know He is coming, Abraham à Frankenberg, Johann Mochinger, the author of *Du Rappel des Juifs,* and Nathaniel Holmes, and Henry Jessey.[41] The rest of the book is a compendium of letters by millenarians about how wise and profound Menasseh is. (Cecil Roth, in his biography, is sheepish about the fact that Menasseh liked Felgenhauer's book, since it is conversionist.)[42] All this indicates that prior to leaving for England, Menasseh was becoming a more and more central figure in a world of millenarians, that he saw his mission in messianic terms, and that he was not uncomfortable operating in a Jewish-Christian world.

There are a series of stories in the millenarian literature, whether true or false, that reflect the theological significance of Menasseh's trip to England. These stories suggest that Cromwell was the Messiah and that Menasseh should look into this. They also report that a delegation of rabbis from all over the world went with him, making the significance of the trip part of a world Jewish conspiracy. As soon as Menasseh and the delegation arrived in London, the stories continue, they rushed off to search the birth records to see if Cromwell had Jewish ancestors and could be from the House of David.[43]

At any rate, Menasseh went to England in September 1655. (He was away from Amsterdam when his star student, Baruch de Spinoza was expelled from the community.) He spent a fair amount of time with Cromwell. The question of Jewish readmission became central for a while with tremendous pressure mounted by both positive and negative sides, each publishing a host of pamphlets. One of the leading opponents of Jewish readmission, William Prynne, gave as one of his reasons for opposing the move that it might have the opposite effect of that expected by millenarians like Henry Jessey and Nathaniel Holmes. Prynne said that "in this giddy, unsettled, apostatizing age . . . they (the Jews) are likelier to gain a thousand *English Proselytes to their Judaisme,* than we one Jewish convert to Christianity."[44] So Prynne suggested that God could convert the Jews in countries other than England if He wanted to start the millennium.[45] As Menasseh waited for a decision, he became personally acquainted with a large number of English millenarian theologians, some of whom like Margaret Fell tried to convert him.[46] The issue of Jewish readmittance became both a tedious legal one (as to what the act of 1290 really entailed) and a theological one. Menasseh wrote an interesting work in answer to the theological controversies, replying to some of the antisemitic material being published. In his *Vindiciae Judaeorum* (1656) he took up the points raised by the opponents one by one. Cecil Roth states, "There is no more of the somewhat inflated messianic speculation of the *Hope of Israel* or the *Humble Address* — Menasseh had learned his lesson."[47] This is not quite true, and the messianic discussion in the work may be quite revealing. Roth and others make it look as if the messianic appeal was to catch the eye of the millenarians and lead them to bring about Jewish readmission on their false hopes of bringing about Jewish conversion. It seems to me that Menasseh was a dedicated messianist. His messianism turned out to be one step away from the Christian millenarian position, which probably accounts for why he was so popular with them. If everything in Menasseh's scenario occurred, *plus* the conversion of the Jews, then the Christian millennium would be here. Menasseh doesn't argue against conversion, but rather ignores it, and stresses prophecies about what is to happen to Jews as Jews. In the *Vindiciae Judaeorum,* after defending the Jews against the charge of idolatry, Menasseh offers a strange view of La Peyrère's as a way of settling the competing messianic claims of Judaism and Christianity. "For, as a most learned Christian of our time hath written, in a French book, which he calleth the *Rappel* of the *Iewes* (in which he makes the King of *France* to be their leader, when they shall return to their country) the *Iewes,* saith he, shall be saved, for yet we expect a second coming of the same *Messias;* and the *Iewes* believe that that coming is the *first,* and not the second, and by that faith they shall be saved; for the difference consists onely in the circumstance of the time."[48] If Menasseh really subscribed to LaPeyrère's two messiah theory and the further claim that it didn't matter whether you believed in the first coming or the second, then millenarianism and messianism became almost the same view, except that the Jews did not have to be converted. This may be a peace treaty he was offering his Christian friends. Sokolow has tried to portray Menasseh as the father of Zionism because of his strong attachment to Jewish messianism and all that it entails.[49] but a good deal of Menasseh's advocacy of this went on in the Christian intellectual world, where Menasseh's evidence was constantly being scooped up to provide ammunition for the millenarians. He doesn't seem to have been shocked or resentful. If he held a view like LaPeyrère's, the differences between Christianity and Judaism weren't very significant, if Jews could fulfill their divine mission as *Jews.*

   Menasseh's attempt to force the next stage in the messianic program failed. The Jews weren't legally admitted to England until the nineteenth century, though Jews were there when he was and thereafter. (So in a nonlegal sense the Dispersion was complete.) Menasseh's son died in England, and he left brokenhearted and died himself on his return to Holland. With his passing, the direct personal link between a Jewish scholar and the English millenarian thinkers broke down. Menasseh had no real successor, an ardent Jewish messianist anxious to communicate with hopeful Christian millenarians.

This didn't stop the millenarians from reading signs in every-thing they heard of in the Jewish world, or from reading signs of the impending coming of the millennium. I will only deal with two of these which play a role in millenarian history.

As mentioned earlier, in spite of great Jewish expectations that 1648 would usher in the messianic age, a frightful, devastating pogrom occurred instead. In the aftermath of the pogrom, the Jewish community had to rebuild. A council was held in late 1650 to deal with the consequences in terms of broken marriages, ille-gitimate children born, and so forth.[50] An English millenarian apparently heard of the council a few years later, and gave it a wildly different significance. In 1655 Samual Brett or Breet pub-lished *A True Relation of The Proceedings of The Great Council of the Jews assembled in the Plains of Adjady in Hungaria . . . to examine the Scriptures concerning Christ, October 12, 1650.* This work was republished with various pamphlets about the Jews several times into the eighteenth century. The account it gives is printed in various histories of the Jews into the nineteenth cen-tury, when the unlikely character of the meeting seems to have become clear.

The author claimed to have been present and says that three hundred rabbis were there. After the catastrophe of the great pogrom, the rabbis were gathered to discuss whether or not the Messiah had actually come. As a council of Jews from all parts of the world they could presumably make a binding decision for the Jewish world. The place has interesting symbolic suggestiveness, namely right on the border between the Turkish and the Chris-tian world. Brett's account comes with speeches by various rabbis. Presumably with all hopes dashed, the rabbis could now seriously consider that they were on the wrong track in refusing to be Christians. The dismal picture of Jewish history, the endless suf-fering, made it evident that Judaism is wrong. After six days of discussion, a rabbi Abraham is said to have raised the point that maybe Jesus of Nazareth was the Messiah. Rabbi Abraham was making some progress in beating down the usual Jewish argu-ments against Jesus' messianic role, when it was decided to con-sult some priests. The priests, not content with just reinforcing rabbi Abraham's reasoning, tried to sell the assemblage on all of Catholic doctrine and practice. The rabbis all rebelled, and dropped the subject, and were going to meet again in three years.[51]

Now there is no evidence whatsoever that any such council ever met. Brett seems to have heard of the actual council that met in Poland to decide the host of legal problems raised by the pogrom. He interpreted it to be something more monumental from a millenarian point of view, a worldwide meeting of Jewish leaders to consider conversion. The evidence for conversion now was supposedly sufficiently overwhelming that the Jews would have converted were it not for the blundering of the Catholic priests. Presumably, English Protestants would have succeeded.

The reissuing of the story of the council suggests a millenarian dream that if the Jews just sat down and looked at their situation they would convert. Basnage's *History of the Jews* is written from that perspective. The fact that the council story could be taken seriously as an actual event for almost 200 years shows that the conversionist hopes were extremely great. Milman says that Menasseh ben Israel shot down the council story when it first appeared.[52] I haven't found such a text, but he obviously didn't prevent it from becoming part of the millenarian lore, indicating that the Jews were on the verge of throwing in the sponge.

The English millenarians continued in the second half of the seventeenth century to pour out works on the need to convert the Jews and the need to bring about the Restoration of Israel. For the last part of the story in this paper, the climax came when word began to filter across Europe that the Jews now believed *their* Messiah had come. In 1666, a year many Christian millenarians had forecast as the beginning of the millennium, reports came out of Turkey that the Messiah of the Jews had appeared. This was coupled with other reports of the emergence of the Lost Tribes and other expected miracles that would accompany the messianic age.

The Jewish messianic movement of Sabbatai Sevi is the most important such movement in *Jewish* history. Its effects are still being felt. In the seventeenth-century context of expectation, what could English millenarians make of the news? Before going into this, a little background may help. The movement out of which Sabbatai Sevi emerged was, as Gershom Scholem has shown, a cabalistic one infused by the cosmic significance of both the tragedy of the Spanish Jews and the catastrophe of 1648. God had withdrawn Himself in preparation for the Redemption. In this atmosphere of exultant hope and utter despair, a young man from Smyrna appeared who impressed some by his actions and interpretations of prophecies and texts. He married a survivor of the 1648 pogrom, who it was said was saved to be the bride of the Messiah. Disciples gathered and insisted Sabbatai Sevi was the Messiah, and finally he proclaimed the messianic age in 1666.[53] There is a constant story, vehemently denied by Scholem, that Sabbatai Sevi derived some of his claim from English millenarian sources. Some of the literature says that Sabbatai Sevi's father worked for some English millenarians, and through them the importance of 1666 as the right year got to the new Messiah.[54] Scholem insists the movement is entirely derived from Jewish sources.[55] Whether it was or not, its impact was swift and immediate on Jewish and Christian millenarian groups. Scholem has shown that the Jewish world overwhelmingly accepted Sabbatai Sevi, not just in Turkey and Persia, but in eastern Europe, in Italy, in Amsterdam, and in England.[56] Much research has been done on the effects of the Sabbatian movement on the various Jewish communities (and much remains to be done, especially on the lingering effects in the eighteenth and nineteenth centuries). The effect on the Christian world has only been touched here and there.

Of course, for the Christian world the purported emergence of the Jewish Messiah poses some monumental problems. If true, what does this do to Christianity? Does it show it to be false? Or is there some relation between the basic Christian claim that Jesus of Nazareth, the Messiah, has already come, and the appearance of a purely Jewish Messiah? The basic account of the whole affair of Sabbatai Sevi that became known in England is by the English consul at Smyrna, Paul Rycaut, in his *History of the Turkish Empire*. Rycaut describes the section on 1666 by starting with the Christian expectations of the time. Sixteen sixty-six was to be a year of wonders, strange revolutions, and particularly of blessings to the Jews. They would either be converted to Christianity or restored to their temporal kingdom. Rycaut pointed out that many Reformers and Enthusiasts believed this, and reported many signs that it was true, ships arriving in Scotland whose sailors spoke only Hebrew, the reappearance of the Twelve Tribes, and others.[57]

If these were the Christian millenarian expectations, namely that something monumental was supposed to happen in the Jewish world in 1666, and Sabbatai Sevi announced in the said year that he was the Messiah, what was one to make of it? Scholem has shown traces of news about Sabbatai Sevi reaching the tiny English Jewish community and creating excitement not only among them but among millenarians. Signs of interest appear in Pepys's diary, and even in a work written in Boston by Increase Mather.[58] The clearest sign of concern appears in some material Scholem did not use, the correspondence of Henry Oldenburg.[59] Oldenburg, a German who settled in England, was secretary of the Royal Society of England. He had been interested in Jewish affairs for a long time and had known Menasseh ben Israel. When news about Sabbatai Sevi reached England, Oldenburg tried to find out what was really going on. He wrote to his epistolary friend, Benedictus de Spinoza: "As for politics, there is a rumor everywhere here concerning the return of the Jews, who have been dispersed for more than two thousand years, to their native country. Only a few here believe in this, yet here are many hoping for it. May it please you to communicate to a friend what you have heard regarding this matter, and what you think of it. As for me, I cannot believe this report until it is confirmed by reliable people from the city of Constantinople, which it touches most of all. *If the tidings prove to be true, it is sure to bring about an upheaval of everything in the world*"[60] (my italics). Unfortunately, this letter from the secretary of the leading scientific society in the world to the foremost critic of revealed religion was either unanswered or the answer is lost. It would be marvelous to see Spinoza's comments, a decade after his excommunication, on the reaction of the Jewish community to Sabbatai Sevi.

Either Oldenburg didn't find out what he wanted to know from Spinoza, or he wanted further data from more enthusiastic sources. His correspondence indicates that he was getting a stream of data from Holland. He wrote Lord Brereton that "The Holland letters continue their stories of the Jewes, and now tell us, yt they have appointed their Rendezevous at Jerusalem by ye first of Aprill, and yt the Jews at Amsterdam as well, as well, as in other places, doe resigne their house, resolved to repair for Palestina with the first conveniency."[61] Two months later he was reporting to Robert Boyle, "The last letters from Holland mention, yt now Christians as well as Jewes write from Constantinople, ye confirmation of ye reports concerning ye motion of ye Israelites and ye great hopes, ye Jewes entertain of recovering their land very shortly."[62] He then quoted from two letters from Constantinople about "le Roy des Juifs" and one from Paris, all giving more details.[63] A week later he sent Boyle more data he had gathered.[64]

Oldenburg exhibited the excitement about the stirring news from Turkey and the confusion about where to put it in his theology. Presumably others were equally or more confused. If 1666 was supposed to bring about some world-shaking development in the Jewish world vis-à-vis the Christian world, something was askew. The Jews weren't becoming Christians and their Messiah seemed to have little to do with the Christian one. (La Peyrère, who had argued that there would be both Messiahs, Jewish and Christian, was totally uninterested in the reports about Sabbatai Sevi.)[65] Fortunately for the Christian millenarians this anomalous situation did not last long. Sabbatai Sevi converted to Islam a few months later. The effect on the Jewish world was horrendous. Most Jews rejected him as a fraud. But the price they paid was great. The centuries of forbearance and hope, the messianic expectation as the justification for the nightmare of Jewish history, all ending in total disillusionment! Some of Sabbatai Sevi's followers tried to make a new religion around the apostate Messiah who had committed the gravest sin to save mankind. (There still are faithful believers, the Donmeh, who are fake Moslems and true followers of Sabbatai Sevi). It has taken almost three centuries until the Jewish world could discuss the matter in a calm manner. And as Scholem, Buber, and others have shown, the effects have been traumatic on the subsequent course of Judaism. For the Christian millenarian world there was probably relief. The anomaly of a Jewish Messiah was gone, and Jewish events could not be put back in a Christian perspective. A letter to Oldenburg from a friend of Menassah ben Israel, Pierre Serrarius, indicates that some millenarians still wanted to believe that God was working His wonders through Sabbatai Sevi. Serrarius, after Sabbatai's conversion, reported, "As for the Jews their hopes revive more and more." Someone who spoke to Sabbatai "found him, not turned Turk, but a Jew as ever in the same hope and expectation as before.... It appears both in regard of Christians and of Jews, that Gods Works ever were a ridle to flesh and bloud, and a stumbling-block to worldy minds."[66] Most others just wrote off the Jews as credulous, and dropped Sabbatai Sevi from divine history. John Evelyn made him a central figure in his book, *The History of The Three Imposters.* The longest section of the book deals with him, and Evelyn pointed out that this case history should have made the Jews realize they were wrong. "[This] *might, one would think at last open the* Eyes, and turne the hearts *of that* obstinate and *miserable* People."[67]

Some have claimed that Sabbatai Sevi ended Jewish messianism as an expectation that a *person* would come to restore Israel and fulfill the prophecies. Except for the continuation deviant movement of the Frankists (Jacob Frank claiming to be the reincarnation of Sabbatai Sevi), the mainstream of Judaism has moved away from hopes of a personal Messiah. Scholem and Buber have shown how Hasidism is an internalizing of the Messianic hopes. Other Jewish strains have centered on the People of Israel being the messianic force, or some generalized activity constituting it. At any rate, Jewish messianism in its literal sense withered away after 1666, and only small groups probably still expect the literal events described in the prayers. (The Reform Jews have dropped most of the prayers about rebuilding the temple and so on.)

Christian millenarianism, however, went on undaunted. Believers might have to recalculate the date of the wondrous year when the millennium would begin if 1666 was not it. The Jews could have an imposter without effecting the Christian perspective. Indeed, the fact that the Jews were taken in by an imposter became a conversionist argument. Charles Leslie tried to show that Jews should become skeptical about their Judaism because they couldn't tell a false Messiah from a true one. Therefore, they should join a religion that has a genuine criterion for messiahship, namely christianity.[68]

The English millenarians went on and on, calculating the ends of days. Based on the theories of Joseph Mede, Isaac Newton, William Whiston, David Hartley, Joseph Priestly, to name but a few, dates were given later and later into the eighteenth century, until millenarians were predicting the beginning of the millennium in 1776 and 1789. Two critical issues for these millenarians were the conversion of the Jews and the rebuilding of Palestine. It is interesting, or amusing, to note how much got written in the seventeenth and eighteenth centuries about these matters and how little got done about them. Few Jews were converted in

England, first, because few lived there, and second, because not much of a conversion effect was attempted. No efforts went into Palestinian reconstruction. It was enemy territory. But the theory that the Jews had to be converted and Palestine rebuilt kept being pushed. Only with the French Revolution and the Napoleonic Wars did the millennialists find a relationship between their theory and their practice. The French Revolution had given citizenship to the Jews. Napoleon had invaded Palestine and invited the Jews to join in rebuilding the temple. In 1806, Napoleon had called the Grand Sanhedrin to meet in Paris, the first time it had met since Titus conquered Jerusalem. The sort of English millenarian reaction is indicated in the title of J. Bicheno's book, *The Restoration of the Jews, the Crisis of All Nations, to which is now prefixed, a Brief History of the Jews from their first Dispersion to the Calling of their Grand Sanhedrin at Paris, October 6th, 1806.* In what was happening in France, the English millenarians saw the culminating events. For most of them Napoleon was the Antichrist, using the Jews. Increased effort had to be employed to convert the Jews to save them and the world from Napoleonic influence. The Society for Promoting Christianity among the Jews took its efforts abroad (since they had had miserable results in England), and sent field teams to eastern Europe and Palestine. Zionism as a Christian view started being pushed not as a theory, but by encouraging Jewish colonization in Palestine.[69] Though this would be another paper, a few words should be said on the subject. From the seventeenth century onward there is in the English literature a Zionist perspective, a call to rebuild Palestine and a call for the Jews to return there. It's part and parcel of the millenarian theory. But it was a hope more than anything else. In the nineteenth century something could be done about it. And the English who were so helpful in early Zionism, plus Lord Balfour, plus some today, are going at it from their Christian millenarian zeal.[70] I have a super-Zionist work written in southern California in 1955 by a fanatic millenarian who sees the state of Israel as the penultimate step before the conversion of the Jews and beginning of the millennium.[71]

This picture of the interplay between Christian millenarianism and Jewish messianism, particularly in the seventeenth century, has tried to show how these movements affected each other. Christian millenarianism was probably more affected by Jewish views than vice versa, mainly because the Christian sought clues and guidance in Jewish sources, and partly by the influence of Menasseh ben Israel. In Menasseh's day it looked as if the Christian millenarian thinkers were saying approximately what Menasseh was. He, himself, may have minimized the difference to avoid conflict and to benefit Jewish hopes in England. The Christians always transformed what he said into a conversionist view and saw the progress toward the messianic age he portrayed as one more sign that the Jews would now convert. The basic misunderstanding that separated the Jewish and Christian view never became clear for the millenarians since they probably couldn't really conceive what the Jewish position was, namely that messianic history had not yet begun. Late in the century a liberal Protestant, Philip van Limborch could debate an ex-Marrano, Orobio de Castro, on the truth of the Christian religion.[72] It is hard to believe the writers of the millenarian tracts could consider such a debate.

If the Christian millenarians could not grasp the Jewish position, they also could not ignore it. For them the conversion of the Jews was central. The Jews could, and usually did, ignore the Christian theory, since no Christian event was crucial to Jewish expectations, whereas some Jewish ones were crucial to the Christian hopes. So one finds the serious Christian millenarians needing to convert the Jews, and constantly misunderstanding what the Jewish view is. For some of the millenarians, God would convert the Jews at the end of time, so the misunderstanding wouldn't matter.

Historically the confrontation of expectations in 1666 should have brought a kind of climax to this story. If Sabbatai Sevi had produced a lasting movement accepted by most Jews, there might have been a bizarre end to the story. If Jewish expectations could be realized in some form independent of Christianity, what effect would this have had on the millenarians? Since Sabbatai Sevi's movement collapsed so fast, it hardly had time to start the confrontation.

The seventeenth-century movements of the Jews and the Christians affected each other to some degree. The century of the greatest millenarian expectations was also the one of the greatest messianic ones. The cross currents had some interesting results, as I have tried to show. The lasting effects include at least the tempering of messianic expectations on the Jewish side, and on the English millenarian side the development of two strands, the British Israelite movement, and a British penchant for Zionism as a prelude to conversion. The first allows for millenarianism without stiff-necked actual Jews. The second combines a now practical venture (within the limits of Arab power and oil politics) with the remaining millenarian hopes that a happy state of Israel will become a paradise of Jewish Christians. The endless calculating that went on from Napier to Faber as to when the millennium will begin can be dropped, and energy can be concentrated on the conversion of the state of Israel.

In conclusion, it's hard to tell if either side gained from the intermixture of the millenarian and messianic views in the seventeenth century. The nature of the former was bound to lead to some interaction. The Jewish contribution to millenarianism in the seventeenth century is significant, especially in the case of Menasseh ben Israel. Both views went through a transformation in the course of the seventeenth century. Messianism changed more because of the debacle of Sabbatai Sevi, but I think millennialism became more practical, though not necessarily more successful in its goal of converting the Jews. And this practicality may have been quite important in developing Zionism.

One last consequence from this interaction and intermixture is probably a skepticism about the claims of both the messianists and the millenarians. The Sabbatian debacle no doubt created many Jewish skeptics. In the Enlightenment, the case was used to suggest that if Sabbatai Sevi said he was the Messiah and he wasn't, maybe others who made the claim also weren't. The culmination of this was the infamous *Three Impostors, Moses, Jesus and Mohammed*. Similarly, if the millenarian experts calculated that 1666 was the crucial year, and nothing happened, then will there really be a crucial year? The energy and force poured into the Jewish and Christian expectations in the seventeenth century probably led to the Enlightenment disillusionment with such a world, and the transformation from eschatological interpretations to secular ones.

NOTES

1. See *Daily Prayer Book*, translated and annotated by Philip Birnbaum (New York, 1949), Morning Service, pp. 50, 62, 70, 76, 90, etc. Page 90 is typical: "Return in mercy to thy city Jerusalem and dwell in it as thou hast promised; rebuild it soon, in our days, as an everlasting

structure, and speedily establish in it the throne of David, Blessed art thou, O Lord, Builder of Jerusalem."

2. Such views have been condemned from Talmudic times down to the present. Projects such as reestablishing a Jewish Holy Land have been condemned by orthodox Jews, and Theodore Herzl met with stern rabbinical opposition when he began his movement for the rebuilding of Palestine. See article "Zionism" in the old *Jewish Encyclopedia*, XII, 672. "It [Zionism] was supposed to be forcing the hand of Providence and to be contrary to the positive teachings of Orthodox Judaism in regard to the coming of the Messiah and the providential work of God in bringing about the restoration." There are orthodox Jewish groups opposing the state of Israel on such grounds.

3. Abba Hillel Silver, *A History of Messianic Speculation in Israel* (Boston, 1927), p. 195, cites Rabbi Jonathan in the Talmud as saying, "Perish all those who calculate the end, for men will say, since the predicted end is here and the Messiah has not come, he will never come." On p. 214 Maimonides is quoted as saying, "It is a fundamental dogma to believe in the coming of the Messiah; even if he is delayed long, wait for him. But no one should attempt to fix the time of his coming." Needless to say, even the great Maimonides tried his hand at calculating when the Messiah would come. The same official view was being stated in the nineteenth century. Rabbi Cologna, a leader of the Paris Sanhedrin, said, "We declare that according to our dogmas, God alone knows the time of the Restoration of Israel," quoted in Henri Grégoire, *Histoire des sectes religieuses* (Paris, 1828), III, 377.

4. See, Silver, *A History of Messianic Speculation,* Parts I and III.

5. By "Jewish messianism" I mean the hope or expectation that the Messiah described in Isaiah will appear in human history, will redeem the Jews, bring them back to their homeland, and produce a better world for everyone. As Silver's book cited above shows, there was and is a wide range of speculation as to whether the Messiah will be one or more persons, or forces, or other possibilities.

6. "Christian millenarianism" covers a wide range of views, as LeRoy E. Froom shows in his massive four volumes on the *Prophetic Faith of Our Fathers* (Washington, 1948-1954). Here I shall use the term to cover views described in Revelation, whether preceded or followed by the Second Coming of Jesus.

7. It is often seen as the initial and crucial event in the millenarian sequence. This was especially true in early nineteenth-century theories, but appeared in most earlier ones. On the nineteenth-century views, see Froom, *Prophetic Faith,* Vol. III; and Ernest R. Sandeen, *The Roots of Fundamentalism* (Chicago and London, 1970), chap. 1.

8. The general facts of Iberian Jewish tragedy, plus a great deal of bibliography appear in Salo W. Baron, *A Social and Religious History of the Jews* (New York, 1969 and 1973), Vols. XIII and XV.

9. On Reubeni and Molko, see Silver, *A History of Messianic Speculation,* pp. 133-135 and 145-150.

10. This work has been translated by Martin A. Cohen and pub-

lished in Philadelphia in 1965 by the Jewish Publications Society.

11. On Luria and his movement, see Gershom G. Scholem, *Major Trends in Jewish Mysticism* (New York, 1969), pp. 244-286; and Silver, *A History of Messianic Speculation,* pp. 137-138.

12. Montalto, a Portuguese who was raised in Italy, became the doctor of Marie de Medici, wife of Henry IV of France. He wrote several anti-Christian works that circulated widely in manuscript. There are copies in the Ets Haim Library in Amsterdam and in many other libraries.

13. See Joseph L. Blau, *The Christian Interpretation of the Cabala in the Renaissance* (New York, 1944); and Francois Secret, *Le Zôhar chez les Kabbalistes chretiens de la Renaissance* (The Hague, 1964).

14. See Cecil Roth, *The History of the Jews in England* (Oxford, 1964), pp. 145-150. Roth cites some extreme cases of people proclaiming themselves king of Israel.

15. On Finch, see Nahum Sokolow, *The History of Zionism* (London, 1919), I, 47-49; and Peter Toon, *Puritans, the Millennium and the Future of Israel, Puritan Eschatology 1600 to 1660* (Cambridge and London, 1970).

16. See Toon, *Puritans,* pp. 56-65. Mede, who is a central figure in the development of English millenarianism, is discussed at length in Ernest Tuveson, *Millennium and Utopia* (Gloucester, Mass., 1972), pp. 76-85, without dealing with the Jewish role in this millennial theory.

17. Toon, *Puritans,* pp. 71-74.

18. See, for example, A. J. Ferris, *God's Education of the Anglo-Saxon Israel Race* (Keston, Kent, n.d.); and E. Odlum, *God's Covenant Man: British-Israel* (London, 1916). For an answer, see W. Lamb, *Anglo-Israelism, True or False?* (Sydney, 1935).

19. See the authors and books mentioned in Sokolow, *History of Zionisn,* Vol. I, chaps. vii and viii; and in Toon, *Puritans,* chap. vii; Appendix III in Toon, by J. Van Den Berg, shows that something similar happened in the Netherlands.

20. The most complete study of Menasseh is Cecil Roth's, *A Life of Menasseh ben Israel* (Philadelphia, 1945).

21. See Roth, *Life of Menasseh,* chaps. vi, vii and viii.

22. See Sokolow, *History of Zionism,* Vol. I, chap. vi.

23. Isaac B. Singer, *The Slave* (New York, 1962).

24. The story of Montezinos's discovery of his reporting it to Menasseh is given in Roth, *Life of Menasseh,* pp. 176-181.

25. Thomas Thorowgood, *Jewes in America, or Probabilities that the Americans are of that Race* (London, 1650), p. 22.

26. On this dispute see Lee E. Huddleston, *Origins of the American Indians, European Concepts 1492-1729* (Austin, Texas, 1967), pp. 130-135. The theory that the American Indians are Jews was still being argued in the nineteenth century.

27. The Latin, Spanish, and Hebrew editions were published in Amsterdam; the English was done by Moses Wall in London. Roth's *Life of Menassah,* pp. 301-303 gives a list of editions down to the twentieth century.

28. Menasseh ben Israel, *The Hope of Israel* (London, 1650), "The Epistle Dedicatory."

29. Ibid., p. 80.

30. This appeared in the second edition.

31. On Wall's theology see Toon, *Puritans*, pp. 118-120.

32. Cf. Menasseh ben Israel, *The Hope of Israel*, 2d ed. (London, 1652), pp. 56-61.

33. This is still the case. See Froom's evaluation of Menasseh in *Prophetic Faith*, II, 232-240.

34. See Cecil Roth, *History of the Jews in England*, p. 156.

35. See Toon, *Puritans*, pp. 117-118.

36. Menasseh ben Israel, *To His Highnesse the Lord Protector of The Commonwealth of England, Scotland, and Ireland. The Humble Addresses of Menasseh ben Israel, a Divine and Doctor of Physick, in behalf of the Jewish Nation* (probably Amsterdam 1651), 2d page.

37. Ibid.

38. See Roth, *Life of Menasseh*, p. 184, and Toon, *Puritans*, p. 118.

39. Cf. R. H. Popkin, "Menasseh ben Israel and Isaac LaPeyrère," *Studia Rosenthaliana* VIII, 59-63. On LaPeyrère's millenarian theology, see R. H. Popkin, "The Marrano Theology of Isaac La Peyrère," *Studi internazionali di Filosofia*, V (1973), 97-126.

40. This point is developed in Felgenhauer's main section, *Bonum Nunciam* (Amsterdam, 1655), pp. 1-86.

41. Letter of Menasseh to Felgenhauer, 1 Feb. 1655, in Felgenhauer, *Bonum Nunciam*, pp. 87-91.

42. Roth, *Life of Menasseh*, p. 156. "Conversionist in tendency though the work was, Menasseh was childishly delighted with the compliment and he presented copies of it complacently to strangers who visited him about this time."

43. See Isaac De Larrey, *Histoire d'Angleterre, d'Ecosse et d'Irlande* (Rotterdam, 1713), IV, 341; and Charles Malo, *Histoire des Juifs* (Paris, 1826), pp. 402-403.

44. William Prynne, *A Short Demmurer to the Jews* (London, 1656), p. 91.

45. Ibid., p. 92.

46. Margaret Fell wrote *For Menasseh ben Israel, The Call of The Jewes out of Babylon which is Good Tidings to the Meek, Liberty to the Captives, and for the opening of the Prison Doores* (London 1656). On Menasseh's stay in London see Roth, *Life of Menasseh*, pp. 248 ff.

47. Roth, *Life of Menasseh*, p. 264.

48. Menasseh ben Israel, *Vindiciae Judaeorum* (London, 1656), p. 18.

49. Sokolow, *History of Zionism*, chaps. iv-vi.

50. The Council of Four Lands met in Lublin in the winter of 1650. On this meeting see Max L. Margolis and Alexander Marx, *A History of the Jewish People* (Philadelphia, 1945), p. 555.

51. Samuel Brett, *A True Relation of the Proceedings of The Great Council of the Jews Assembled in the Plains of Adjady in Hungaria*, in [Nathaniel] Crouch, *Two Journeys to Jerusalem* (London, 1709), pp.

107-117. An example of the way this purported council got taken as fact is the account of it in Malo, *Histoire des Juifs,* pp. 355-357.

52. Henry Hart Milman, *The History of the Jews* (London, 1903), pp. 579-580.

53. All of this is set forth in full detail in Gershom Scholem's superb *Sabbatai Sevi; The Mystical Messiah* (Princeton, 1973), chaps. 1 and 2.

54. One of the basic sources of the Sabbatai Sevi story, the account in Paul Rycaut, *The History of the Turkish Empire from the Year 1623 to the Year 1677* (London, 1687), p. 174, gives some of these claims.

55. See Scholem, *Sabbatai Sevi,* pp. 101-102.

56. Ibid., chaps. 4, 5, and 6.

57. Rycaut, *History of the Turkish Empire,* p. 174.

58. Samuel Pepys, *Diary* for 19 Feb. 1666. Increase Mather, *The Mystery of Israel's Savation explained and applied* (London, 1669), prefatory epistle by John Davenport.

59. Scholem used some of Oldenburg's material, but not that included in the recent edition of Oldenburg's correspondence.

60. Benedictus de Spinoza, *Letters,* no. 33, as translated in Scholem, *Sabbatai Sevi,* p. 544. The letter has no date.

61. Oldenburg to Lord Brereton, 16 Jan. 1665/6, in *The Correspondence of Henry Oldenburg,* trans. A. Rupert Hall and Marie Boas Hall (Madison, 1966), III, 23.

62. Oldenburg to Robert Boyle, 6 March 1665/6 in ibid., p. 49.

63. Ibid., pp. 49-50.

64. Oldenburg to Boyle, 13 March 1665/6 in ibid., p. 59.

65. The Bible scholar, Richard Simon, tried to interest LaPeyrère in the Sabbatai Sevi movement and in meeting an adherent. There is no evidence that LaPeyrère cared. Richard Simon, *Lettres choisies* (Rotterdam, 1703), II, 14.

66. Peter Serrarius to Oldenburg, 5 July 1667, in Oldenburg, *Correspondence,* III, 447.

67. John Evelyn, *The History of Three Impostors* (London, 1669), 6th and 7th pages.

68. Charles Leslie, *A Short and Easy Method with the Jews,* in *Theological Works* (London, 1721), I, 52.

69. A lot of this literature is described in Froom, *Prophetic Faith,* Vol. II, chaps. 33-35 and Vol. III, chaps, 15-24; Sokolow, *History of Zionism,* Vol. I, chaps. ix-xvii.

70. I am working on a study of Christian roots of Zionism that will go into all of this.

71. David L. Cooper, *The Eternal God Revealing Himself to Suffering Israel and to Lost Humanity* (Los Angeles, 1955), esp. pp. 330-331.

72. Philip van Limborch, *De Veritate Religionis Christianae Amica Collatio cum Erudita Judaeo* (Gouda, 1687).

IV
POST-PURITAN ENGLAND AND THE
PROBLEM OF THE ENLIGHTENMENT

J. G. A. Pocock

In this paper I intend to raise some questions about the relations between England and the Enlightenment and about the proper use and scope of the latter term; and I shall suggest some solutions in terms of the changing patterns of thinking which are visible as England passes from the Puritan to the Whig ascendancy. The particular "problem of the Enlightenment," about which I hope to say something, arises from the fact that though we speak with facility about a French, a German, an Italian, or a Scottish Enlightenment, to try to articulate the phrase "the English Enlightenment" is to encounter inhibition; an ox sits upon the tongue. Why is this? The first phase of the Enlightenment in France coincides with the era of Anglomania; England is a crucially important model to Enlightenment thinkers. At the outset of the whole movement we find a group of English Deists — Toland, Collins, Blount — who obtain a European reputation and are visibly engaged in that semiclandestine diffusion of ideas subversive of revealed religion which we recognize as the Enlightenment's central feature. There was an Enlightenment, and England and the English had much to do with it, and yet the phrase "the" (or "an") "English Enlightenment" does not ring quite true.

We have a problem; one perhaps of the same order as Leonard Krieger has recently shown to exist in the case of the phrase, "enlightened despotism."[1] We must start by defining what we think this "Enlightenment" was which we find it hard to say can be found in England.

For Peter Gay,[2] whom we may well allow to state our antithesis for us, the Enlightenment is identical with the existence of a *troupeau des philosophes* and their crusade against Christianity; and it is observable that he is in the habit of speaking in terms of "Britain" and "British philosophers," although the Union of 1707 inaugurates a century in which the advance of the Scottish intellect was massive and autonomous.[3] We have no trouble in pronouncing the words "the Scottish Enlightenment," though how far it consisted of *philosophes* may be another question. But Gay's linguistic practice, though it involves him in such occasional infelicities as "In Great Britain the Anglican Church...,"[4] has the advantage that it enables him to bracket and present two authentic giants among Anglophone philosophes: David Hume and Edward Gibbon. The year 1976 marked, *inter alia,* the bicentennial of the death of the one and the first major publication of the other, each a significant event in the history of the Enlightenment. But Hume was a Scot, and Gibbon a good deal of an expatriate; and just as Gibbon was a philosophe at Lausanne and a placeman at Westminster, so there is a sense in which Hume was more significantly a philosophe in Paris than in Edinburgh.

When we speak of the Scottish Englishtenment, that is, we are talking about a marvelous explosion of ideas in moral philosophy and historical sociology, one more evidently related to the national and social consciousness of those who took part in it than to their religious belief or lack of it. It can of course be argued that the destruction of the biblical scheme of sacred history was a necessary condition of this triumph of secular historiography; but Hume is not writing to destroy Bossuet, as Voltaire and perhaps Gibbon are, because in Protestant culture this task was scarcely necessary. Images of national history, part apocalyptic and part secular, had long ago taken the place of the *histoire universelle,*[5] and it was with them that the philosophical historians of north and south Britain had to reckon. Consequently, it was not from the Voltairean *guerre de course* against miracle and revelation that Ferguson, Stewart, Smith, and Millar learned to understand the history of civil society, and even Gibbon has a different insight into the social character of barbarism from that he has into the character of religion.[6]

I have begun, I suspect, to outline an explanation of why, if there is Enlightenment in England, it is enlightenment sans philosophes; in post-Puritan and Whig England, philosophes were not much needed. I hope to trace some reasons why this was so from their late-Puritan beginnings; but before I make this attempt, I must take notice of two other important contributions to the understanding of our problem. Franco Venturi, for whom there is no English Enlightenment but there is a Scottish one, has offered a suggestive link between the anticlerical Enlightenment and the growth of historical sociology in the eighteenth century by stressing the ties between deism and theoretical republicanism.[7] The English deists, who helped spark the continental Enlightenment, were mostly English commonwealthmen, and from that aspect of their political beliefs, which I call neo-Harringtonian, may be traced ideas about the problematic relations between land and commerce, politics and culture, which formed one major source of the eighteenth century's understanding of history. This is one of the themes which can be traced back through Whig to Puritan antecedents; but we cannot do so without attending to the critique of H. R. Trevor-Roper[8] who, arguing against the theses of Marxian or Weberian descent, has contended that the roots of Enlightenment are to be found not in Calvinism but in an Arminian tradition whose antecedents were Erasmian and humanist. He tends to exclude radical Protestantism on these grounds from the prehistory of the Enlightenment, though he would have had little difficulty in particularizing how much of radical Puritanism was Arminian and even Socinian rather than Calvinist, and developed brands of tolerance and enlightenment rather less Erasmian, courtly, and critical than Trevor-Roper has sought to emphasize.

There is an antinomian and spiritualist strain in the story we have to tell, and it is related in a rather elusive way to the association between deism and republicanism stressed by Venturi. But it is important to give Trevor-Roper's argument its proper weight, and I propose now to begin from an episode in late-Puritan intellectual history in which the various themes I have so far outlined seem to appear in an intelligible relation with one another, and in which — as an added bonus — the role of science in the English pre-Enlightenment (for I will venture to use that term) also presents itself.

The pioneer theorist of English republicanism, James Harrington, published his *Oceana* in 1656 and by 1658 was defending it against the criticisms of Matthew Wren.[9] We think of *Oceana* as the affirmation of the supremacy of landed property in determining the distribution of political power in England, and as the blueprint of England as an agrarian and republican utopia. But Wren, the son of a Laudian bishop and just then a member of that Oxford scientific circle we find near the origins of the Royal Society — it was at the instance of John Wilkins that he had undertaken to criticize *Oceana*[10] — had fastened on the core of Harrington's strictly political theory: the assertion that the relations of debate and result, whereby one actor determines the choice to be made and the other makes it, are natural among human beings and make them essentially republican political animals. Harrington had insisted that, as constituted by this relationship, the body politic was indeed a creature possessing a soul and organized by a form, and had continued to use medieval and even Platonic language concerning it. Wren, bishop's son though he was, had skeptically observed that all this must wait until people knew what the soul was and what philosophy should attend it; and he had insisted that human beings in society were individuals engaged in driving exploitative bargains with one another according to the measure of their strength, needing the supremacy of an absolute sovereign, whose interests could never be identical with those of the subject, to regulate the bargaining process. Wren, in short, conforms perfectly to C. B. Macpherson's model of the possessive individualist,[11] who presupposes (as Wren did) a commercial rather than a natural economy in order to reduce politics to that pursuit of private interests under public authority which modern theorists insist on calling liberalism. It is a little disturbing to our received ideas to discover that he wrote as an upholder of both monarchy and clergy, but it is this fact which makes the episode a revealing one in the history of English thinking.

According to conventional wisdom, the great master of possessive individualism was Thomas Hobbes, and we might expect to find Wren regarding Hobbes as an ally and Harrington considering him an enemy. But, in fact, we do not. To Wren the differences that did exist between Hobbes and Harrington were super-ficial and a little surprising—"Leviathan and Oceana," he observed, "whose names might seem to promise a better agree-ment..."—Harrington developed the work he began in 1658 as a reply to Wren into a defense of Hobbes, not indeed against Wren, who had declined to enter upon this part of the argument, but against the neo-Laudian Henry Hammond.[12] And this was not because Harrington had failed to understand the difference be-tween his political philosophy and that which was Wren's and which he might have seen as Hobbes's. As long as he continued writing, he continued to assert that the republic was a relation between soul and body, and to denounce "mathematicians"—a term of opprobrium as he used it—who sought to reduce it to a series of mechanical operations; but he nowhere suggests that Hobbes is one of the mathematicians. It is true that about this time Hobbes was quarreling with the Oxford group to which Wren and Wilkins belonged on matters so purely mathematical as the squaring of the circle; but any ideological dimension to the difference between Hobbesian and Oxford mathematics would, I fear, be beyond my powers to discover. The area of agreement between Harrington and Hobbes as against Hammond and as discerned by Wren, lies elsewhere. Both men were intent on destroying any but a political origin for the orders of Christian priesthood, and adopted what were to them and their adversaries all but identical means of doing so. Both, that is, insisted that the Mosaic theocracy in Israel had possessed a rigorously political character, which Christ would restore at his second coming, and both insisted on the Roman and civic authority under which the apostles had carried out the first Christian ordination. The fact that Israel was a republic to Harrington and a monarchy to Hobbes,[13] that Roman authority was that of the Asian munici-palities to Harrington and that of Caesar and his legates to Hobbes, is mentioned by neither man nor by their adversaries. (It should be added that we have no comment from Hobbes on his relation to Harrington.)

Now what is the significance of all this in the history of the English pre-Enlightenment? It is that a driving thrust in the de-velopment of English Protestantism, from its beginnings under Henry VIII to its stabilization a century and a half later, had been and was to be a ruthless determination to do away with any claim by the clergy to other than a strictly social authority, and that various forms of argument based on the structure of Christian prophecy—on the relation between Old Dispensation and New, between Israel and Christ—had figured prominently among the means of reversing these claims.[14] Hobbes and Harrington stood in a succession reaching back to Foxe, Bale, and even Wyclif. And English Protestantism regularly entered upon phases of violent dissension when groups within its ranks—bishops, presbyters, or saints of the inner light—showed signs of asserting a jure divino authority over their fellows. During the Interregnum, private judgment and private spirituality, which had been mobilized by Parliament against the king and the hierarchy, developed conflicts of their own with the secular authority to whose supremacy over popes, priests, and presbyters they were so profoundly committed; and it is this which gives the articulate life of the period its extraordinarily complex texture, at once deeply conformist and deeply radical, deeply secular and deeply spiritual. English anticlericalism had far too many roots in religious and social life, was far too skilled in the combination and permutation of secular and spiritual argument, to require the aid of a philosophe intelligentsia in expressing itself; and any philosophe-like or Enlightenment-like characteristics it developed must be seen as evolving from the logic of the long alliance and long debate between saint and sovereign. The story I now hope to outline is how it came about that in Whig England there was little need of Voltairean philosophes, while the critical intelligentsia that took shape was critical of secular society and its history, in ways as likely to prove Tory as radical.

I want next to explore the interrelations between secular, prophetic, and spiritual in the thought of Harrington and of Hobbes, partly with a view to setting the arguments of Wren in their proper perspective. Of the two former, it is Harrington who is in one important respect closer to the mind of radical Puritanism. He insists, as we have seen, that the commonwealth is not a mechanism, but a union of soul and body; and he presents the Mosaic theocracy as a commonwealth or republic, of which the restoration will be the restoration of the kingdom of Christ. His republicanism is millennial, and there is something about his program for associating the distribution of property with the distribution of land—and so rooting in land the restoration of Christ's kingdom and the union of soul and body—not altogether remote from the far more radical and spiritualist utopia of Gerrard Winstanley,[15] for whom the restoration of social justice in the earth was coterminous with the resurrection of Christ in the body or of universal spirit in universal matter.

It can be debated forever whether Winstanley's spiritualist materialism is the final form of his thought or simply a halting place on the way to an unmediated and irreligious perception of social relations merely as themselves; and once we recognize that since the radical Franciscans of the fourteenth century, the kingdom of the spirit could be identified with the perfection of human capacities in human bodies,[16] we may decide that the debate is incapable of solution. Once men are fully spiritualized, the godman sees no more than human eyes may see; we are getting near that branch of the history of Western atheism which declares less that God does not exist than that men have become God. In the spiritualist tradition, furthermore, spirit could be identified with reason, and the resurrection of spirit in body could mean the perfect union of God with his creation, of spirit with matter through reason and love. To Winstanley the distinctions between spiritualism, rationalism, and materialism were of very little account, and his doctrine of God was full of a hylozoistic pantheism, which many found it hard to tell from atheism. There are spiritualist roots to the Enlightenment, and—given especially the crucial if puzzling role played by Spinoza—it is not surprising to find in the next century philosophers such as Hartley, Priestley, and Rush,[17] to whom rational materialism was wholly compatible with exegesis of that Biblical edifice of prophecy which the philosophes sought above all things to destroy. Radical Puritanism, then, is one of the phenomena of the pre-Enlightenment, though we may concede to Trevor-Roper that Calvin had less to do with the matter than Joachim of Fiore and Jacob Boehme.

But Harrington was not a Winstanley, and there are further ambivalences to his brand of republican spiritualism. If the republic was the union of soul and body, that union could only take a political form; Christ was the type of the republic, and Oceana was the Bride of Christ.[18] Since Israel had been a theocracy—a republic to Harrington, a monarchy to Hobbes—the magistrate took precedence over the priest, and the clergy could lay claim to no authority, even at the point where their mission expressed most perfectly the union of God with man, which did not come to them from the political relations between men; and these in turn were what gave soul to the body politic and displayed the action of spirit in history. To affirm that the clergy possessed an independent charisma and jurisdiction was to set up a false spirit[19] — very like the Antichrist of the older Puritans — which, by speaking to some men but not to others, operated against the true, political nature of man. Such had been the Talmudic rabbis, the Romish hierarchy, the Laudian episcopate, and the Scottish presbyters; and such was the contemporary attempt to set up the rule of the saints as a spiritual elite. Because Harrington was the closer of the two to the radical Puritans, he argued against Vane and Milton,[20] where Hobbes argued mainly against Bellarmine and Bramhall.

Both men, however, interpreted Israel as a theocracy in order to politicize the reign of the spirit, to identify man the child of God with man the political animal, and to argue that the kingdom that had been and would come again was literally a political as well as a peaceable kingdom. They found means of turning the apocalyptic structure of Christian thought not merely in an anti-clerical direction, but in one that exalted the political over the clerical by reducing spirit to politics. But to do this, as their adversaries saw,[21] contained implications that were certainly anti-trinitarian and might go much further. If the perfection of man's relation with God was theocracy, and if theocracy had been realized in Israel, under the Old Dispensation and in the reign of the Father, what remained for the Son or the Spirit to do, under the New Dispensation or in the kingdom of the Resurrection, but to restore what had essentially existed then? It became hard for Christ to add anything to Moses. And the logic of Harrington's argument drove him to identify spirit with politicized reason and to insist that the orders of the Israelite commonwealth were the work less of Moses, speaking with the voice of revelation, than of Jethro the Midianite, speaking with the voice of the being naturally political.[22] If the commonwealth had been the kingdom of the Father, what could Christ add to what he restored? If the kingdom of the Father had been a natural and rational phenomenon, what had there been for the covenant to promise its peculiar and holy people?[23] There was clearly a tendency for spirit to empty itself of content, for the sequence of apocalyptic types and Joachite persons to resemble the serpent that swallows its tail. We may here be looking at a corner of a larger pattern: the relative absence of Christ from the Christianity attacked by the Enlightenment, defended by apologists, or analyzed by the Enlightenment's historians. The Socinian effect — if that be the word for what we have isolated here — was not only a consequence of liberal and enlightened scholarship and criticism; it was additionally a kind of Hegelian mystery in the self-development of spirit, against which Methodist and Moravian insistence on the personal reality of Christ as savior was a reaction and a protest.

But the attenuation of spirit was merely a consequence of its politicization and did not prevent Harrington from retaining the concept in order to politicize it. He continued to insist that the commonwealth was not a mechanism as the mathematicians affirmed, but a union of soul and body. Hobbes, on the contrary, set out to deny the independent operation of spirit and, indeed, its very existence. To him the Mosaic theocracy had not been a republic but a monarchy. It consisted not in a community of relations between men, but in an empire of command over the movements of bodies and the articulations of speech, and will was central for him in a way that reason was not. He did not hesitate, therefore, to extend his denial of spiritual authority to the clergy into a radical denial of the autonomous existence of spirit.[24] But the apocalyptic structure did not disappear for that reason; on the contrary, it remained as a pattern of words spoken, and of command exercised through the speaking of words, in a time-frame that prophecy constituted and which Hobbes was careful to retain in the structure of his own thought. Spinoza, twenty or so years later, endeavored in the *Tractatus Theologico-Politicus* to reduce all truth to philosophy, and prophecy to a mere allegorization of philosophy suited to the understanding of the vulgar; but Hobbes, the radical nominalist for whom words were commands, was hardly less suspicious of the independent role of philosophy than of that of spirit. He, therefore, took pains to leave Leviathan the exercise of the empire of the word, and consequently left the prophetic word a necessary element of Leviathan's empire. It might be the sovereign's command that invested the prophetic word with authority and interpreted its meaning, but for this very reason the sovereign could not annihilate the word, or convert belief in it into some other mode of knowledge, without annihilating a part of his own authority.

Spinoza, the quasirepublican, may have thought of philosophy

as supporting the sovereign, of the sovereign as protecting philosophy, and of revelation as dangerous to both; but to say this
would be to assert that Spinoza was a protophilosophe and that
Hobbes was not. He retained the prophetic and scriptural structure just as Harrington did, and with the same aim of undermining the clerical claim to authority; and this is clearly the reason
why it never occurred to Harrington to consider Hobbes a mathematician in the same sense as Wren. He could see that the Oxford
circle were clerics. He could never quite believe that Wren was
not, in fact, in orders.[25] And he could see that those who denied
his thesis of the naturally political relations between men were
also those who denied the typical role of Israel which he, and
Hobbes, were using as a means of establishing the supremacy of
the political over the clerical. It followed for him, therefore, that
mathematicians were not only partisans of a mechanized and
privatized society under sovereign authority, but also upholders
of an independent clerical authority—jure divino men in disguise, emissaries of that kingdom of darkness and unreal attributes so trenchantly analyzed by Hobbes. His suspicions were in
no way dispelled when he learned that John Wilkins was the
author of a book entitled *Mathematical Magic*.[26]

Harrington would be very wrong if he could not tell the difference between the Oxford scientists and the Laudians, or between
the younger Matthew Wren and his father; but he was not wrong
in detecting that his critic's philosophical skepticism, his dismissal
of Israel as nontypical and irrelevant, and his interest in the politics of a commercial society were aspects of a campaign to restore
authority to the clergy. The church of the Restoration was to be
Arminian rather than Calvinist, but Erastian to a degree that dispelled many of the suspicions formerly attached to the Laudians.
That is, it laid much less emphasis on jure divino episcopacy than
on jure divino monarchy, and was able to combine its insistence
on the duty of nonresistance with many of the arguments with
which the mid-century radicals had affirmed the supremacy of
the secular power and the secular character of clerical authority.
Only after 1688 did a handful of extremists on the fringe of the
nonjuring secession follow out the Anglo-Catholic implications of
an apostolic church under an illegitimate monarch;[27] and among
the leading figures of Restoration Anglicanism, we find latitudi-
narians who could uphold both a rational religion, in which the

apostolic and the prophetic were alike reduced in role, and the need for authority in church, state, and cosmos. It is of importance to the history of Enlightenment in England that these beliefs could go together, and that as part of the great campaign against enthusiasm that characterizes post-Puritan England, the clergy could find it to their purposes to act as patrons of the New Philosophy. We are learning from the work of Margaret Jacob[28] and others that in the concept of an ordered universe, moving under laws entirely compatible with the presence of a directing intelligence, they found the expression of a clear separation between the universe and its creator, between the rational subject and the authority he acknowledged, which could not be merged in that hylozoistic pantheism, upheld in one way by Winstanley and in another by Spinoza, in which the late seventeenth century was most likely to recognize (however mistakenly) the combination of atheism and materialism. The subject of a Newtonian universe was not likely to find God and spirit immanent in the universe or in his own body and perceptions; he would be free from the smallest tincture of enthusiasm.

Though this was a way of thinking which neo-Laudian and Tory clergy, like Thomas Sprat, could very well endorse, its combination of moderation with authoritarianism puts us on the highroad toward the Anglicanism of the Whig ascendancy. Once the issue ceased to be that of a jure divino clergy, capable of being seen as a threat to the secular establishment, there was less need of the radical eschatology by which both Harrington and Hobbes had sought to politicize the operations of the spirit; the church by law established could claim to have performed that task, and so to have returned to an English mainstream it had never truly left. Hobbes, therefore, could be seen in his true colors, as a secularized Puritan who wanted only a preaching ministry and saw little need for any hierarchy of authority within it, and this may help explain why the University of Oxford in 1683 was as anxious to condemn his doctrines as those which endorsed the legitimacy of resistance.[29] To us it may seem evident that he was an enemy of enthusiasm, that his brand of materialism could never be mistaken for any kind of pantheism, and that his politics stood close to that egoistic rationalism and acceptance of the need for a sovereign authority of which Matthew Wren had been the forerunner. But his retention of a radical, if unspiritual, eschatology forbade the Restoration Anglicans, as it had forbidden Wren, to recognize him as a supporter, and helps account for the ambivalence of his position vis-à-vis Spinoza.[30] On the one hand, Spinoza's reduction of revelation to philosophy weakened the prophetic structure as Hobbes had never attempted to do; on the other, his philosophy seemed to restore that alliance of materialism with pantheism, and of atheism with enthusiasm, from which the Restoration intellect never fully detached what it meant by "Hobbism." A brutally godless cynicism was only part —though a conspicuous one—of what it feared.

We are beginning to confront the problem that whereas the radical secularism of the Puritan era employed the patterns of Christian eschatology as one of its chief weapons, the secular radicalism of the philosophes thought nothing so important as the undermining of the structure of Christian prophecy and revelation on which eschatology depended. That the quasirepublican Spinoza should have engaged in this venture is not surprising, since in Holland — as he would appreciate both as a citizen and as a Jew — the authority of the republican councils rested on secular foundations to which Protestant spiritualism and apocalyptic presented an obvious threat. But in England apocalyptic was the ally of secular authority far more often than its enemy, and the threat of a rule by the saints had not led Harrington or Hobbes to alter this strategy. Yet once we reinspect Venturi's thesis of the alliance between republicanism and deism at or near the foundations of the Enlightenment, we encounter the paradox that John Toland, the most striking among the deist commonwealthmen, was simultaneously the editor of the works of Harrington and the author of *Christianity Not Mysterious*. If there is one thing I have labored to emphasize in this paper, it is that it was not self-evident, in an English context, that the destruction of prophetic authority was the best means of undermining the position of the clergy, of maintaining the supremacy of secular politics, or of presenting politics in a republican guise. On the contrary, the assertion of an eschatological and prophetic pattern in history was traditionally a means that radical secularists adopted of doing all these things; and some explanation of the reversal of strategy discernible between Harrington—or Hobbes—and Toland will have to be found.

It is by no means certain that one yet exists, and I may be

rather stating an agenda than solving a problem. We may underline the paradox we find ourselves in by repeating that, in the tradition descending from Wren through the clerical endorsers of Newtonian science, a rational religion that deemphasized prophecy and typology had appeared as an effective means of defending the church against enthusiasts, and that if we define the Enlightenment as the replacement of prophecy by rationality, this was, to an increasingly Whig and Erastian Anglicanism, an ideology rather supportive than subversive of clerical authority. To say this is to rejoin Trevor-Roper in emphasizing the Erasmian and Arminian origins of an Enlightenment conducted by liberal and tolerant rulers, whether secular or clerical, who found, in the liberal tradition, that their tolerance increased their authority. It was in this tradition that Locke wrote, and the rational religion of *The Reasonableness of Christianity* may by some be opposed to the radical deism of *Christianity Not Mysterious*.[31] There was an Enlightenment of the Establishment, as well as an Enlightenment of the philosophe underground. Yet to give an exclusive emphasis to the former not only fails, I suggest, to give full weight to the critical secularism developed by means of radical eschatology in the Puritan era but also fails to explain the disappearance of radical eschatology from the thought of the deist commonwealthmen and, to that extent, leaves the conjunction of deist and republican ideas without a full explanation.

Voltaire, and I suspect Gay as well, would offer us a dialectical explanation. They would point out, with unconcealed relish, that if it was the Erastian and antienthusiastic churchmen who developed the idea of a rational and decreasingly prophetic religion, from which typology and apocalyptic tended to disappear, they had only themselves to thank if there arose a deism, which realized that anticlericalism had no longer any need of the eschatological patterns so heavily criticized, that rational religion could be attacked by eliminating the content of revelation altogether, and that radical thought could secularize its own spirituality most effectively by following the paths pointed out by Spinoza. There is an element of exaggeration in this. The abandonment of apocalyptic by latitudinarian Anglicans was not as complete as we have so far suggested. Some of them had returned with relief to a tradition, discountenanced by the Laudians, of insisting that the Pope was Antichrist and of developing an apocalyptic to go with the doctrine; and their very concern for a rational religion led to renewed exegesis of the prophets and the tradition of prophetic scholarship. In fact, it is from Anglicans of this generation, as well as from the mutation of English Presbyterianism into its Arian, Socinian, and Unitarian forms, that we can trace what Ernest Tuveson has studied under the title *Millennium and Utopia:*[32] the development of the idea that human capacities would be millennially perfected by the providentially directed perfection of philosophy, science, and society in the course of secular history. Along this line of growth we can discern the resumption of the spiritualist tradition by the Arminian and enlightened upper clergy of the Anglican and dissenting, as well as Scottish and American, establishments; and much that we vaguely recognize as deism can be located on a spectrum that allows of its retaining its own kind of millennialism.

This was clearly a long way from employing apocalyptic as a deliberate instrument of anticlericalism; but before we can explain the phenomenon of a deist anticlericalism that had abandoned the use of apocalyptic altogether, we need to ask ourselves why, especially in the conditions obtaining after 1688, there should be a radical anticlericalism in England at all. Here it may be possible to restate the interpretation I have attributed to Voltaire and Gay in a somewhat more precise form. There is some reason to suspect that deism was directed against Anglicanism less in its rigorous than its moderate shape. Certainly, there was a Tory Anglicanism that was High Church, nonjuror, nonresistant, and in a very few cases Anglo-Catholic; but at least one astute contemporary[33] thought that the deist attack was occasioned less by right-wing dissentients such as these, than by indignation against Tory conformists, such as William Sherlock, who were prepared to take oaths of allegiance on the grounds that submission to a de facto regime was justified. To thinkers and ideologues in the commonwealth tradition, it seemed a greater insolence than nonjuring itself that clerics should presume to distinguish between government de jure and de facto, to grant the latter a conditional obedience of their own defining—purely Jesuitical behavior, this—and finally to be received as brethren by clergy who had taken the oaths on grounds which they said were different from those of Sherlock's persuasion, but which must clearly be regarded as no less suspect. Deism, if there is substance to this interpretation, was therefore directed against a latitudinarianism that had come in its own way to stir up the sleeping furies of English Erastianism. Like other features of the commonwealth ideology during these post-1688 years, it was directed against aspects of the Revolution compromise; and it employed the image of the commonwealth or republic as that of a society in which the independent role of the clergy had been reduced to a minimum, one indeed below that accorded it by the establishment in law of the Church of England.

If we think of deism as directed against latitudinarianism, we can restate the dialectical interpretation of its antiprophetic character in the following way. Given that the target was no longer a jure divino clergy claiming an authority independent of the civil power, there was little point in reiterating the theses in political eschatology by which Hobbes and Harrington had sought to demonstrate the subordination of clergy to commonwealth. Given that the clergy, since the end of the Protectorate, had been expounding a rational rather than a prophetic conception of religion as part of their case for religious authorization of the civil power and their own share in it, there was not much point in denying the prophetic character of religion—which a Christian clergy must somewhere include in the most rational and enlightened conception of their creed—as a means of denying that they had any role in the civil order at all; but this did not mean reinvesting the civil order with the prophetic significance Harrington and Hobbes had given it. If we must find a philosophical patron for the theologicopolitical positions adopted by the English deists of the 1690s, his name would be Spinoza rather than Hobbes; elements of a hylozoistic pantheism are to be found in the philosophy of Toland;[34] but if we seek explanations for the disappearance of apocalyptic from English political discourse after 1660, we must find them to some degree in the arguments of latitudinarian clergy under the Restoration, but even more in the changed dialectical situation brought about by the Erastian resurgence of which these arguments were the symptom.

If we can accept that what would otherwise have been termed Enlightenment in England was promoted as much conservatively, by the clergy of a legally established church, as radically, by deists no longer Christian but representing the secularization of elements in revolutionary Puritanism, then we can understand why Enlightenment in England is so far from being associated in our minds with the activity of a philosophe intelligentsia that we find it difficult to call it an Enlightenment at all. In a Protestant, Erastian, and Whig society, there was not much occasion for a philosophe intelligentsia to emerge; and to the extent to which there was such an intelligentsia, its character was muted and rendered less dramatic by the existence of a complex of shared attitudes toward church and prophecy, science and society, from which it could never emerge as an embattled *troupeau*. In England there was—to run the risk of simplifying Enlightenment attitudes by taking one Voltairean phrase as expressing the whole —simply no *infâme* to be crushed. Gibbon did not writhe under clerical tyranny at Oxford; he flirted with Catholicism because he was bored. Bentham did suffer by being obliged to subscribe to the 39 Articles against his beliefs, but it is significant that we begin to think of a philosophe movement in England only when he and his associates pit a new philosophy against the entire weight of a tradition, by then overwhelmingly secular. And their style is by no means Whig.

In conclusion, let us glance back at the question of the Scottish Enlightenment, and ask whether we find it easy to use that term because in Scotland there was—as Buckle and Trevor-Roper have suggested[35]—the need to shake off the yoke of a Calvinist clergy, or even whether Edinburgh, like Geneva, passed through a relatively dramatic peripeteia as a Calvinist clergy and laity secularized and enlightened themselves. I would like to suggest a rather different perspective, if not actually an interpretation, based on a perception of what was happening among English intellectuals—to whom Scots and Anglo-Irish may be added— belonging to the commonwealth tradition. So far we have been stressing that the image of the commonwealth or republic appears in English thought with Harrington as a weapon in the armory of apocalyptic anticlericalism; but it is at the same time, and was recognized far earlier as being, a device for explaining a political revolution by positing a long-term process of historical change. Harrington was one of the first thinkers to find ways of doing this, in England or elsewhere; and the relation between this and the anticlerical aspect of his thinking is easier to work out in terms of configuration than of causation. He had thought mainly of long-term changes in the structure of landholding; but I have emphasized elsewhere[36] that the restatement of his thought in the next generation, which I have termed neo-Harringtonian, became a means of positing the transition from a world of land-holding to one of parliamentary patronage, professional armies, and public credit, and of diagnosing and deploring that displacement of land by commerce which Matthew Wren had applauded for his own purposes. It can be shown how, even before 1700, there was a dawning realization that, according to contemporary moral and intellectual categories, the historical process that produced the arts, enlightenment, culture, and the specialization of labor was incompatible with the maintenance of liberty and led in consequence to the corruption of society. The republican ideal thus became a means of stating the quarrel of Western man with his own history; and the English, Anglo-Irish, and Scottish intellectuals of the commonwealth tradition were engaged in this quarrel for reasons only contingently related to the pursuit of the philosophes' quarrel with Christianity. They felt themselves cast off by history before they knew they had cast off God; and they saw the destruction of virtue by progress worked out in the Greco-Roman world that Peter Gay insists was the paradigm for the rebirth of modern paganism. An analysis of Gibbon will show, I believe, just how fragile he knew his golden age of the Antonines to be and how deeply rooted in the eighteenth-century dilemma his reasons were for thinking so.

As for the Scots, Franco Venturi, conceding that the student of the Enlightenment who looks to England finds himself a stranger there, adds that when he turns his gaze to Edinburgh and Glasgow, he sees at once the Enlightenment he knows and understands.[37] It is with the greatest hesitation that any other student of the Enlightenment presumes to disagree with Professor Venturi, and I will confine myself to suggesting an alternative emphasis. If we may focus on what is called the Scottish Historical School, as distinct from the Scottish Common Sense Philosophy—a difficult distinction about which there is debate—it can be argued that the great Scottish social philosophers were North Britons, children of the Union of 1707, whose social and national consciousness was so far dominated by acceptance of English political and historical conventions that they had no recourse but to understand English history, and the dilemma of virtue and progress which the English had discovered, better than the English did themselves, and to use this transformed understanding to restate their theory of Scottish, English, European, and human history on a scale that no Englishman, not even Gibbon, would find it necessary to attempt, and which only Germans continued to exceed. English thought, I am arguing, was at once larger than the philosophe Enlightenment and larger than England itself could contain. Its Erastianism was so complex as to bypass the paganism of the philosophes and to set out toward post-Christian thinking by routes of its own; its republicanism helped produce a new secular history, and understanding of the quarrel with history, which was exported to the British and European worlds and left to them to work out. The deists and commonwealthmen, if not the scientists, had builded greater than they cared to know.

It might seem, then, that there are two lines along which enquiry into this problem might be advanced. First, it has been my general strategy to suggest that the term *Enlightenment* is difficult to use where philosophes and their characteristic modes of activity are not present, as does not seem to have been the case in England before the time of the Philosophic Radicals. We might return to this purely lexical problem and decide either to use the term boldly for what did, in fact, go on in England, or, while employing it sparingly, if at all, to break down the usual connotations of Enlightenment — a replacement of typological by critical interpretation of prophecy, an ebullient expansion of epistemology and psychology in nontraditional directions, a movement in favor of Moderns over Ancients in humane letters, an explosion of both the physical and social sciences — and trace the progress of all these things, in England as well as Scotland, with relative indifference as to whether we use the word *Enlightenment* or not. There are undeniable advantages to such a strategy.

Second, given that the nonpresence in England of what we term philosophes has been established and in part explained, we might pursue the subject of the formation of intelligentsias as secular dissenting groups in eighteenth-century society. That the *encyclopédistes* constituted an early (though not the earliest, even in France) group of such a kind seems plausible, and the social history of their formation, as of their activity, is no doubt accessible. In England, while we do not find encyclopédistes or philosophes, it does seem that we encounter at least two groups, distinguishable if overlapping, of secular intellectuals marked by a discontent with society and its history—a portent in the growth of Western modernity. The "commonwealthmen," whose lineage has been traced by Caroline Robbins, form one such group, and another is furnished by the so-called "Tory satirists," active in the reign of Anne and again in that of George II, and including so many of the age's men of letters as to make Walpole's ministry a paradigm of the warfare between a politician grown symbolically important and an organized troupeau of intellectuals. It is in the differences between these two coteries and the philosophes proper that we have located the difficulty in speaking of an English Enlightenment; and to explore the formation, roles, and activities of the various secular clerisies emerging in post-Puritan England might tell us much—as comparable studies of the "Scottish Enlightenment" in terms of the regrowth of a provincial patriciate are already doing.[38] In this paper I have attempted to map the ideological strategies of England after 1649 with a view to seeing what roles radical dissenters might perform. To study them in terms of the changing politics and sociology of the higher literacy might be informative in other ways.

NOTES

1. Leonard Krieger, *An Essay on the Theory of Enlightened Despotism* (Chicago: University of Chicago Press, 1975).

2. Peter Gay, *The Enlightenment: an Interpretation. The Rise of Modern Paganism* (London: Weidenfeld and Nicolson, 1967).

3. There is no recent history of the eighteenth-century Scottish intellectual movement, though works by Duncan Forbes and Nicholas Philipson are expected. Gladys Bryson, *Man and Society: the Scottish Enquiry of the Eighteenth Century* (Princeton: Princeton University Press, 1945) is valuable.

4. Gay, *Enlightenment: an Interpretation*, p. 343.

5. See Orest Ranum's preface to Ranum, ed., *National Consciousness, History, and Political Culture in Early Modern Europe* (Baltimore: Johns Hopkins University Press, 1975), pp. 10-11, and his forthcoming introduction to Bossuet's *Histoire Universelle* (Chicago: University of Chicago Press).

6. J. G. A. Pocock, "Between Machiavelli and Hume: Gibbon as Civic Humanist and Philosophical Historian," *Daedalus* (Summer, 1976).

7. Franco Venturi, *Utopia and Reform in the Enlightenment* (Cambridge: Cambridge University Press, 1971).

8. H. R. Trevor-Roper, "The Religious Origins of the Enlightenment," in *The European Witch-Craze of the Sixteenth and Seventeenth Centuries and Other Essays* (New York and Evanston: Harper Torchbooks, 1969).

9. Matthew Wren, *Considerations upon Mr. Harrington's Commonwealth of Oceana* (London, 1657); James Harrington, *The Prerogative of Popular Government*, Bk. I (London, 1658). For further analysis, see J. G. A. Pocock, ed., *The Political Works of James Harrington* (Cambridge: Cambridge University Press, 1977), and "Contexts for the Study of James Harrington," *Il Pensiero Politico*, XI, 1 (1978), 20-35.

10. Barbara Shapiro, *John Wilkins, 1614-72: an Intellectual Biography* (Berkeley and Los Angeles: University of California Press, 1969), pp. 116-117.

11. C. B. Macpherson, *The Political Theory of Possessive Individualism: from Hobbes to Locke* (Oxford: Clarendon Press, 1962).

12. Wren, *Considerations*, p. 14, for the quip about *Leviathan* and *Oceana;* Harrington, *Prerogative of Popular Government*, Bk. II, for the polemic against Hammond.

13. J. G. A. Pocock, "Time, History and Eschatology in the Thought of Thomas Hobbes," in *Politics, Language and Time: Essays in Political Thought and History* (New York: Atheneum, 1971).

14. William Haller, *Foxe's Book of Martyrs and the Elect Nation* (London: Jonathan Cape, 1963); William M. Lamont, *Godly Rule: Politics and Religion, 1603-60* (London: Macmillan, 1969).

15. *The Law of Freedom in a Platform, or, True Magistracy Restored* (1652); modern editions by Robert W. Kenny (New York: Schocken Books, 1973) and Christopher Hill (Harmondsworth: Penguin Books, 1973). G. H. Sabine, ed., *The Works of Gerrard Winstanley* (Ithaca: Cornell University Press, 1941); Hill, *The World Turned Upside Down* (New York: Viking Books, 1972).

16. Gordon Leff, *Heresy in the Later Middle Ages* (Manchester: Manchester University Press, 1967).

17. Donald J. D'Elia, *Benjamin Rush: Philosopher of the American Revolution; Transactions of the American Philosophical Society*, 64, 5 (Philadelphia, 1974).

18. John Toland, ed., *The Oceana and Other Works of James Harrington* 4th ed. (London, 1771), pp. 187-188.

19. Harrington, *A Parallel of the Spirit of the People with the Spirit of Mr. Rogers* (London, 1659). This was John Rogers, the fifth monarchist preacher.

20. Vane published in May 1659 *A Needful Corrective or Ballance in Popular Government, expressed in a Letter to James Harrington...*, and Harrington's *Aphorisms Political* (August and September) are concerned partly with this and partly with Milton's *Considerations Touching the Likeliest Means to Remove Hirelings out of the Church* (August).

21. See J. W. Packer, *The Transformation of Anglicanism, 1643-60* (Manchester: Manchester University Press, 1969), pp. 179-180.

22. Toland, ed., *Oceana and Other Works,* pp. 48, 74 and passim.

23. Hobbes, *Leviathan,* III, 41, contains Hobbes's dealing with this question.

24. Ibid., p. 34.

25. It would be wearisome to rehearse the shafts directed at Wren's supposed clericalism scattered through Harrington's writings.

26. Toland, ed., *Oceana and Other Works,* pp. 558-559.

27. See *The Constitution of the Catholic Church and the Nature and Consequences of Schism . . . by the late . . . Dr. George Hickes* (London, 1716).

28. M. C. Jacob, "John Toland and the Newtonian Ideology," *Journal of Warburg and Courtauld Institute* xxxii (1969); "The Church and the Formulation of the Newtonian World View," *Journal of European Studies* I (1971), 2; *The Newtonian and the English Revolution* (Cornell University Press, 1976); "Newtonianism and the Origins of the Enlightenment, a Reassessment," *Eighteenth Century Studies* 11, 1 (1977), 1-25.

29. The eleventh, twelfth, and thirteenth propositions then condemned are Hobbesian, and the seventh may be; there are twenty-seven in all; cf. D. Wilkins, ed., *Concilia,* 4 vols. (London, 1737), IV, 610-612.

30. Spinoza's role in English thought awaits full-length study; see meanwhile Rosalie Colie, "Spinoza and the Early English Deists," *Journal of the History of Ideas* xx (1959), and "Spinoza in England, 1665-1730," *Proceedings of the American Philosophical Society,* 107 (1963).

31. Jacob, "John Toland," and Gay, *Enlightenment; an Interpretation,* p. 327.

32. E. Tuveson, *Millennium and Utopia* (Berkeley and Los Angeles: University of California Press, 1949).

33. William Stephens, *An Account of the Growth of Deism in England* (London, 1696).

34. Jacob, "John Toland."

35. H. T. Buckle, *On Scotland and the Scotch Intellect* (see edition by H. J. Hanham [Chicago: University of Chicago Press, 1970]); Trevor-Roper, "The Religious Origins of the Enlightenment."

36. Pocock, *The Machiavellian Moment: Florentine Political Thought and the Atlantic Republican Tradition* (Princeton: Princeton University Press, 1975), chaps. xii-xv.

37. Venturi, *Utopia and Reform in the Enlightenment,* pp. 132-133.

38. Nicholas Philipson, "Culture and Society in the 18th Century Province: the Case of Edinburgh and the Scottish Enlightenment," in Laurence Stone, ed., *The University in Society* (Princeton: Princeton University Press, 1974), II, 407-448; "Towards a Definition of the Scottish Enlightenment," in P. Fritz and D. Williams, eds., *City and Society in the 18th Century* (Toronto: University of Toronto Press, 1971).

V

JOHN DRYDEN'S PLAYS AND THE CONCEPTION OF A HEROIC SOCIETY

John M. Wallace

We probably agree that Dryden towers above most of his contemporaries as the most representative speaker for the passions and opinions of his age, and the most skillful interpreter of them. Other writers like Bunyan, Fox, or Traherne are better spokesmen for the varieties of religious experience (although one remembers *Religio Laici*) and the court wits wrote better comedies than he did, but Dryden tried his hand at many of the literary genres with conspicuous success; in his great satires, especially, the literary and political cultures are so enmeshed that many a reader has obtained his sole acquaintance with the turmoil of the Restoration years through an annotated edition of Dryden's works. We accept that just as the court's cynicism and profligacy pass into Rochester's poems and Restoration comedy, or that the gossip of Whitehall and the interests of the virtuosi are truthfully reflected in the diaries of Pepys and Evelyn, so is the experience of an essentially ordered if fearful culture expressed in Dryden's *oeuvre*. In an old-fashioned sense his works could be called criticisms of life which faithfully reproduce, albeit in heightened and artistic forms, the actual feelings and thoughts of the time. It is hence inherently unlikely that the old clichés about heroic drama can be true. Although they have been challenged recently by a growing number of scholars, the author of the standard literary history of the period can still say of *Tyrannick Love* that "Dryden, in fact, has taken leave of reality before the play begins," and the historian David Ogg remarked that heroic drama "depicted a world infinitely remote from the actualities of the present." Another critic has declared that "Dryden does not deny heroism so much as he embalms it, memorializes it in the form of terminal tragedy. His heroic stage is a museum of vital feelings honored lest they be forgotten but securely preserved from present use"; while Anne Righter in a brilliant polemic has damned heroic tragedy as flattering "exactly those romantic notions and grandiose dreams of the self which comedy sets out to deflate." The plays, she continues, "were essentially frivolous... literary and hollow. Behind them, as behind the painted gardens and palaces of the scenery, there was nothing at all."[1] Those of us who have questioned these views, or have thought that the excellent studies by Kirsch, Rothstein, and Waith[2] have underestimated the importance of Dryden's ideas in his plays, have invoked notions of debate or "plays of ideas"[3] and called in Hobbes or Filmer to substantiate our claim that heroic drama should be taken seriously, but we have not succeeded in showing (nor indeed have we advanced) that the subject of Dryden's plays were matters of urgent and topical concern. To read them in this light, I now believe, is to realize that Dryden was as totally committed in his drama to political and constitutional positions as he was in his great nondramatic poems, and that the issue at stake for him was no less than the survival of the Restoration settlement itself.

We need first of all a model for the heroic play, and the best example is probably Dryden's first tragicomedy, *The Rival Ladies*. Produced in 1664, it is a beginner's work, but it thus reveals, like an oversimplified sketch, a pattern that Dryden was to elaborate throughout his dramatic career. He became increasingly sophisticated and, later on, much gloomier in his analysis of political structures, but the play remains a genuine precursor of his later triumphs and a true indicator of his main concerns. As usual, it is necessary to study the plot closely because the details of the action sustain the theme, and the barest summary might run as follows. The shipwrecked Gonsalvo rescues a brother and sister from two robbers (one of whom is instantly converted into an honest man by Gonsalvo's generosity to him) and falls in love with the sister, Julia, who takes an aversion to him. At the same time Gonsalvo is followed by two girls disguised as boys who are both in love with him. After a series of exciting adventures, fights, more pirates, and a dramatic escape from a ship, Gonsalvo relinquishes his love for Julia, reconciles the jealousies between the two other male characters, and proposes to one of the disguised girls, Honoria, who has done him endless service. The play concludes with the line "Beauty but gains, Obligement keeps our Love."[4] It has been obvious long before this, however, that the theme of the play is "obligement" (and I write in full knowledge of, and partial disagreement with, Richard Levin's recent pronouncements about the inadequacy of thematic criticism).[5] Love itself creates obligations of duty and obedience to the beloved, but in this play, like all the others, obligations are also created by any number of favors that one man or woman can do for another: saving or sparing his life, setting him free from imprisonment, giving him gifts or rendering him service, protecting his person, pardoning him, returning him kindness for an ill deed, repealing him from banishment, ransoming him, giving him a relative in marriage, and so on almost ad infinitum. No character in *The Rival Ladies* is exempt from obligations that he or she has incurred from the good offices of others, although it tortures Julia that her aversion to Gonsalvo prevents her from returning his benefits. Gonsalvo himself is taught by her rejection of him that he must continue giving without hope of return, even when his mistress is formally surrendered to him by her brother. Love forces him to be generous when the law would permit him to claim her hand, so he overcomes the hope of recompense and learns that the true reward for giving a benefit is a good conscience. Since Honoria is in the same plight, and as both are willing to sacrifice their lives for their loves, they have earned each other by the end of the play, and their mutual obligement will carry them into a happy future. It takes Almanzor ten long acts to learn the same lesson in *The Conquest of Granada*.

The ethic Dryden's plays expound, and of which *The Rival Ladies* is an especially clear example, is an undiluted Stoicism, although it derives from a branch of that philosophy which has been relatively little studied, even by classical scholars. Cicero's famous *Offices* (I. 42 ff.) are part of the background, but the cru-

cial documents are Seneca's *De beneficiis* and his brief redaction
of similar ideas in his eighty-first *Epistle*. The seven rambling
books of *De beneficiis*, full of difficult cases of conscience concerning benefits, offer an extraordinary clarification to anyone
who is immersed in Dryden's plays. Seneca returns again and
again to certain principal ideas and then discusses the apparent
exceptions to the rules. A benefit is "the act of a well-wisher who
bestows joy and derives joy from the bestowal of it, and is inclined
to do what he does from the prompting of his own will."[6] The free
will of the giver and the intention to give pleasure to the recipient
are all-important, because gifts donated under pressure or services performed grudgingly do not qualify as gifts and do not
oblige the receiver. Similarly, a virtuous recipient will not only
instantly recognize his obligation but also will wait for years if
necessary to repay the favor with interest. The state of mind of
both parties is an essential factor, since the gift itself is only the
sign of a benefit, not the substance. The generosity of one (or, as
Dryden often called it, the "kindness") is balanced by the gratitude of the other, and while the giver should seem to forget his
benefit, the receiver should remember it forever; one should hold
his tongue while the other publishes his thanks. Benefits conferred with the hope of repayment are not true gifts, and an
ungrateful receiver should be bombarded with further benefits
until he relents — as Gonsalvo continues to shower Julia with good
turns until he learns the other (the giver's) lesson that nothing is
to be redemanded. Generosity is its own reward and ingratitude
its own punishment, and as men rebuild houses and cities on the
very sites where they have been destroyed, so a virtuous man will
maintain his hopes in human nature and continue giving "to re-
edify and re-attempt the ruins that were past."[7] An unthankful
man should not be accused because "the complaint of the loss of
our benefit, is a sign it was badly given" (p. 310)—a reflection
that immediately puts Almanzor or any number of Dryden's pro-
tagonists in their place. On one hand, while ingratitude appears
to be the least of the outrageous sins and is rarely punished (p.
148), yet are all tyrants, thieves, adulterers, and church-breakers
"children of ingratitude, without which scarcely any evil enterprise hath been plotted or performed" (p. 20). On the other hand
the virtue of generosity or benefiting "constitutes the chief bond
of human society" (Loeb ed., p. 19), and Roger L'Estrange in his

very popular abstract of *De beneficiis* castigated all the rebels of his times as ingrates and stated that "the whole Business (almost) of Mankind in Society, falls under this Head [of benefiting]: The Duties of Kings and Subjects; Husbands, and Wives; Parents and Children; Masters, and Servants"; it was "the very Ciment of all Communities."[8]

A history of the influence of *De beneficiis* on English thought would be a sizeable undertaking, especially as Christian homiletics are also much concerned with gratitude, but it would show the consistent and widespread diffusion of the ideas that permeate Dryden's plays. In the first edition of his popular *Treatise of Morall Phylosophie* (1547), William Baldwin entitled one chapter "Of benefyttes, and of unthankfulness," which he soon expanded into a longer essay "Of giving and receiving." By the end of the seventeenth century Saint-Evremond could ask rhetorically, "Is there a dispute about the acknowledgment of a good turn, a thousand Men refine upon the *Discourses of Seneca?*" Catholics and Puritans alike tended to ally the mutual obligations of children and parents with similar ties between rulers and ruled. Essayists expounded the theme, and writers on friendship could hardly avoid it. Thomas Gainsford in 1616 summarized the clichés in his handbook, including the reflection that "benefits have sometimes a taste of bribery," and Nicholas Caussin made gratitude the tenth motive for stirring up people of quality to seek Christian perfection; he scattered his pages with metaphors for the power of benefits. "Benefits are sharp-pointed Arrows, which thoroughly penetrate the heart of Tygers and Lions.... Good turns are golden Nets, which catch the swiftest gliding Fishes.... O how strong bird-lime is a benefit all generous birds are taken with it." Clarendon found the fourth psalm an occasion for a brief discourse on the subject. In the political realm, as we might expect, patriarchalism best expressed the universal wish for a society united like a happy family, with each member gladly acknowledging his indebtedness to the others. Edmund Bohun defended Filmer with the claim that Adam was a kind of father to his wife

that Marital as well as all other Power, might be founded in Paternal Jurisdiction. That all Princes might look upon the meanest of their Subjects as their Children: and all Subjects upon their Prince as their common Father: And upon each other as the Children of one Man, that Mankind might not only be united in one common Nature, but also be of one Blood, of one Family, and be habituated to the best of Governments from the very Infancy of the World.

Were this well considered, as there would be no Tyrants, so neither would there be any Traytors and Rebels, but both Prince and People would strive to out do each other in the offices of Love and Duty.[9]

To this traditional emphasis upon the good feelings and the good turns which "cemented all communities" Descartes was to make an important contribution. It is an interesting one for our purposes because it brought to bear on an emotional drama the full weight of the seventeenth-century psychology of the passions. In *Les passions de l'âme* (1649), translated into English in 1650, he substituted generosity for Aristotelian magnanimity or scholastic prudence as the greatest of all the virtues, and hence the most appropriate for heroic figures. Yet he was working, as Father Levi has shown,[10] from well within a neo-Stoic tradition, and it comes as no surprise to find that yet another French influence was operative in the heroic plays. Generosity, Descartes said, was "the key of all the other virtues, and a generall remedy against all the irregularities of Passions."[11] It "causeth a man to set himself at the highest rate he justly may" and consists "in knowing that there is nothing truly he can call his own, unless this free Disposition of his Wills [sic], nor wherefore he ought to be praised or blamed, unless for using that well or ill." A generous man will restrain himself from condemning others, and because he does not think himself much inferior to another with more wit, knowledge, beauty, or honors, he is less inclined to think himself much superior to those whom he surpasses. Generosity thus consorts with a virtuous humility while naturally inciting men to perform great deeds. It would be hard to find a better description of Aureng-Zebe. The generous, moreover, are also the most pitiful, "for it is a part of Generosity to bear good will to every man," although their pity is not bitter and is reserved rather for the weakness of those who cannot bear afflictions than for the grievousness of the ills themselves. Descartes defined gratitude, the proper response to generosity, as "a sort of Love, excited in us by some Action of him to whom we offer it.... So it includes all that Goodwill doth, and this besides, that it is grounded on an Action we are very sensible of, and whereof we have a desire to make a requitall. Wherefore it is far more strong, especially in Souls never so little noble and generous." He followed Seneca, too, in his claim that gratitude was "one of the principall bonds of humane society."[12]

It is also the bond that unites all the successful societies in Dryden's plays, from the happy marriages at the end of *The Rival Ladies* to the concluding lines of his last drama: "Let thanks be paid; and heaven be praised no less/For private union, then for public peace" (VIII, 474). One of the most characteristic scenes in any play by Dryden is an encounter between two people who are profoundly obliged to each other either by love or by some great service that one of them has performed: Montezuma and Cortez, for example, in *The Indian Emperour,* Antony and Cleopatra in *All for Love,* Arimant and Indamora in *Aureng-Zebe,* and many more. Stresses arise either when one party is ungrateful, like most of Dryden's senile and libidinous old emperors, including Ptolemy in *Cleomenes,* or when a conflict of obligations makes right action difficult to determine; e.g., Acacis in *The Indian Queen,* Cortez again, and married or betrothed women like Almahide and Indamora. A main feature of the plot in *Don Sebastian* is that the hero, that "great and grateful" loser, has been apparently ungrateful to his follower Dorax, who has broken all the Senecan rules by harboring a grudge about it for many years. They are reconciled in an "ecstacy of joy" and generosity at the end of Act IV, when Dorax may be said to have learned the truth he had stated earlier: "All must be Rapine, Wars, and Desolation/When trust and gratitude no longer bind" (XV, 111-112). The gloom of the later plays is caused largely by their characters' sense that gratefulness has declined from former days and that the court view of gratitude, "so much for so much," now prevails (*Cleomenes,* VIII, 296). The "ungenerous usage" that Cleomenes has suffered in Alexandria leads him to more Senecan declamation: "Believe me, Ptolemy, a noble soul/Does much that asks: He gives you power to oblige him. / Know, sir, there's a proud modesty in merit, / Averse from begging; and resolved to pay / Ten times the gift it asks" (VIII, 294). His predicament is worsened by Cassandra who offers him herself, although he responds with the proper maxim "Immoderate gifts oppress me, not relieve; / Nor dare I take what ruins you to give" (VIII, 326).[13] Similar unwanted and improper presents are rejected in

Tyrannick Love, which is also the play that demonstrates most unequivocally that force has no power over generous minds, nor can it persuade them to succumb to the baser passions.

Another classical situation in which Dryden's characters are sometimes placed is that of being unable to repay the obligations they profoundly feel. Almahide, for instance, exclaims, "How much, Almanzor, to your aid I owe, / Unable to repay, I blush to know; / Yet, forced by need, ere I can clear that score, / I, like ill debtors, come to borrow more" (IV, 210). She might have spared her blushes because Seneca had taught that "anxiety becometh not a grateful mind" (Lodge trans., p. 271) and that while occasions of restitution were to be observed, they were not to be sought. The desire to requite a benefit speedily was the mark of ingratitude "because a benefit is a common bond, and linketh two together" (p. 270). "Shall I always be indebted? Thou shalt be indebted, but openly indebted, but willingly indebted, but with great contentment shalt thou behold the gage laid up by thee" (p. 271). Dryden's heroic lovers are all schooled in the precept that "it is no less proper to a noble heart to owe, than to give" (p. 272) and they would have agreed with Seneca that it was a more laborious occupation since the keeping of things required more diligence than giving. "But 'tis thy fate to give, and mine to owe," says the emperor to Aureng-Zebe, although his reprehensible behavior in returning malice for kindness raises the still further question of whether the obligation conferred by a former benefit can be extinguished by subsequent cruelty, a problem faced not only by Aureng-Zebe but by the recipients of the erratic favors of Montezuma in *The Indian Queen* and of Almanzor. Seneca himself seemed to think that it could, although he was careful to point out that as a benefit was an action it could not be taken away, although it might be overpressed or drowned (p. 225). Benefits can remain but they may not be due. Aureng-Zebe, in another important scene occurring (as so often) at the end of Act IV, proposes the ideal solution. The emperor has finally repented: "my cruelty / Has quite destroyed the right I had in thee. / I have been base, / Base even to him from whom I did receive / All that a son could to a parent give: / Behold me punished in the selfsame kind; / The ungrateful does a more ungrateful find." Aureng-Zebe will have none of it, however: "Accuse yourself no more," he replies, "You could not be / Ungrateful;

could commit no crime to me. / I only mourn my yet uncancelled score: / You put me past the power of paying more" (V, 276-277). This Senecan kind of casuistry permeates both the plots and the language of all Dryden's heroic plays. It creates ties of obligation which the noble characters spend their lives trying to fulfill, and which the baser sort attempt to escape at their peril. Abenamar's stubborn mind melting into "headlong kindness," Melesinda's devotion to her husband in spite of his ingratitude, Duke Ferdinand's "obliged and grateful mind," maxims like, "And they shall overcome who love the best," "Each gains the Conquest which the other gives," or "Honor I sought, the generous mind's reward" — even the images of the three graces that seem to appear in the early plays, together with the pirates, robbers, and shipwrecks with which Seneca's pages are also sprinkled: countless incidents and lines of this sort establish a view of perfect relationships and a stable society that closely follow the Senecan model. Yet Dryden was naturally aware of the mutability of all human systems, which was one of the principal reasons why Seneca thought that men should be kind and compassionate to each other. "The thought of human chance should make us kind," as Zulema remarks. Heroic drama is tinged with the sadness of an unattainable ideal, as others have noted, but the nostalgia has been overstated, and it would be fairer to Dryden to exempt him from Seneca's condemnation of the fabulists and to class him with the moralists who "speak seriously and employ their utmost forces" to heal men's disfigured and vicious minds, and to "maintain faith in human things" by engraving the memory of good turns in the hearts of men (p. 12).

If Dryden's vision of a heroic society, united by bonds of natural obligation, was as unreal as some of his critics have claimed, then Clarendon's conception of England's noble past, now corrupted by the effects of two civil wars and the Interregnum, must be called equally fanciful. In a well-known passage from his *Life*, he mourned a decline from a national ideal which Dryden shared:

In a Word, the Nation was corrupted from that Integrity, good Nature and Generosity, that had been peculiar to it, and for which it had been signal and celebrated throughout the World; in the Room whereof the vilest Craft and Dissembling had succeeded. The Tenderness of the Bowels, which is the Quintessence of Justice and Compassion, the very Mention of good Nature, was laughed at and looked upon as the Mark and Character of a Fool; and a Toughness of Manners, or Hardhearted-ness and Cruelty was affected. In the Place of Generosity, a vile and sor-did Love of Money was entertained as the truest Wisdom. . . . There was a total Decay, or rather a final Expiration, of all Friendship; and to dis-suade a Man from any Thing He affected, or to reprove him for any Thing He had done amiss, or to advise him to do any Thing He had no Mind to do, was thought an Impertinence unworthy a wise Man, and received with Reproach and Contempt. These Dilapidations and Ruins of the ancient Candour, and Discipline, were not taken enough to Heart, and repaired with that early Care and Severity that they might have been. . . . So that, much of the Malignity was transplanted, instead of being extinguished, to the Corruption of many wholesome Bodies, which, being corrupted, spread the Diseases more powerfully and more mischievously.[14]

Dryden's heroic plays, as well as his satires, were his contribu-tion to the "Remedies" that Clarendon called for, but while the ex-chancellor had at the time of writing very personal reasons for feeling disheartened by the state of the nation, he did not exag-gerate the magnitude of England's problems. Historians of the Restoration, although they try to maintain their impartiality, point to a continuing decline of responsible government, at least until 1688—an alienation of the governors from the governed which Professor Hurstfield has recently declared to be almost inevitable, over time, as the rulers try to govern successfully and yet perpetuate their own power.[15] Professor Browning refers to consistently bad leadership, unprincipled and disillusioned poli-ticians, "astonishing variations" of policy, and a situation after 1667 when Charles's deliberate fomentation of the rivalries among his ministers led not so much to his personal government as to the insurance "that nobody should be in control at all." Blackmailed by France, extravagant and wasteful at court, Charles lost the national confidence and brought "discredit [to] the existing system." By 1678, Browning continues, "the whole policy of the government was discredited"[16]—a process vehe-mently exposed in Marvell's *Account of the Growth of Popery and Arbitrary Government* and, I think, by Dryden's *All for Love*. As society became less rigidly hierarchical, we learn, the fluidity and competitiveness within the political nation were increased.[17]

The enormous competition for office and emoluments is a theme of everyone who writes about the period. Clayton Roberts entitles his chapter on the years 1660-1674 "The Breakdown of the Balance of Government," and his chapter on the years 1674-1688 "The Crisis of Confidence."[18] The "unresolved equilibrium" of the constitution in 1660 had led to "paralysis of government" in 1679 and to arbitrary power and the "Stuart revenge" in 1681. Even by 1665 the mood of the House of Commons was similar to its mood in 1641, and two years later a flood of opinion existed for parliamentary supervision of the executive.

In the sixties the attack on reputations was even more serious than the attempt to bring enemies to trial, although the struggle for office does not really begain until the fall of Clarendon in 1667. Politics, as Roberts reminds us, "was a desperate and hazardous game in the seventeenth century, played for the highest stakes, and exacting the severest penalties from the loser,"[19] and J. R. Jones comments that the success of the revolution in 1688 was the more remarkable "when set . . . against the background of chronic political crisis, instability and lack of mutual trust which characterized the period after the Restoration." The court, he says of the years 1667-1688, "lived in what may best be described as a Hobbesian state of nature. . . . There was no sense of unity or collective responsibility, all were constantly disturbed by intrigue and manoeuvres."[20] In the country as a whole, Christopher Hill has evidence to show that the animosities between the gentry and the "ordinary sort of people" were increasing and that the "sharpening class divisions . . . made Parliamentary leaders think twice about pushing their quarrels too far."[21] The oppressive nature of government is another of Hill's themes, and one recalls Ogg's warning that we hear too much of the rights and liberties of seventeenth-century Englishmen and not enough of the many duties that were silently enforced. "The state was then thought of not as an instrument of social service, nor as an establishment for the political education of the masses; but as the armed force providing ultimate sanction for the enforcement of law and order. . . . 'Authority is the main point of government,'" as a contemporary remarked.[22]

These are but samples, drawn from standard sources, of the conflicts of interest that flourished in every segment of society and across the whole hierarchy of orders and degrees with which it was obsessed. Even looks and glances carried much surreptitious meaning, because the face was supposed to be unable to hide the characters of the passions, and Clarendon's *Life* is full of the "countenances" that were reserved, darkened, withdrawn, or cloudy toward him. One gets the impression from texts as varied as Restoration comedy or Sir Keith Feiling's history of *British Foreign Policy 1660-1672* that the entire system was an elaborate charade of deception and chicanery in which only the most acute, who could read the smallest signs correctly, had any chance of survival or success. The vocabulary of this world reflected its eternal suspicions, and no single word captured them more often than "jealousy." I do not know the exact moment when the word *jealousy* entered political discourse but it was in common use before the civil war. Then, in the early months of 1642, shortly after the Attempt on the Five Members, the phrase "fears and jealousies" entered popular speech and became the single most frequent slogan to explain the causes of the war. They were, said Clarendon in his *History,* "the new words which served to justify all indispositions and to excuse all disorders."[23] Charles resented them very much and they were so overused that many men must have abandoned them, but nevertheless they remained, either singly or together, as staple epithets to describe any kind of political suspicion or antagonism. One cannot read more than a few pages of the parliamentary debates, the political documents, or contemporary annals without coming across them, and they have often been absorbed, perhaps only half-consciously, into the language of modern historians.

It was inevitable sooner or later that the jealousy that had for centuries occurred in dramatic literature, and of which *Othello* and *The Winter's Tale* contain the most memorable examples, should reflect the new status of the word. As I have tried to show in an earlier essay,[24] it was in fact less than six months after the coinage of the phrase that John Denham wrote his play *The Sophy* to expose the danger of fears and jealousies. It was published less than three weeks before the king raised his standard at Nottingham, although there is no certain record of its performance before the closing of the theatres. In December 1660 the rights to the play passed to the Duke's Company, and I presume it was acted before its only recorded performances in 1670 and 1674. It was reprinted in Denham's *Collected Poems* in 1668. It may not have been a coincidence that Dryden should have praised Denham in the dedication to his first play, because in *The Rival*

Ladies the astounding jealousy of Roderick encountered the incredible generosity of Gonsalvo, and another of the basic conflicts in all Dryden's serious plays was established.

In *Secret Love, or The Maiden Queen,* the queen herself is racked with jealousies, on the one hand for her prerogatives and on the other for her chief adviser, who has no inkling until the end of Act IV that she has fallen in love with him. If Charles II, who called it "his play," was adept at reading morals, he would have seen that secrecy was partly the cause of jealousies on both sides, and they lead in the play to an abortive rebellion. The queen loses her power until she decides to break her attachment to her counselor and to remain in a celibate enjoyment of her glory for the rest of her reign. Charles had no interest in celibacy, but it did so happen that in the year of the play's first production the jealousies of the early years of the Restoration came to a head in the impeachment and fall of Clarendon, and Charles was left alone to begin what were supposed to be his years of personal rule. The subplot of *Secret Love* concludes the play with a young couple deciding to be open with one another, and unjealous. Twenty-three years later Dryden was to return to a similar theme, and since in *Don Sebastian* the incestuous tragedy occurs because the lovers have hidden their origins from each other and performed a secret marriage, and since every other character has engaged in some act of concealment, I assume that the danger of secrecy is the moral that Dryden assured his readers he had "couched under every one of the principal parts and characters" for judicious critics to observe.[25] Dryden's own secretiveness was in keeping with his plot.

Both *The Indian Queen* and *The Indian Emperour* contain scenes of jealousy, and in the latter Cydaria becomes "jealous to the last degree" of Cortez's deceased mistress, and Almeria is so tortured by this passion that she stabs her rival in the final moments of the play. Many of Cortez's troubles are also caused by the jealousies of Odmar and Orbellan, although the play ends with the "generous exiles" of the young lovers and the expression of "loud thanks" by Cortez for the double blessing of conquest and of love. In *Tyrannick Love* the action is initiated by the jealousy that Placidius feels for Albinus and his not unjustifiable sense that the emperor has ungratefully rewarded him for the victories he has won. Jealousies and ingratitude are constantly linked in the plays, as they should be, because Seneca had said that the most "powerful and insistent" of all the causes of ingratitude was jealousy, "which disquiets us by making comparisons."[26] In *The Conquest of Granada* the factions that threaten to bring anarchy to the state are "grounded on a grudge, / Which all our generous Zegrys just did judge: / Thy villain-blood thou openly did place / Above the purple of our kingly race" (IV, 41). The effects of these jealousies were no less dire than those inspired by Lyndaraxa, which eventually cause her death, or the jealousy of Almanzor himself over the scarf that induces him at a crucial moment to betray his trust to Almahide. Jealousy also plays an important role in *All for Love,* where the politicians deliberately incite it, but it is of *Aureng-Zebe* and *Love Triumphant* that one may say it forms the mainspring of the dramas. The open warfare between the four brothers in *Aureng-Zebe,* the injustice of the emperor to his noble son, and the struggles that Aureng-Zebe undergoes in winning Indamora are all brought about by jealousies that must be cured before the country can return to sanity and stability. In *Love Triumphant* the "Song of Jealousy"—that "tyrant of the mind"—holds a central position in the play and the jealous conflict between Veramond and Alphonso constitutes the main action, which is resolved only when both men confess their sins and recognize the gratitude they owe to the other's generosity.

Jealousy is the single most disruptive passion in Dryden's plays as it was in the political language of the Restoration, and Dryden's audience could not have escaped the connection. Ingratitude was not considered to be a passion, as no motion of the spirits excited it, but it shared with jealousy the distinction of being a mortal enemy of generosity. Another brief foray into the theory of the passions should help to explain further the rationale of the emotional structures that Dryden designed. This time, however, it will not be necessary to turn to Descartes or to other French moralists like Senault, La Chambre, and de Courtin, all of whom were translated into English, because Dryden's own honored friend, Walter Charleton, wrote a book in which the main principles of heroic drama might be said to be expounded. There is some confusion about his *Natural History of the Passions* (1674) as the *D.N.B.* and the *B.M.* catalog state that the book is based on Senault's *Use of the Passions,* but a good deal of it is a virtual translation of Descartes, whom he honorably mentions as "incomparable." He makes the usual distinction that jealousy is a sub-species of fear, not envy (a fear of losing a good that belongs to us), castigates ingratitude as the vice of men who are either fool-ishly proud, sottishly stupid, or of weak and abject minds, and observes (as Dryden's heroines often demonstrate) that love attends on gratitude as hatred is an adjunct of ingratitude. He concludes that against all vain desires there are two general reme-dies, a tranquil dependence on divine providence and, chiefly, true generosity:

For, that noble and heroic habit of the mind, which is called *Generosity*, and which seems to comprehend all other Virtues; though it animateth Men to great and honorable enterprises, doth yet at the same time re-strain them from attempting things which they conceive themselves in-capable to effect; inspiring *courage*, not temerity. Then by teaching, that nothing is either more worthy of, or more delightful to a spirit ele-vated by love of virtue, above the vulgar, than to doe good to others; and in order thereunto, to prefer beneficience to self-interest: it makes us perfectly charitable, benign, affable, and ready to oblige every one by good offices, when it is in our power to do so. Again, being insepara-ble from virtuous *Humility*, it makes us both to measure our own Merits by the impartial rule of right reason, and to know that we can have no just right to praise or reward but from the genuin and laudable use of the freedom of our Will. And from these and other the like excellent effects of this divine Virtue, it is that the *Generous* attain to an absolute dominion over their exorbitant passions and desires. They conquer *Jeal-ousie* and *Envy*, by considering, that nothing whereof the acquisition depends not wholly upon themselves is realy valuable enough to justify their earnest desire of it. They exempt themselves from *Hatred* towards any, by esteeming all as worthy of love as themselves. They admit no *Fear*, by being duly conscious of their own innocency, and secure in the confidence of their own Virtue. They banish *Grief*, by remembring that while they conserve their *will* to doe *good*, they can be deprived of noth-ing that is properly theirs. And *Anger* they exclude, because little esteeming whatsoever depends upon others, they never yeeld so much to their Adversaries, as to acknowledge themselves within the reach of their injuries. It is not then without reason, that I fix upon *Generosity*, as one of the universal remedies against our inordinate Cupidities. [pp. 175-177]

This was the essence too of Dryden's conception of a heroic soci-ety; Stoic in its origins, French by immediate extraction, but nat-uralized in England, and attributed by Clarendon to the genius of the English people from time immemorial. If it was unreal,

then it was no more so than any other image of national character
and virtue with which countries have consoled themselves, and
gone to battle to defend. The exaggerations of heroic language
can be readily admitted, and Dryden defended them on grounds
that were then perfectly reasonable, but the ethic that underlies
them was rooted in a classical idea of a just society and the contemporary psychology of the passions, and it was intended to
counteract the myriad causes of jealousy which disturbed the
Restoration peace.

Keeping the peace was also the overriding concern of the greatest English political philosopher, but to turn from Dryden's plays
to the *Leviathan* is seemingly to pass from one world to another.
It is true that the language of "benefits" awakens many familiar
echoes and that the fourth law of nature, gratitude (it had been
the third in *De Cive*), is high up on the list of laws that bind at
least *in foro interno;* but the essential difference of course is that
Hobbes's society was a contractual construct whereas Dryden's
was founded on principles of natural obligation in which benefits
flowed reciprocally between the ruler and the ruled but could not
be claimed or redemanded. Hobbes was well aware of the difference. Service performed "in hope to gain the reputation of charity, or magnanimity; or to deliver his mind from the pain of compassion; or in hope of reward in heaven; this is not contract, but
GIFT, FREE-GIFT, GRACE: which words signify one and the
same thing."[27] To Hobbes, however, these "benefits oblige, and
obligation is thraldom . . . but to receive benefits, though from an
equal, or inferior, as long as there is hope of requital, disposeth to
love: for in the intention of the receiver, the obligation is of aid
and service mutual; from whence proceedeth an emulation of
who shall exceed in benefiting; the most noble and profitable
contention possible; wherein the victor is pleased with his victory,
and the other revenged by confessing it" (p. 67). Seneca never
described better the rivalry between the obliger and the obliged,
and of which he wished to learn the secret. Hobbes's system, as
many have complained since Clarendon's *Brief View and Survey
. . . of Leviathan,* leaves little room for this contention of generosity, but there has in recent years been some disagreement as to
the role in *Leviathan* of those generous natures who glory in
appearing not to need to break their word, and whose pride
exempts them from the fear of the consequences of breaking it,

by which most men are persuaded to keep their contracts. "This latter," said Hobbes, "is a generosity too rarely found to be presumed on" (p. 92).

Leo Strauss discounted the significance of generosity to Hobbes, attributing it to the passing influence of Descartes, and Keith Thomas has concurred to the extent that he too finds that "one can recognize in the man of generosity Hobbes's ethical ideal without making him an essential part of Hobbes's political structure." Hobbes's aristocratic ideal was one to which "only a select minority can aspire" and his ethical assumptions, Thomas believes, "may well prove to be more closely associated with the refined heroic code of the Great Tew than with any other identifiable milieu."[28] Perhaps this is true, but the background I have been discussing suggests that Hobbes was certainly aware of a much larger context in which the principles of generosity and reciprocity were norms rather than aberrations, and from which his own system was a deliberate departure. Consequently, Thomas has not altogether disposed of Michael Oakeshott's interesting speculations about Hobbes's generous natures. Such men "with a touch of careless heroism" about them achieve by themselves and contribute to the common life "a complete alternative to what others may achieve by means of agreement inspired by fear and dictated by reason." Their kind of pride (and "*Pride* and *Generosity* consist equaly in *Self-esteem,* differing only in the injustice and justice thereof")[29] was "capable of generating an endeavour for peace more firmly based than any other and therefore (even in the *civitas,* where it is safe to be just) the surest motive for just conduct." Although Hobbes's was the philosophy of the tame man, he concludes, and although "he felt constrained to write for those whose chief desire was to 'prosper,'" he himself "understood human beings as creatures more properly concerned with honour than with either survival or prosperity."[30]

Much has been written about Dryden's indebtedness and opposition to Hobbes, and it is often pointed out that the evil tyrants in his dramas proclaim a kind of Hobbesian absolutism, but there exists this small corner in the *Leviathan,* reserved for the elite, where Dryden's heroes and Hobbes's friend, Sidney Godolphin, could have shaken hands. If Howard Warrender's thesis about Hobbes were true—than "men could never by valid covenant bind themselves to obey a human ruler unless they were already

obliged to obey the laws of nature[31] — then one could claim much
more, because the law of gratitude would become one of the cor-
nerstones on which a contractual society rested. Dryden's view of
Hobbes, however, was more likely to have resembled Clarendon's
and he was probably unaware that in a rigorous analysis of the
system, Hobbes was "moving from the principle that promises
oblige towards the principle that benefits oblige," and that in the
keeping of all covenants there were always two principles operative: "that of keeping a promise and that of gratitude for the consideration involved."[32]

John Locke refers to the "generous Temper and Courage" of
the English nation in the very first sentence of his *Two Treatises
of Government,* but for him also it was a generosity not to be presumed upon, except within the confines of the ordinary family,
where it ruled as the order of the day: "honour and support, all
that which Gratitude requires to return for the Benefits received
by and from them is the indispensible Duty of the Child, and the
proper Priviledge of the Parents. . . . The *Duty of Honour . . .*
remains never the less entire to them; nothing can cancel that."[33]
There is much more of the same kind, none of it the least new,
but Locke's complete divorce of political power from the uncon-
tractual arrangements of the family nailed down the old parliamentary positions with an authority his work has never lost. The
length and severity of his preliminary assault on Filmer was required if he was to dispose once and for all of natural obligation
as the foundation of government. Filmer himself, with whose
ideas Dryden's are often compared, had no significance whatever
in the development of Dryden's thought, in my opinion. *Patri-
archa* appeared long after Dryden's position had been fully established, and Filmer's tracts of the late forties and early fifties had
no particular impact at the time. There had always been a strand
of moderate patriarchalism in English discussions of kingship,
and the idiosyncrasies of Filmer's extreme statement of it would
have seemed to Dryden unnecessary. Andrew Marvell (who never
promoted contract theory in his life, Whiggish though he was)
was closer to Dryden than Filmer when he concluded his definition of the English limited monarchy with the statement that
"nothing comes nearer in Government to the Divine Perfection,
than where the Monarch, as with us, injoys a capacity of doing all
the good imaginable to mankind, under a disability to all that is

evil."[34] What the example of Dryden's plays suggests, and what the Filmer phenomenon confirms, is that theories of natural obligation had taken far deeper root in English soil than critics, historians, and political scientists have recognized. We have been obsessed with the contractual schemes of Hobbes and Locke and have insufficiently explored the appeal of much older ideas that were thought to be the cement of all societies, and which flourished in the eighteenth century as the principles of benevolence. It was the great achievement of Locke and his parliamentary predecessors to have erected an enduring alternative to the principles of natural obligation, but as Dryden looked back on the seventeenth century, he recorded only the failure of its aspirations and the faithlessness of the times. In his distress he may have taken some comfort from the last line of De beneficiis: "It is not the action of a generous mind, to give and lose; this is the mark of a mighty mind, to lose and give."

NOTES

1. The references for these quotations are James Sutherland, *English Literature of the Late Seventeenth Century* (Oxford, 1969), p. 60; David Ogg, *England in the Reign of Charles II*, 2d ed. (Oxford, 1967), p. 706; R. J. Kaufmann, "On the Poetics of Terminal Tragedy," in *Dryden: A Collection of Critical Essays*, ed. Bernard Schilling (Englewood Cliffs, N.J., 1963), p. 89; Anne Righter, "Heroic Tragedy," in *Restoration Theatre*, Stratford-upon-Avon Studies 6 (London, 1965), p. 138, ibid., p. 135.

2. Arthur C. Kirsch, *Dryden's Heroic Drama* (Princeton, 1965); Eric Rothstein, *Restoration Tragedy* (Madison, 1967); Eugene Waith, *The Herculean Hero* (New York, 1962) chap. 6, and *Ideas of Greatness: Heroic Drama in England* (London, 1971).

3. Notably Anne T. Barbeau, *The Intellectual Design of John Dryden's Heroic Plays* (New Haven and London, 1970). See also John A. Winterbottom, "The Place of Hobbesian Ideas in Dryden's Tragedies," *JEGP* LVII (1958), 665-683 and two essays by Michael Alssid, "The Design of Dryden's *Aureng-Zebe*," *JEGP* LXIV (1965), 452-469 and "The Perfect Conquest: A Study of Theme, Structure, and Characters in Dryden's *The Indian Emperor*," SP LIX (1962), 539-559.

4. *The Works of John Dryden*, gen. ed., H. T. Swedenberg, Jr. (Berkeley, Los Angeles, London: University of California Press 1956-), VIII, 179. In this paper the California edition is used for *Rival Ladies*, *Indian Emperour*, *Indian Queen*, *Tyrannick Love*, *Secret Love*, and

Don Sebastian. Volume and page numbers are cited in the text. For all other plays the edition used is *Works,* ed., Sir Walter Scott, revised by George Saintsbury (Edinburgh, 1882-1893), with references also cited in parentheses.

5. From a long series of articles the following can be selected: "Some Second Thoughts on Central Themes," *MLR* LXVII (1972), 1-10; "Third Thoughts on Thematics," *MLR* LXX (1975), 481-496; "My Theme Can Lick Your Theme," *College Enlish* XXXVII (1975), 307-312; and a forthcoming article in *MP.* Levin's articles are an excellent antidote to the excesses and the frequent narrow-mindedness of thematic criticism, but he has yet to dispose of the fact that renaissance readers delighted in deriving precepts (or themes) from all kinds of literary and historical works, and that many authors explicitly proclaimed their concern with the morals of their works. For partial answers to Levin's criticisms, see a review by Aubrey Williams in *PQ,* LIII (1974), 676-680, and John M. Wallace, " 'Examples are Best Precepts': Readers and Meanings in Seventeenth-Century Poetry," *Critical Inquiry* I (1974), 273-290.

6. *Moral Essays,* trans. John W. Basore, Loeb Library ed. (London, 1899), III, 23.

7. *Seneca on Benefits,* trans. Thomas Lodge, Temple Classics ed. (London, 1899), p. 313. Subsequent references to Lodge's translation are incorporated in the text.

8. *Seneca's Morals by Way of Abstract* (London, 1678), pp. 2-3. There were no less than ten editions of this book in the next twenty-one years.

9. *A Defence of Sir Robert Filmer* (London, 1684), pp. 13-14. References for the preceding paragraph are as follows: Saint-Évremond, *Miscellaneous Essays* (London, 1692), p. 258; [Gainsford], *The Rich Cabinet Furnished with a Variety of Excellent Descriptions* (London, 1616), sig. $10^V - 12^V$; Caussin, *The Holy Court* (London, 1663), pp. 93-94; Clarendon, *A Collection of Several Tracts* (London, 1727), pp. 388-390. See also this assortment from varying sources: Owen Felltham, *Resolves* (London, 1661), nos. 10, 41, 54 ("Of Gifts and their Power"); Daniel Tuvill, *Essays Politic and Moral,* ed. John L. Lievsay (Charlottesville, Va., 1971), pp. 106-114 ("Of Gifts and Benefits"); Henry Percy, Ninth Earl of Northumberland, *Advice to His Son,* ed. G. B. Harrison (London, 1930), pp. 107-127; Thomas Wright, *The Passions of the Minde in Generall* (London, 1630), pp. 239-260; N. Remond des Courts, *The True Conduct of Persons of Quality* (London, 1694), chap. 74; Sir T[homas] C[ulpeper], *Morall Discourses and Essayes* (London, 1655), pp. 182-184; Robert Johnson, "Of Greatness of Mind" and "Of Liberality," in *Essaies, or, Rather Imperfect Offers* (London, 1613); William Ames, *Conscience with the Power and Cases Thereof* (n.p., 1639), pp. 153-169 (on mutual obligations).

E. Catherine Dunn, *The Concept of Ingratitude in Renaissance English Moral Philosophy* (Washington, D.C., 1946) remains a useful and well-documented study of the evils that were alleged to occur if benefits were not recognized. Since no good study of the theory of patronage in England appears to exist, I have avoided the topic. Patronage, however, when it was not overtly bought or sold, was a practical manifestation of a noncontractual basis for society.

10. Anthony Levi, *French Moralists: The Theory of the Passions 1585 to 1649* (Oxford, 1964), esp. chap. 10.

11. René Descartes, *The Passions of the Soule* (London, 1650), p. 135.

12. Ibid., p. 157. Information cited in this paragraph will be found on pp. 126-128, 152-153. The discussion of generosity arises naturally from the initial consideration of Estimation and Contempt. The generous man's just estimation of himself and of the virtues and vices of others brings equanimity and the control of his passions. He is free of all desires except the desire for virtue.

13. Cf. *De beneficiis*, Loeb Library ed., p. 19 ("thoughtless indulgence that masquerades as generosity") and p. 63 ("That is no benefit which I am not able to think of without a blush").

14. *The Continuation of the Life of Edward Earl of Clarendon* (Oxford, 1759), II, 41-42.

15. Joel Hurtsfield, "The Politics of Corruption in Shakespeare's England," *Shakespeare Survey* XXVIII (1975), 21.

16. Andrew Browning, introduction to *English Historical Documents 1660-1714* (London, 1966), p. 12; see also pp. 7-8.

17. J. R. Jones, *The Revolution of 1688 in England* (New York, 1972), p. 26.

18. *The Growth of Responsible Government in Stuart England* (Cambridge, England, 1966).

19. Ibid., p. 161. The preceding information is also from Roberts.

20. Jones, *Revolution of 1688*, p. 24.

21. *The Century of Revolution 1603-1714* (Edinburgh, 1962), p. 233.

22. David Ogg, *England in the Reign of Charles II*, 2d ed. (Oxford, 1955), p. 486.

23. *The History of the Rebellion and Civil Wars in England*, ed. W. Dunn Macray (Oxford, 1888), I, 493; see also I, 535.

24. See the article cited in note 5. Much earlier, however, R. Nannini in *Civill Considerations upon Many and Sundrie Histories* (London, 1601), p. 65 had made the connection between state and domestic jealousy: "Forasmuch as Princes concerning their estates are like lovers towards their Mistresses; and as for iealousy they are equal and march with like pace: for as a man may easily lodge iealousy in the heart of a lover; even so may a man with great facilitie put a doubt and suspicion into the heart of a Prince, by reason of his estate." The chapter is entitled "A man ought not neither in iest or by other meanes to put a Prince in iealousie of his estate, for that it is a matter full of danger."

25. See his preface to the play in California edition, page 71. Douglas Canfield in a review in *PQ* LIII (1974), 699 asserts that the secret moral

"is that subjects (Dorax) should never violate their trust in their king (Don Sebastian), just as he, in the face of inexplicable misery, must trust implicitly in Providence." Because secrecy destroys trust the different morals we discover in the play are more related than they at first seem.

26. *De beneficiis,* Loeb Library ed., p. 105.

27. Thomas Hobbes, *Leviathan,* ed. Michael Oakeshott (Oxford, 1947), p. 87.

28. "The Social Origins of Hobbes's Political Thought," in *Hobbes Studies,* ed. K. C. Brown (Cambridge, England, 1965), p. 207; previous quotation from p. 204. An article that supplements Thomas's fine essay and supports some of my own claims is Jerrilyn Green Marston, "Gentry Honor and Royalism in Early Stuart England," *Journal of British Studies* XIII (1973), 21-43.

29. Walter Charleton, *Natural History of the Passions* (London, 1674), pp. 99-100.

30. Michael Oakeshott, *Rationalism in Politics* (New York, 1974), p. 294; previous quotations from pp. 290, 293.

31. *Hobbes Studies,* ed. Brown, p. 76.

32. Howard Warrender, *The Political Philosophy of Hobbes* (Oxford, 1957), pp. 233, 235.

33. *Two Treatises of Government,* ed. Peter Laslett (Cambridge, England, 1960), p. 331.

34. *The Growth of Popery and Arbitrary Government,* in *Complete Works,* ed. Alexander B. Grosart (n.p., 1872-1875), IV, 250. In writing this essay I have been deeply indebted to Mr. Quentin Skinner, Dr. Derek Hirst, and my colleagues Dr. Richard Strier and Dr. Jay Schleusener for long conversations about the theory of natural obligations. I have also profited from discussions in seminars at the Clark Library, Washington University (St. Louis), Purdue University, and the British History Club at the University of Chicago.

VI

ISAAC NEWTON IN CAMBRIDGE: THE RESTORATION UNIVERSITY AND SCIENTIFIC CREATIVITY

Richard S. Westfall*

The question to which I address myself is straightforward. Isaac Newton spent thirty-five years in Cambridge, from 1661, when he enrolled as an undergraduate, until 1696, when he departed for London. During those years, he invented the calculus, discovered the composition of light, and composed the *Principia*. Although he would publish his *Opticks*, specimens of his fluxional calculus, and two amended editions of the *Principia* in London, his achievement in science had essentially been completed by the time he left Cambridge. I seek to investigate what contribution the Cambridge environment, from which it emerged, made to that achievement.

Let me be clear that I am not engaged in the current debate on the relation of the universities to the scientific revolution.[1] Although it is impossible wholly to avoid the issue if I consider Newton in Cambridge, I shall confine myself to the relative security of a few judgments delivered *ex cathedra* in passing. Coward

*The author gratefully acknowledges the support of the American Council of Learned Societies which made possible the research on which this paper is based.

135

that I am, I intend to emulate Newton in his fear of controversy and pass by the questions central to the debate. As my title attempts to suggest, I shall concentrate on the one institution in its relation to the one man. I think I may be engaged in a sociological inquiry. As far as I know, I have never committed sociology before, and what looks to me like sociology may look to sociologists like something they would rather not name. Call it what you will. I intend to commit it in any case.

At first glance, I may appear to be intent on a problem that does not exist. What could be less surprising than Newton in an academic environment? We are accustomed to the notion that the university is the primary home of theoretical science. Every year, Professors Who and What at the Universities of Here and There smile with satisfaction as they adjust their Nobel laurels. Why belabor the obvious in the case of Newton? The problem, of course, lies in the well-known fact that the present pattern in the relation of science and the university is less than two centuries old. It cannot be traced in any significant sense beyond the founding of the École polytechnique in 1795. In calling my assertion a well-known fact, I realize that I have delivered my first pronouncement ex cathedra. I shall pause to justify it only by noting that Newton was the only prominent figure of the scientific revolution who pursued his career with a university.[2] In the seventeenth century, he was the anomaly rather than the rule. As such, he requires investigation.

Let me begin with what I take to be the most basic fact about Cambridge University in the second half of the seventeenth century. Newton's career there roughly coincided with the most calamitous decline in the history of the university. Within the limits of my knowledge, it is the most calamitous decline ever suffered by any university that has survived as an important institution. The tiny medieval institution along the river Cam had grown during the Elizabethan and Jacobean age at a rate reminiscent of the manic expansion of higher education in America after the second World War. Increasing in numbers by a factor of five or six until the early 1620s, the population of Cambridge reached a size it would not know again for another two centuries. A survey of the university undertaken in 1622 showed a total of 3050, a number that included students, fellows, and servants. This year was very near the peak of the university's expansion. In

1623, the highest year, 290 students commenced bachelors of arts. Over 450 students matriculated, and if the usual divergence between admissions and matriculations held, the colleges admitted about 550 students. From that point a steady decline set in, encouraged initially no doubt by the policies of the church, especially under Laud, and continued by the upheaval of the civil war and the Interregnum. A brief resurgence accompanied the Restoration, bringing the size of the university back to about 2,500 by 1672. The following decline was all the more precipitous. By 1690 matriculations numbered less than two hundred per year and bachelors of arts about 145. No one was thoughtful enough to do a survey of the entire university in that year, but extrapolation from the earlier figures implies that it had shrunk to barely more than half its maximum size in the 1620s.[3] Oxford went through a similar cycle with less extreme fluctuations. Early in the seventeenth century, as Puritanism waxed, the junior institution surpassed it in size for a brief time. Correspondingly, the decline at Oxford was less radical; at the end of the century it was about fifty percent larger than Cambridge.

Mere numbers offer the crudest measure of any institution's vitality. If we speak instead of morale and vigor, of intellectual vitality, the available evidence indicates that Cambridge declined even more dramatically in these respects than in size.[4] Perhaps the decline was inevitable, given the course of English history. Cambridge had been the pulsing heart of English Puritanism; it was bound to beat more slowly once the great crusade lost confidence in its mission. Probably the greater decline of Cambridge stemmed from its connection with Puritanism. The similar if less pronounced decline of Oxford inclines one to look for further causes as well.

Intellectually speaking, both universities were adrift. The scholastic curriculum established by acts of Parliament continued to have legal force. It had ceased to command allegiance. An "arid feast of brambles and sow thistles," in the words of Milton, it attempted to perpetuate the philosophy of Aristotle in an age when he no longer claimed the assent of European philosophers.[5] Piecemeal changes in the curriculum, whereby some of the *litterae humaniores* crept in under the guise of rhetoric, had undermined the coherence of the old curriculum without providing a consistent alternative. The medieval universities had generated their own vitality by leading European thought. Restoration Cambridge, in contrast, repeated by rote the formulas of another age.

Considerable evidence indicates that the curriculum had ceased even to command the allegiance of those with a vested interest in enforcing it. Repeatedly Cambridge received orders from Charles II, presumably prompted by some conscientious official of the university, that the exercises and disputations of the curriculum be performed. In 1668 the monarch imposed a fine on those failing to keep their divinity acts. Eight years later, after inquiries by the chancellor had established that exercises were not being performed, Charles sent a letter to the vice-chancellor admonishing him to see that all exercises whatsoever prescribed by the statutes were observed. Another eight years later, alas, he had to order the same for exercises required of the masters of arts.[6] When repeated orders to the same purpose have to be given, one can only assume that they produce no effect. At the very same time, as though it knew very well where Charles's attention was really focused, the university was itself ensuring that his orders were not enforced. The climactic exercises of the undergraduate career had been the public disputations during the Lent term of a student's final year, what was called standing *in quadragesima*. In 1681 a decree by the Heads, recognizing that nonresidence during the final Lent term had become the established practice of the university, dispensed with required residence during that term.[7] Long before this, the university senate had taken to passing the grace, which granted degrees, at the beginning of the Lent term, which I understand to be a tacit admission that the Lenten exercises had ceased to have any significance. The statistics for degrees during the plague years offer vivid testimony on the state of the university. From the summer of 1665 to the spring of 1667, Cambridge hardly functioned for the better part of two years. One can scarcely see a ripple in the statistics for commencing bachelors of arts.[8] Studies or no, the degree mill ground on.

The counterpart of the relaxation of requirements for students was the relaxation of duties for professors. Cambridge had a number of university professorships, and three more were established during the Restoration. All of them carried stipends for the incumbents, and the statutes for every chair required the attendance of a particular class of students. Most of the chairs were converted into sinecures. The very creation of the Adams Professorship of Arabic in 1666 was an irresponsible act by the university, which seemed concerned only that the money being offered not escape. Arabic had no relation to the curriculum of the university. After the initial novelty wore off, the first incumbent found himself without auditors and promptly made his position a sinecure, which it remained for a century and a half. Early in the eighteenth century a second professorship in Arabic was established. From the beginning its stipend was used to alleviate whatever distress might afflict the holder of the Adams chair.[9] In contrast with Arabic, moral theology was directly related to the acknowledged functions of the university. Nevertheless, the Knightsbridge Professorship of Moral Theology, established in 1682, was treated as a sinecure from the moment of its creation; no Knightbridge Professor lectured before the nineteenth century.[10] Early in the eighteenth century Conyers Middleton, a fellow of Trinity College and a bitter opponent of the efforts of the master, Richard Bentley, to reform the college and to suck it dry at the same time, used Bentley's neglect of the Regius Professorship of Divinity as a stick with which to beat him. Earlier professors of divinity, he claimed, had put up notices of lectures, showed up, "and actually read a theological lecture whenever they found an audience to attend them, which was sometimes the case."[11] When the Woodwardian Professorship of Geology was created shortly thereafter, the same Conyers Middleton, who knew nothing about geology, did not hesitate to secure the chair for himself and after an inaugural lecture (on the content of which it is impossible not to speculate) to enjoy the income for three years without further performance.[12] In 1710, a German traveler, Zacharius von Uffenbach, visited Cambridge. Even when we compensate for Uffenbach's tendency to denigrate everything English, it is difficult to imagine an attractive reality behind his depressing account. He visited the university library and those of the colleges. Without exception, he found them in a state of neglect and confusion. Books and manuscripts were covered with mold and dust; he had to wear an apron in order not to ruin his clothes. It was no use in any case; the libraries were in such disorder that nothing could be located. Clearly, scholars did not frequent them. He was told about the state of the university "which is certainly very bad." Uffenbach was amazed to find that no lectures were being given. It was summer. In the winter, he was told, three or four lectures were given—"to the bare walls, for no one comes in."[13]

To his account of university lectures, Uffenbach added the comment that instruction was given in the colleges by tutors. Certainly anyone would be misled who attempted to judge Restoration Cambridge by the university's lectures and exercises. By 1660 the conquest of the university by the colleges was nearly complete. One reason behind the decline of university lectures was the rise in the colleges of the tutorial system, which appears consciously to have seen university lectures as a rival and to have striven to destroy them. One looks to the colleges in vain, however, for the spark of vitality so absent from the university. Quite the contrary, they present a spectacle all too similar. A fellowship was looked upon as a freehold to be enjoyed without corresponding duties. A small minority saw in tutoring a source of additional income. The great majority looked upon it as an imposition to be evaded. They referred to the active tutors derisively as "pupil-mongers," while they themselves accepted their stipends and dividends as rights that involved no obligations whatever. Scholarship was no more their business than tutoring. Already in 1663, William Sancroft, the master of Emmanuel College, complained that he could not find "that old genius and spirit of learning generally in the college that made it once so deservedly famous. . . ."[14] By the end of the century, reformers such as William Whiston and Humphrey Prideaux (of Oxford) were proposing means to retire fellows who neither tutored nor lectured. Prideaux suggested a sort of almshouse, suitably named "Drone Hall," where they could live on a pittance.[15] In 1754, Samuel Johnson visited Pembroke College, Oxford, where he had been a student nearly thirty years before. There he and his companion, Wharton, met the Reverend Mr. Meeke, a fellow, whose learning Johnson had envied when they were students. "About the same time of life," Johnson told Warton after they left, "Meeke was left behind at Oxford to feed on a Fellowship, and I went to London to get my living: now, Sir, see the difference in our literary characters!"[16]

More than adequately, if less than sumptuously supported and divested of any serious function, the average Cambridge fellow of the Restoration found himself with only two weapons to fend off boredom, the table and the tavern. In Roger North's splendid phrase, they became "wet epicures," surrendering to a corpulent lethargy liberally flavored with alcohol.[17] To be sure, it was only late in the eighteenth century that one of their descendants, Dr. Ogden, remarked that the goose was a silly bird, too much for one and too little for two[18] — but this was lack of wit on the part of Restoration dons, not lack of capacity. Whiston told of a fellow student at Clare in the 1690s who observed the conduct of the fellows carefully and concluded that heavy drinking was the way to gain a fellowship.[19] Early in the eighteenth century, a French visitor to Cambridge, a Huguenot to be sure but also a friend of Diderot and not likely to be excessively fastidious, wrote that "whoever is ignorant of the art of drinking a lot and smoking a lot is very unwelcome in this University. . . ."[20] Fellows cultivated idiosyncrasies and adopted adolescent standards of behavior. Roger North's brother John, a fellow of Jesus College, installed in his room an organ which he played when he could not sleep. When the bellows hit the floor, they awakened "a morose and importune master of arts" who lived in the room below. Realizing that there was no point in appealing to North's sense of decency, he attacked his problem by indirection. He repaired to the green outside North's window where he played at bowls, generating even more noise than the organ. North gave up the organ, and the morose and importune master of arts, at least, got his sleep.[21]

By the early eighteenth century, the air of Cambridge and Oxford was filled with satires — of practices established during the Restoration.

> Within those walls, where thro' the glimmering shade
>   Appear the pamphlets in a mould'ring heap,
> Each in his narrow bed till morning laid,
>   The peaceful Fellows of the College sleep.
>
> The tinkling bell proclaiming early prayers,
>   The noisy servants rattling o'er their head,
> The calls of business, and domestic cares,
>   Ne'er rouse these dreamers from their downy bed.
>
> Oft have they basked along the sunny walls,
>   Oft have the benches bow'd beneath their weight;
> How jocund are their looks when dinner calls!
>   How smoke the cutlets on their crowded plate![22]

There is universal agreement on the decline of Cambridge and Oxford during the Restoration. There is less than universal agreement as to its cause. Inevitably, among academic historians, students have been a popular target. According to this argument, the universities were taken over during the seventeenth century by a new class of students, the sons of the ruling class, who came to the university for whatever polish they could acquire while they pursued their customary pleasures. A hard drinking, hard gaming, hard wenching crew, they established themselves as the dominant class in the two universities and set the tone of student life.[23] Certainly one cannot mistake the presence of the fellow commoners and pensioners in Restoration Cambridge. No longer could the Puritan tone by maintained. University authorities kept themselves busy issuing orders against the frequenting of taverns. They forbade students to enter certain houses in Barnwell and even in Cambridge inhabited by women of ill repute. The orders were very specific, naming the houses in question precisely, to the considerable benefit of any students, if such they were, who had failed to locate them on their own.[24] The repetition of such admonitions indicates that they were roughly as effective as the king's orders to observe academic exercises. In fact, the university was powerless to control its wealthy students, on the favor of whose parents it was dependent. Such discipline as there was fell primarily on the sizars, the poor students who were servants to the wealthy and to the fellows, who found the recreations of their bettors attractive but lacked the influence to avoid the consequences. One can readily understand how the socially dominant class of students, especially such a class and in such an age, could alter the tone of a university.

Nevertheless, I wish to argue that they were only a secondary factor and that another feature of Cambridge common both to students and to fellows played a much larger role in the intellectual decline of the university. Careful statistical studies have shown that the proportion of sons of gentlemen among the student body did not alter appreciably during the seventeenth century. The proportion of another class did increase dramatically, the sons of professional men, of doctors, lawyers, and especially clergy.[25] We need to remember as well that less than half of the sons of gentlemen who entered Cambridge bothered to graduate. A degree held no significance for them. Many of them went on, after a couple of years, to the Inns of Court for training in the law, which would be significant. For what alone was a degree all important? A career in the church. Roughly three quarters of all university graduates during the Restoration did in fact go on to ecclesiastical careers. More than the playground of the aristocracy, the universities became the breeding pens for the other branch of the establishment, the Anglican church. One seems to see a hereditary clerical class emerging. Narrowly vocational in outlook, their attention focused upon preferment, they were supremely interested in degrees, much less so in education.[26] The realities of the age confirmed their choice. The precise nature of the universities' decline appears to coincide with their interests.

Moreover, their interests were identical with those of the majority of fellows in the colleges, and the interests of all meshed smoothly with another prominent feature of both universities, the role of patronage. Together, Cambridge and Oxford were the largest reservoir of patronage in England. No Church Catholic stood as a buffer between them and the secular powers that wished to exploit their resources. Intrusions of the government in the affairs of the universities had become common after the Reformation. They had increased steadily in the seventeenth century, first with the efforts of Laud to control the universities, then with the wholesale evictions on ideological grounds that came with the civil war and the Restoration. Charles II, returned from his travels, was concerned to construct a network of clients to buttress his power. Hence both universities received a stream of letters mandate such as they had never known before, ordering them to admit someone to a degree or to elect someone to a fellowship, "local statutes notwithstanding." Masterships were significant positions. Nominations to several of them were in the Crown's hands. Almost all of those supposedly elective were filled by letters mandate from London. Fellowships were much smaller pickings, but they were suitable for younger sons, for the clients of clients, and for aspiring men who might use them as their first stepping stone and continue to hold them as supplements to other preferments.[27]

Faced with continual external pressures, the colleges made faint gestures of resistance. On occasion, they tried to preserve the appearance of independence by replying that they had already elected the man in question. On other occasions, they tried to forestall mandates by actual preelections designed to keep all of the fellowships full. In 1677, Pembroke College simply outsped the crown. At 2:00 A.M. on the morning of 20 August, Robert Maptetoft, the master of Pembroke had convened the fellows to choose his successor, and the new master was inducted at 6:00 A.M. Charles allowed them to have their way this once.[28] To understand why the colleges did not protest more, one has only to look at the ritual volumes of verse that the university churned out on every occasion that touched the Crown. There was a volume for Charles's restoration in 1660, a volume in 1661 on the deaths of his brother and sister, a volume in 1662 on his marriage, a volume in 1669 on the death of his mother. For each of them, every ambitious man in the university ponderously tortured his muse for his quota of Latin verses. *Lacrymae Cantabrigienses* was the title of the 1670 edition for the death of Charles's sister, a hideous composite of sycophancy unmoistened by any suggestion of a real tear. Cambridge was populated with men in search of patronage. They were not likely seriously to oppose the wishes of their own best hope. When Andrew Marvell characterized the master of St. John's as "this close youth who treads always upon the heels of Ecclesiastical Preferment,"[29] he sketched the portrait of the whole university. As it appears to me, the prime reality of Restoration Cambridge was its symbiotic relation with the monarchy. On the one hand was a king who sought to bolster his position by judicious patronage. On the other hand was a group of men seeking to rise in the world by preferment in the church. It was not a relationship calculated to promote a vigorous intellectual life.

It is misleading, however, to speak continually about Cambridge University as a collectivity. By the Restoration, the university hardly existed. The reality of Cambridge was the group of sixteen colleges. For Newton, Cambridge was primarily the most important of the sixteen, Trinity College, to which he belonged. Trinity was also one of the two largest. Together with its neighbor, St. John's, it comprised a good third of the entire university. The statutes of Trinity made provision for sixty fellows. During the Restoration, a fellowship was worth at least £650 per annum when all of its perquisites were taken into account. To put that sum into perspective, recall on the one hand that in 1658 Samuel Pepys was living in London with a wife on a salary of £50. On the other hand, skilled workmen such as stone masons who worked on the Trinity library in the 1670s received between 20 and 24 pence a day, which would come to between £26 and £31 for the year if they worked six days a week, fifty-two weeks of the year. Actual earnings were more likely between £15 and £20 per year, on which sum most of them were supporting families. Unskilled laborers received half as much.[30] With the exception of the incumbents of two specific fellowships, all the fellows of Trinity were required to take orders in the church within seven years of incepting masters of arts. It is hardly surprising that nearly all of them intended to pursue a career in the church. They fell into two categories. Most of them regarded the fellowship as temporary support until they found a living. The college itself controlled extensive patronage. It held the advowsons of nearly fifty churches into which it inducted its own members, primarily on the basis of seniority. It might take as long as twenty years to wait out a desirable living, but once he had done so, the erstwhile fellow could escape from enforced celibacy and support a wife on an adequate income. Those to whom marriage promised no delights, for whatever reasons, could stay on in the college where benefits of a different sort awaited them. With sufficient seniority, they were appointed college preachers, positions that carried the privilege of holding a college living near Cambridge without surrendering the fellowship.

The year 1661, when Newton entered Trinity as a student, marked the final triumph of seniority as the governing principle of the college. Seniority had always been important, but in the statutes it had competed with the rival principle of achievement. A fellow with an advanced degree received from the college a stipend nearly double that of a master of arts, and as long as the stipend mattered, this provision operated as an effective inducement to continued study. By the mid-seventeenth century, however, inflation had reduced the value of the stipend, set by the statutes of 1560, to insignificance. As the college's income also increased, a new system was hit upon to restore the value of a fellowship, the dividend, literally the division of the annual surplus. The same device was adopted throughout Cambridge and Oxford during this period. As it happened, 1661 was the year in which Trinity College established its definitive pattern of division. Advanced degrees, diligence in tutoring, achievement or performance of any sort played no part in the division. Seniority, and seniority alone, determined the size of one's dividend. Seniority in turn was measured from the day of one's admission to the college as an undergraduate, which established an immutable order of privilege (for those who advanced to fellowships) which no achievement could alter.[31] Not only the dividend but many other perquisites were bestowed by the same immutable order—choice of chambers, appointment to college offices, nomination (which was tantamount to election) by the college in its turn to university offices (additional income being involved for both college and university offices), above all eligibility for the coveted livings in the college's gift. Almost at once, with the full victory of seniority, Cambridge dons ceased to take advanced degrees.

In 1664, 1667, and 1668, Trinity College held three elections in which a total of forty-one men were named to fellowships. Newton was one of those elected in 1667. The average tenure of the forty-one was seventeen and a half years; twenty-one of them stayed at Trinity more than twenty years. The presence of Newton raises the intellectual tone of any group. If we examine the other forty, however, the tone drops rather abruptly. One of them, Robert Uvedale, became an educator and horticulturist who was well known in his own time although he is scarcely remembered today. Another, John Battley, was a reasonably prominent antiquarian; he is remembered even less than Uvedale. Several of the group published a few sermons; one published a lot.[32] One became a stalwart Anglican polemicist ready at all times to expend his ink against any slightest deviation to right or to left; happily, he too has long since sunk into oblivion. Newton aside, they were not a distinguished group of intellectuals by any standard. Perhaps they served their college well as tutors? Not entirely. Of the forty-one, four chose the role of pupil-mongers, in the pejorative phrase of the day; that is, they were active as tutors. Of the other thirty-seven, only ten ever tutored as many as one student, and these ten tutored a total of sixteen.[33] Four of the forty-one remained in the college more than forty years. Patrick Cock, George Modd, Nicholas Spencer, William Mayor— one of them proceeded on to a bachelor of divinity degree after thirty years; none of them published a scrap of writing; none of them tutored a single pupil. By their superior powers of survival alone, they became in the end senior fellows of the college, who plucked its ripest rewards. Modd and Cock bitterly opposed Bentley's efforts to reform the college until, under threat that he would expose the scandal of their lives, they found it prudent rather to reach an accommodation. Modd eventually became Bentley's pliant tool. He died finally in 1722, the last of the forty-one still holding a fellowship. It was said of George Modd that he attended morning prayers in the chapel daily at 6:00 A.M. until he was more than eighty.[34] To the profane eye of the twentieth century, it hardly seems an adequate recompense for the benefits he enjoyed.

The question of Newton in Cambridge is leading to a rather different resolution than someone with the current organization of science in mind might have expected. Is there any legitimate sense in which we can speak of a scientific community in Cambridge which encouraged, stimulated, and nurtured Newton's achievement? I am unable to perceive any scientific community in Cambridge.[35] I am not even sure there was an intellectual community. There had been. In the first half of the century, when Cambridge was the center of English Puritanism, it had furnished the ferment in English intellectual life. From that earlier period, the Restoration university inherited the Cambridge Platonists. No one replaced them as they died off, and by the 1680s Cambridge was becoming an intellectual wasteland. Who besides Newton left any perceptible trace on the intellectual history of England?

We need to define his relation to the university in different terms, keeping both Newton's genius and the nature of the institution clearly in mind. As for Newton, the scope of his genius rendered him independent of his immediate surroundings. The community that stimulated and nurtured him was the church invisible of seventeenth-century natural philosophy. Its members were present to him in their published works. He required no more. As far as Cambridge is concerned, it is necessary to realize that Newton's work contributed as little to its overt purposes as the inactivity of the average fellow. It is true that Newton held a university chair in mathematics. If we think that the university deliberately created the chair as part of a conscious educational plan, however, we shall be deceived. The Lucasian Professorship of Mathematics, like the Adams Professorship of Mathematics, like the Adams Professorship of Arabic which was established two years later, came to the university unsought. It never occurred to a group of men whose foremost thought was preferment that they might reject a gift. Both chairs were established for the sole reason that they were offered. The one was as little concerned with the reality of the institution as the other; neither produced any perceptible effect on the university in the seventeenth century.

That is, Newton exploited Cambridge almost as much as George Modd. The mere fact that time and change have validated his activities in our eyes should not mislead us. When we judge his activities in terms of the seventeenth-century institution, we are forced to conclude that they contributed nothing to its functions. The significance of Cambridge for Newton was not its stimulation but its laxity. The circumstances of his election to a scholarship and then to a fellowship are hidden from us. Since he had abandoned the recognized curriculum to pursue his own interests, he may have owed his elections to a patron within the college; if that was so, no more than hints of their relation have survived.[36] Once he held a fellowship, it was as much a freehold for him as it was for the others. By good fortune, he impressed Isaac Barrow on the eve of his resignation from the Lucasian chair; and scarcely a year beyond his master of arts degree and his fellowship, he found himself the incumbent also of the third richest professorship in Cambridge. Although the Lucasian statutes prescribed a lecture a week when the university was in session, the chair did not intrude on his time any more than the fellowship. Apparently he did lecture, at least part of the time, for eighteen years during the period when other professors were converting their positions into sinecures.[37] Since he presented work he was doing anyway, and even then frequently to the walls, he cannot have found it a heavy burden.[38] For nearly thirty years, Cambridge gave to Newton what it gave to Patrick Cock, George Modd, Nicholas Spencer, and William Mayor—provision for his needs, access to books, and unencumbered leisure. They ignored the books and used their leisure to bask along the sunny walls, bowing the benches a bit more each year beneath their growing weight. He devoured the books and devoted his leisure to the studies of his choice. The arrangement does not appear to me to be a promising prescription for a flourishing intellectual or scientific community. For Newton, whose genius isolated him in any case, it chanced to be an ideal arrangement.

He must have appeared a strange figure indeed to the other fellows. They took their ease; he studied without intermission to the point of endangering his health. And what studies! They would find mathematical diagrams drawn in the walks of the garden. Be it said to their credit that they walked around the diagrams so as not to disturb them.[39] He kept a furnace at which he experimented endlessly at what could only have appeared to be alchemy, as indeed it was. If he came to the hall, he was likely to show up disheveled, in his surplice instead of his gown, and to sit there lost in thought, neither speaking nor eating. They must have found the last peculiarity strangest of all. Newton's chamberfellow Wickins would have told them also that he frequently forgot to eat the dinners sent to his room. Who could be too busy to eat?[40]

> How jocund are their looks when dinner calls!
> How smoke the cutlets on their crowded plate!

Nevertheless, eccentricity was becoming a way of life in Cambridge, and Newton's eccentricities were not demonstrably more subversive, say, than holding a fellowship in absentia or supplementing a fellowship with a prosperous church living. To retain his place he had only to abstain from the three unforgivable sins —crime, marriage, and heresy. To the first he had no inclination, to the second positive aversion. He was in fact inextricably involved in the third, but to his good fortune heresy could be concealed.

In its very triviality, however, Cambridge was a threat. Recall the Reverend Mr. Meek, whom Johnson had considered his superior as a student, but whom Oxford reduced to a nonentity. The various factors that served to isolate Newton from his surroundings played a critical role in his career. The first of these factors operated during his undergraduate career. Although his mother was a wealthy woman,[41] she sent her son to Cambridge as a sizar, a servant either to a fellow or to another student, a servant who awakened him in the morning, emptied his chamber pot, carried food and coals for him, and dressed his hair. Sizars were not allowed to eat with the other students; they dined after the hall was cleared on what the fellows left. Newton was the heir to the lordship of a manor, albeit a minor one. He was used to being served, not to serving. His own records from his undergraduate days show him attempting to associate with the pensioners, the more prosperous students from the better classes. The one anecdote from his undergraduate days that is not concerned with his studies, Wickins's story of how they met, reveals a young man, alienated from his surroundings, walking alone and dejected in the college paths. Significantly, Wickins, who remained his chamberfellow for twenty years, was a pensioner. More than thirty years later, when the chance came to leave Cambridge for the world of fashion in London, the one-time sizar grasped it avidly. Already before he came to Cambridge, Newton had found it difficult to get along with the other boys in grammar school. It is hard to believe that the social stigma of being a sizar, so unnecessarily imposed on him, did not operate to isolate him further.

The Lucasian Professorship, which he obtained almost immediately after his student career, functioned in the same way. The statutes of the professorship forbade the incumbent to hold any college office. This provision helped to cut Newton off from influence in his college at a time when the vitality of Cambridge had come to reside in the colleges. To be sure, most regulations in Restoration Cambridge existed in order to be violated. The regius professors were under the same limitation, but regius professors held offices in Trinity. Nevertheless, Newton chose to observe the prohibition and hence to cut himself off from the other fellows.

Most important in this respect was a third factor. Sometime in the early '70s, within five years of his master of arts degree, Newton became a heretic. Apparently he felt no similar leanings in 1668 when he signed the three articles required of every incepting M.A. By the third article, he explicitly accepted the creed of the Anglican church. So also, under the Act of Uniformity, Anglican orthodoxy was a condition of his fellowship in the College of the Holy and Undivided Trinity. The holy and undivided trinity was exactly what Newton came to reject in the early 1670s. His theological manuscripts indicate that he embraced antitrinitarianism about that time.[42] Heresy is the only explanation I can imagine for an action he apparently took in 1673. One of the two fellowships in Trinity which were exempt from the requirement of ordination fell vacant; Newton tried to get it.[43] Unfortunately, Robert Uvedale, his senior by two years, also wanted the exempted fellowship. Uvedale was almost completely nonresident, but the rule of seniority was absolute. In two years, Newton faced the certainty of eviction from his fellowship unless he were ordained. This rule appears to have been the only one invariably observed in Restoration Cambridge. I do not know of any exception.[44] One can understand why. The ladder of seniority was filled with men eagerly climbing toward preferment. They would not tolerate anyone above them who could be evicted on grounds that did not threaten them. Ordination held no terrors for them; it was a necessary means to the preferment they sought. Ordained Newton could not be, however—or would not be. Perhaps he could have retained his chair without his fellowship, though I do not know of anyone in that status. The threat lay in the exposure of his heresy. Embarrassing questions could not have been avoided. Why was he refusing ordination when of itself it entailed no duties? Suspicion of the truth would have arisen, and heresy was not tolerated in Restoration Cambridge.[45] In the end, Newton was rescued, probably by the influence at court of Isaac Barrow, who obtained a royal dispensation exempting him from the requirement. He was able to stay on in Cambridge, but only at the price of silence. It must have been a powerful influence separating him from his peers.[46]

Thus Newton was in Cambridge but not of Cambridge. For thirty-five years he was a member of Trinity College. Twenty men admitted at about the same time were his potential companions, first as students, then as fellows, for over twenty-five years. There is no evidence that he formed a friendship with any of them except one. He shared a chamber with John Wickins for twenty years. Even they did not maintain any relation once Wickins left the college.[47] After Newton left Cambridge in 1696, he never wrote a single letter (so far as we know) to anyone he had known there. It is worth recalling that a genius for friendship was hardly lacking in the age. One thinks, for instance, of Samuel Pepys and John Locke. The Cambridge Platonists frequently dedicated books to each other in which they publicly presented bouquets of mutual esteem. Newton's life in Cambridge was devoid of such embellishments. The factors isolating him served to confirm his neurotic tendencies, which were pronounced in any case. Their combined effect on his personality was disastrous—unless perhaps one considers immortality worth a neurosis.

The story does not end on this note, however. An unexpected final chapter began with the effort of James II to intrude Father Francis into the university, apparently as a first step toward its catholicization. The timing was almost providential. When James II succeeded to the throne in 1685, Newton had just seriously embarked on the *Principia*.[48] The two years necessary for the crisis to reach the university were almost exactly the time he needed to complete his masterpiece. When the crisis struck in the spring of 1687, he was completing the manuscript of the third and final book and was free to turn his attention elsewhere as he would not have been a year earlier. The terms of the challenge were equally providential. An advanced heretic, concerned primarily to avoid theological issues in order to conceal his beliefs, is not a likely candidate to lead the defense of orthodoxy. As it happened, however, he had convinced himself that the doctrine of the trinity was an invention of the papacy fostered by the willful perversion of the Scriptures during the early history of Christianity. Newton was a man of passionate convictions. Against the papacy he directed the full force of his hatred. James's challenge was exactly the one he could and, indeed, must accept.

Moreover, he was free to accept it as few in Cambridge were. In avoiding ordination, he had also foresworn the scramble for preferment to which most of Cambridge devoted itself. Not many members of the university cared to risk their prospects by challenging the principal source of patronage. William Lynnet, a senior fellow of Trinity, let it be known that he was unwilling to oppose His Majesty's pleasure, "which will be interpreted as unbeseeming presumption in us, who in our Constitution so immediately depend upon His Majesty's good Grace."[49] Marvell's "close youth" knew all too well that he could not at once tread upon the heels and step on the toes of ecclesiastical preferment. Having directed his career down other channels, Newton was immune to such considerations. The details of his actions have mostly been lost. The principal surviving account of the Cambridge case is a pamphlet written by the leaders of the resistance as propaganda and published immediately after the Revolution. Newton participated in its production.[50] What cannot be doubted is that Newton, who had been anything but prominent in university affairs, and who in the spring of 1687 was not yet a famous philosopher, suddenly emerged as one of the leaders of the university. senate. When others hesitated in fear and held back, he must have spoken out and rallied the resistance. Almost at once, he was chosen to represent the senate, and in April and May of 1687, while Halley was seeing the *Principia* through the press, he was one of six representatives of the university who appeared before Judge Jeffries to be berated for their disobedience.

When the Glorious Revolution ratified his courage, he suddenly found himself one of the most prominent men in Cambridge. His name began to appear on the tax commissions for Cambridgeshire appointed by Parliament to oversee the collection of specific levies. William proposed to appoint him provost of King's College; though when King's protested that a provost from outside the college would violate their charter, William drew back from imitating the example of James. Nevertheless, Newton was not forgotten, especially by some Whig grandees who had wit enough to realize that one of the men who had committed himself irrevocably to the Revolution by overt resistance to James was also one of the leading intellects of the age. Newton was in line for patronage of a different order from that to which most Cambridge fellows aspired.

The final act of Newton's career in Cambridge helps to put the whole into its proper perspective. I suggested earlier that he exploited the university to his own ends quite as much as the average fellow. By our standards, his life at Cambridge was the very epitome of an academic career well spent. By the standards of seventeenth-century Cambridge, his work was irrelevant to the life of the institution. Apparently he did lecture, at least during the first eighteen years of his tenure as Lucasian Professor. There is no evidence that he lectured after 1687 though he continued to hold the chair for another fourteen years.[51] With the possible exception of those on algebra, his lectures could hardly have been conceived in a form less likely to reach the students, as the stories of empty lecture halls indicate. In this respect, they contrasted with Whiston's successful efforts to pitch the same material on a plane that was comprehensible. Newton did not establish the scientific tradition at Trinity and Cambridge. That tradition was primarily the work of Richard Bentley with men who were Newtonians but who had not been students of Newton. For Newton, as for the rest of the academic world of Restoration England, the university was an institution to be exploited rather than served.

Barred by his heretical stance from exploiting it through the church, he demonstrated a further dimension of his genius by finding a new way to do so. Once preferment was offered him, he was tenacious in his pursuit of it.

By the mid-1690s, Patrick Cock, George Modd, Nicholas Spencer, and William Mayor were approaching the coveted status of senior fellows in Trinity College. They had already begun to reap the rewards of their longevity. They were securing the college's nomination in its turn to university offices such as proctor and taxor, which brought additional income. More important, they had become eligible for the lucrative benefices in the environs of Cambridge which fellows with sufficient seniority could hold. As they basked along the sunny walls, they must have reflected in satisfaction on careers well planned. How startled they must have been when that strange creature Newton, who drew diagrams in the walks, sweated over his furnaces, neglected his meals, and spoke out on dangerous issues, was appointed warden of the mint. They measured their preferment by tens and hundreds of pounds. He measured his by hundreds and thousands. The sizar of yore stepped briskly into the upper establishment, glancing back at Cambridge only when it suited his purposes to run for Parliament. Cambridge had supported him in solitude during his years of discovery. It had never entered his soul. He left in 1696 without perceptible regret.

NOTES

1. Various views on science and the universities can be found in Martha Ornstein, *The Role of the Scientific Societies in the Seventeenth Century* (Chicago: University of Chicago Press, 1928); Phyllis Allen, "Scientific Studies in the English Universities of the Seventeenth Century," *Journal of the History of Ideas* 10 (1949), 219-253; William T. Costello, *The Scholastic Curriculum at Early Seventeenth-Century Cambridge* (Cambridge, Mass.: Harvard University Press, 1958); Mark H. Curtis, *Oxford and Cambridge in Transition, 1558-1642* (Oxford: Clarendon, 1959); Hugh Kearney, *Scholars and Gentlemen: Universities and Society in Pre-Industrial Britain* (London: Faber, 1970); Barbara J. Shapiro, "The Universities and Science in Seventeenth Century England," *The Journal of British Studies* 10 (1971), 47-82; and Edward G. Ruestow, *Physics at 17th and 18th-Century Leiden* (The Hague: Hijhoff, 1973).

2. Galileo does not appear to me to constitute an exception. He used his first significant publication as a vehicle to effect his escape from the University of Padua (what appears to me as a symbolic act) and followed his career henceforth as a client of wealthy patrons, especially the grand dukes of Florence.

3. Statistics on matriculations are found in the *Historical Register of the University of Cambridge*, ed. J. R. Tanner (Cambridge: Cambridge University Press, 1917), pp. 988-989. James Bass Mullinger, *A History of the University of Cambridge* (London: Longmans Green, 1888), presents an eloquent graph of B.A.'s by year. Mullinger also has statistics on seventeenth-century Cambridge in *The University of Cambridge*, 3 vols. (Cambridge: Cambridge University Press, 1873-1911), 3:679. In 1622, 1651, and 1672, surveys of the university entitled *The Foundation of the University of Cambridge* were published. They go through the university college by college, listing the number of officers, fellows, scholars, sizars, and other students and servants. I have accepted their figures, which seem reasonable in comparison with the statistics on matriculations and degrees. David Arthur Cressy, "Education and Literacy in London and East Anglia, 1580-1700" (Cambridge, Ph.D. dissertation, 1972), p. 219, gives solid statistical evidence based on the records of several colleges for the percentage of admitted students who did not matriculate. In a MS that apparently dates from 1736, when matriculations and degrees had both declined further, Thomas Baker set the size of the university at 1,400 (Cambridge University Library, Baker MSS, Mm. 1. 48, p. 461). Since fellows and masters constituted a core of about 400 which did not fluctuate, the size of the university did not vary directly with the number of students.

4. Oxford went through a similar decline. Its historian calls the period of the Restoration "the days of its degeneracy..." (Charles Edward Mallet, *A History of the University of Oxford*, 3 vols. [London: Methuen, 1924-27], 2:433). Two differing interpretations of the decline, which overlap only slightly, can be found in Kearney, *Scholars and Gentlemen*, pp. 141-173, and Curtis, *Oxford and Cambridge*, pp. 272-281.

5. *Of Education*, in *Complete Prose Works*, gen. ed., Don M. Wolfe, 5 vols. to date (New Haven: Yale, 1953-), 2:377. Newton's undergraduate notebooks show that Aristotle and seventeenth-century peripatetics were the primary substance of the reading he was given (Cambridge University Library, Add. MS 3996). Locke complained that he was taught nothing else at Oxford (Maurice Cranston, *John Locke, A Biography* [London: Longmans Green, 1957], p. 39). Years later, in 1704, the heads of the colleges at Oxford tried to suppress Locke's philosophy at Oxford because it "had much discouraged the noble art of disputation (or hog-shearing as we call it)." The irreverent comment was made by his friend James Tyrrell, who informed Locke of the incident (Cranston, *Locke*, pp. 466-468).

6. Cambridge University Library, Baker MSS Mm. 1. 53, ff. 38-39.

Charles Henry Cooper, *Annals of Cambridge,* 5 vols. (Cambridge: War-
wick, 1842-1908), 3:572, 600.

7. D. A. Winstanley, *Unreformed Cambridge* (Cambridge: Cambridge University Press, 1935), p. 42. See pp. 58-61 for the relaxation of
residence requirements for degrees in civil law and medicine. Mallet,
Oxford, 2:439, and A. D. Godley, *Oxford in the Eighteenth Century*
(London: Methuen, 1908), pp. 12, 176-179, tell the same story for the
sister institution.

8. Mullinger, *Cambridge,* 3:679. Bachelors of arts had a stroke of
luck, it is true. The plague abated in the spring of 1666 at the right
moment for them to be present to receive their degrees, though not to
keep the Lenten exercises. In 1667 the plague abated later. Never mind.
The university procured a letter mandate from the king that no one
should "lose his year" merely because he could not perform the required
exercises (Cooper, *Annals,* 3:522). That is, the perquisites that went
with seniority were the prime consideration. As long as they were safe-
guarded, mere academic requirements were readily dispensed with.
Masters of arts were less fortunate. Their degrees were awarded in July,
and in 1666 the plague returned in June with the result that the number
of M.A.s dropped about 40 percent that year. They got no mandate,
but I do not know of anyone who lost his year as a result. Compare the
account of Thomas Fuller of the earlier plague of 1630 which also
forced the university to disperse: "But this *corruption* of the aire proved
the *generation* of many Doctours, graduated in a clandestine way, without keeping any Acts, to the great disgust of those who had fairly gotten
their degrees with publick pains and expence. Yea, Dr. Collins, being
afterwards to admit an able man Doctour, did (according to the pleas-
antnesse of his fancy) distinguish *inter Cathedram pestilentiae,* &
Cathedram eminentiae, leaving it to his Auditours easily to apprehend
his meaning therein" (*The History of the University of Cambridge since
the Conquest* [London: Williams, 1655], p. 166). No one would have
laughed in 1667; no one would have thought to try the jest. To be sure,
his story is about advanced degrees instead of B.A.s and M.A.s, but the
decline in advanced degrees was one aspect of the change whereby the
joke of yore had ceased to be funny.

9. Winstanley, *Unreformed Cambridge,* pp. 132-135.

10. Ibid., pp. 137-138.

11. British Museum, Add. MS 33491. f. 13; quoted in ibid., p. 98.

12. Ibid., pp. 167-168. His successors treated it as a sinecure. The
latter half of the eighteenth century falls somewhat beyond my range.
Nevertheless I cannot resist repeating the vicissitudes of some of the
chairs as a cautionary tale. In 1764, Leonard Chappelow, holder of the
two chairs in Arabic seemed to be dying. Samuel Ogden of St. John's
College sought to succeed him. True, Ogden did not know Arabic, but
in compensation he urged his seniority, which created a right of preferment. Before Chappelow died, however, Ogden secured the Woodwardian chair of geology for which he had, if anything, less qualifica-

tion. Chappelow held on until 1768, when John Jebb and Samuel Halifax competed for the position now empty at last. Neither one of them knew Arabic. Halifax was frank in stating that he only wanted it temporarily until the chair in law might be vacant, and by courting the Heads, who controlled the appointment, he won it (ibid., pp. 135-136). Winstanley discusses the conversion of various professorships into sinecures in the late seventeenth and early eighteenth centuries (ibid., pp. 61, 101). Godley indicates that the same thing was happening in Oxford (*Oxford in the Eighteenth Century*, pp. 40-47).

13. J. E. B. Mayor, *Cambridge under Queen Anne* (Cambridge: Cambridge Antiquarian Society, 1870), pp. 124-181. Uffenbach's account of Cambridge is one of three items that comprise Mayor's volume.

14. In a letter to his former tutor, Ezechiel Wright, 17 January 1663; quoted in E. S. Shuckburgh, *Emmanuel College* (London: Robinson, 1904), p. 111.

15. William Whiston, *Memoirs of the Life and Writings of Mr. William Whiston* (London: Whiston, 1749), p. 47; see also Godley, *Oxford in the Eighteenth Century*, pp. 75-76. The original charter of Emmanuel had included a limitation on the time a fellowship could be held in order to insure that the college would send men out into society. During the period of Laud, the fellows got the provision revoked; it was restored under the Puritan ascendancy but revoked definitively with the Restoration. Complains about the laziness of fellows, both in Oxford and in Cambridge, filled the air by the end of the century. Uffenbach supported Jean LeClerc's condemnation; "enjoying such large *beneficia* and noble libraries, they produced very little in the way of learning; which is only too true, with a few exceptions" (quoted from his *Reisen* in Mayor, *Cambridge under Anne*, p. 427). In 1715, John Edwards, who had been elected a fellow of St. John's (Cambridge) in 1659, delivered a devastating critique of the whole university which cannot be dismissed merely as senile moralizing (James Bass Mullinger, *St. John's College* [London: Robinson, 1901], pp. 203-205). Edwards wrote in earnest. In 1726, Nicholas Amherst of St. John's (Oxford) was no less devastating in writing satire. "When any person is chosen fellow of a college, he immediately becomes a freeholder, and is settled for life in ease and plenty. . . . He wastes the rest of his days in luxury and idleness: he enjoys himself, and is dead to the world: for a senior fellow of a college lives and moulders away in a supine and regular course of eating, drinking, sleeping, and cheating the juniors" (quoted in Godley, *Oxford in the Eighteenth Century*, p. 77). Somewhat earlier, a defender of James II in his confrontation with Magdalen College (Oxford) found an effective line of attack by comparing the fellows' performance with the statutes. According to him, fellowships were bought and sold "so that it was grown to a by-word, that an election at St. Mary Magdalen, was a Magdalen Fair" (Nathaniel Johnston, *The King's Visitorial Power Asserted* [London, 1688], p. 341).

16. James Boswell, *The Life of Samuel Johnson, L.L.D.* (New York: Dent, 1949), p. 161.

17. Roger North, *The Lives of the Norths,* ed. Augustus Jessopp, 3 vols. (London: Bell, 1890), 2:272.

18. Quoted from Gunning's *Reminiscences* in D. A. Winstanley, *The University of Cambridge in the Eighteenth Century* (Cambridge: Cambridge University Press, 1922), p. 8.

19. Whiston, *Memoirs,* p. 129.

20. Louis de Jaucourt to Diderot, 24 April 1727; quoted in Arthur M. Wilson, *Diderot* (New York: Oxford University Press, 1972), p. 481. Mallet has the same story to tell of Oxford, with many of the details drawn from Anthony à Wood. The master of Exeter had frequently to be taken home drunk by the bachelors of the college. On one occasion, the Act had to be postponed because the vice-chancellor was sick from drinking. There were excesses of dress as well, periwigs, scented clothing, painted faces. And, of course, there was plenty of gaming, gambling, and wenching (Mallet, *Oxford,* 2:422-423). Johnston, the defender of James II in the case of Magdalen, did not fail to bring up such matters (Johnston, *Visitorial Power,* pp. 337-339). There had been complaints from early in the seventeenth century about laxity in Cambridge. See the report of the condition of the university sent to Laud in 1630. "We know not what fasting is" [sic!] (cited in John Venn, *Caius College* [London: Robinson, 1901], pp. 114-115). To be sure, frequenting of taverns was also mentioned. Nevertheless, moralists of the Restoration would have regarded the complaints of 1630 as sure evidence of a state of grace.

21. North, *Lives,* 2:284-285.

22. I cheat a bit; the verse dates from 1760, in a collection called the *Oxford Sausage* (quoted in Godley, *Oxford in the Eighteenth Century,* pp. 76-77).

23. See Mallet, *Oxford,* 3:65-66; Godley, *Oxford in the Eighteenth Century,* pp. 155-161.

24. Cambridge University Library, Mm. 1. 53, f. 98. Printed in Cooper, *Annals,* 3: 571.

25. Cressy, "Education and Literacy," p. 273. Cf. Joan Simon, "The Social Origins of Cambridge Students, 1603-1640," *Past and Present,* no. 26 (Nov. 1963), 60.

26. As an example, see *The Diary and Letter Book of the Rev. Thomas Brockbank,* ed. Richard Trappes-Lomax (Manchester, 1930). See the statistics in Robert K. Merton, *Science, Technology & Society in Seventeenth Century England* (New York, 1970), pp. 32-37, based on men eminent enough to appear in the D.N.B. At the beginning of the century, nearly 8 percent of those eminent enough later to be included in the D.N.B. followed a religious vocation; nearly all of them were university graduates. By the final decade of the century, only about 2 percent of the eminent men of England followed religious vocations. Moreover, between a third and a half of the latter group were Catholics and

nonconformists who were excluded from the universities. I decided that I should check the proportion of university and nonuniversity men at the two ends of the century. I went through two volumes (4 and 13) of the D.N.B., noting the men who chose a religious vocation during the first and the last decades of the century. By a strict calculation of percentages, I should have found 9 percent of the men who figured in Merton's statistics; in fact I found 14 men for the first decade (against an expected 18) and 11 for the final decade (against an expected 6). In both cases I restricted myself to Englishmen. Since it is a rough check in any case, I shall leave it to statisticians abler than I to determine if my check by sampling is valid. Meanwhile, of the 14 from the first decade, 2 were Jesuits trained abroad; all of the rest were clergy of the Church of England and products of Oxford and Cambridge. Of the 11 from the last decade, 2 were Jesuits trained abroad and 2 were nonconformists who were not educated at Oxford or Cambridge. There is no evidence that the number of clergy declined. What these statistics reveal is a decline in quality, and a decline that coincided with the establishment of a university degree as a requirement for appointment in the church. That is, the statistics support the picture of a radical decline in the quality of the universities, and the decline was even worse than Merton's statistics reveal because of the presence at the end of the century of a larger number of nonconformists excluded from the universities.

27. See the following examples. Benjamin Laney, who accepted exile during the Interregnum, was reinstalled as master of Pembroke in 1660. He received as well the deanery of Rochester, the bishopric of Peterborough, and a canonry at Westminster, all of which he held with the mastership (Mullinger, *University of Cambridge,* 3:366-367). Peter Gunning became a chaplain to Charles in 1660 and received the prebend of Christ's Church in Canterbury. He was also inducted into two parsonages by prominent courtiers. He was created doctor of divinity at Cambridge in 1660 by letter mandate and the following year made master of Corpus Christi College and Lady Margaret Professor of Divinity. Later that year, he was moved by letter mandate to the mastership of St. John's and appointed Regius Professor of Divinity. When the king appointed him bishop of Chichester in 1669, he resigned as master of John's, but was allowed by the "special favor" of the king to keep the Regius chair for four years to pay the first fruits due from the bishopric (Thomas Baker, *History of the College of St. John the Evangelist Cambridge,* ed. John E. B. Mayor, 2 vols. [Cambridge: Cambridge University Press, 1869], p. 236). A somewhat similar if less lucrative pattern of patronage marked the career of John Covell (Mayor, *Cambridge under Anne,* p. 471). Roger North's account of the life of his brother John illustrates the flood of preferment that automatically descended on the sons of the powerful. At the beginning of his career, when he was a fellow of Jesus College, a master of arts there "used to say that he would give all he was worth to be a lord's son; meaning that such a one, of ordinary learning and morality, could not escape being, early or late, well

preferred" (North, *Lives,* 2:276). The rest of his life amply confirmed the judgment; meanwhile the master of art's own aspirations were also clearly enough revealed. In 1667 and 1669, Lady Fanshawe used her position to obtain letters mandate for the election of her son to a fellowship at Christ's College; in this case the college managed to resist on both occasions by invoking other influence. One Wormley Martin obtained a letter mandate for a fellowship in Pembroke through the influence of Joseph Williamson, the secretary of state, because of his father's assistance to Williamson. Pembroke did not want him, but the master had need of a royal dispensation himself in order to hold a rectory with the mastership. Martin was elected; the master got his dispensation (E. F. Churchill, "The Dispensing Power of the Crown in Ecclesiastical Affairs," *Law Quarterly Review* 38 [1922], pp. 312-313). In the eighteenth century, the duke of Newcastle pursued the chancellorship of Cambridge for over a decade, and when he finally procured it used the patronage he now controlled as a major foundation of his political power (Winstanley, *Cambridge in the Eighteenth Century,* passim). Newcastle's use of Cambridge belonged to the new age of parliamentary dominance, but the system of patronage he utilized was that built in the seventeenth century.

28. Aubrey Attwater, *Pembroke College Cambridge: A Short History* (Cambridge: Cambridge University Press, 1936), p. 80.

29. *Mr. Smirke: or the Divine in Mode,* in *The Complete Works of Andrew Marvell,* ed. Alexander B. Grosart, 4 vols. (Private Circulation, 1872-75), 4:11.

30. Trinity College, MS 0. 4. 47.

31. For example, see the misfortune of Thomas Brockbank. In 1687, he arrived in Oxford with three friends. They all got themselves entered in Queen's that night. Brockbank was not entered until the following morning and therefore found himself irreversibly and forever their junior (Brockbank, *Diary,* p. 3).

32. John Allen's one publication was a sermon, *Of Perjury* (London: Tooke and Atkinson, 1682). I sometimes wonder if he applied the theme to the duties he swore to so solemnly at various times as he proceeded toward his fellowship. I confess that my curiosity has not been sufficient to impel me actually to read it.

33. Newton was one of the ten; he accounted for three of the sixteen pupils. St. Leger Scroope, George Markham, and Robert Sachaverel were all fellow commoners, the richest students. By the Lucasian statutes he was confined to fellow commoners, though one needs to understand that rules of that sort were broken every day in Restoration Cambridge. None of the three graduated. No trace of a close relation with any one of them has survived. Newton's chamberfellow, John Wickins, tutored two, leaving a total of eleven for the other eight.

34. James Henry Monk, *The Life of Richard Bentley, D.D.,* 2d ed., 2 vols. (London: Rivington, 1833), 2:242n.

35. There may have been an alchemical community that fostered

Newton's extensive interest in alchemy. He noted on one MS that he had received it from "Mr. F." (King's College, Keynes MS 33). In Cambridge, "Mr." referred to "Magister" and thus implied a fellow in some college. There was one Ezekiel Foxcroft in King's at this time who was connected with Hartlib's circle in London. The alchemical treatises of Eirenaeus Philalethes, to which Newton had access before they were published, circulated initially within this circle. There is one other piece of evidence, admittedly tenuous, that supports the supposition that the "Mr. F" on the MS was Foxcroft and hence suggests some connection, now probably forever beyond exact definition, between them (Betty Jo Dobbs, *The Foundations of Newton's Alchemy, The Hunting of the Greene Lyon* [Cambridge, Cambridge University Press, 1975], pp. 111-112).

36. A tenuous case can be made for Humphrey Babington, a fellow high on the seniority ladder, who also enjoyed the king's favor enough to receive a dispensation to hold the living of Boothby Pagnell with his fellowship. Boothby Pagnell was in Lincolnshire, less than five miles from Newton's home. While a schoolboy in Grantham, Newton lived with the family of Babington's sister. Newton's undergraduate accounts contain a couple of payments to "Mr. Babington's woman." Newton visited Boothby Pagnell when he was home during the plague. It was there, according to his account, that he calculated the area under an hyperbola to 52 places. Several surviving records associate the two in the years when Newton was also a fellow.

37. A haze of uncertainty does hang over his lectures. As the Lucasian statutes required, he deposited four manuscripts of extended series of lectures in the university library. The deposited *Lectiones opticae* (Cambridge University Library, MS Dd. 9 67), which comprise series of lectures duringhis first three years, differ in organization from an earlier MS that is also divided into lectures and dated (Add. MS 4002). He did not deposit further lectures for another decade. The MS on algebra which he then presented, drawn up in 1684, was later printed as *Arithmetica universalis* (MS Dd. 9 68). In 1674, when John Flamsteed was in Cambridge, he obtained a paper with notes on it which, according to his own note, was the content of a lecture in midsummer of that year. The notes do correspond to a section of the deposited MS, but there it is divided between two lectures and given a date of October 1674. The MS also includes six lectures for the autumn of 1679 when, in fact, Newton was in Lincolnshire settling his mother's estate. The third MS he deposited, the so-called *Lectiones de motu,* is a draft of Book I (with a few propositions that later became the core of Book II) of the *Principia* (MS Dd. 9. 46). Part of the MS contains two successive drafts; Newton blandly presented the whole as two annual series of lectures. He may have lectured on these topics in the years 1684-85, but what he deposited as his lectures was merely an available MS that he no longer needed. So also the fourth, supposedly lectures in 1687, was the first draft of Book III (MS Dd. 4. 18).

38. See the comments of his amanuensis, Humphrey Newton, on his audience in the '80s (King's College, Keynes MS 135). It is noteworthy that Newton presented both his optical and his dynamical work in his lectures, if his deposited MSS are reliable. There is no testimony that anyone understood their import and hence some doubt that anyone heard them at all.

39. William Stukeley, *Memoirs of Sir Isaac Newton's Life*, ed. A. Hastings White (London: Taylor & Francis, 1936), p. 61.

40. See the letter of Wickins's son, Nicholas, to Robert Smith after Newton's death (King's College, Keynes MS 137). No single peculiarity of Newton more consistently attracted attention from his youth to his old age. In Grantham, Stukeley heard stories about it from Newton's boyhood (Stukeley, *Memoirs*, p. 48). John Conduitt, the husband of Newton's niece, heard the servants talking about it when he was an old man (King's College, Keynes MS 130.5, sheet 1). Wickins, Stukeley, and Humphrey all reported it from Cambridge. Clearly, food was not a trifling matter to the average seventeenth-century man.

41. If the stories about the estate of her second husband, the Reverend Barnabas Smith, were true, and if Gregory King's delineations of wealth in England at the end of the century were correct, Hannah Ayscough Newton Smith's household was among the fifteen hundred wealthiest in England. Her first husband, Isaac Newton *père*, was a prosperous yeoman whose father had purchased a small manor of which he was the lord with all the legal rights of a lord. From his will and the inventory of his goods, his estate appears to have been worth at least £150 per annum (C. W. Foster, "Sir Isaac Newton's Family," *Reports and Papers of the Architectural Societies of the County of Lincoln, County of York, Archdeaconries of Northampton and Oakham, and County of Leicester*, 29, Part I [1928], pp. 45-47). The Reverend Mr. Smith was said to have an estate of £500 per annum. There is no way to check the story, but certainly his will and the later will of hs widow are of a different order from that of Newton's father (ibid., pp. 50-54). Whatever the exact amount, Newton's mother was a wealthy woman.

42. See, *inter alia,* Jewish National and University Library, Jerusalem Yahuda MSS, Newton MSS 5, 12, and 14, and King's College, Keynes MS 2. The early 1670s are also the time when Newton began serious study of the biblical prophecies. The coincidence in time suggests a connection between the two. As far as I know, no one has attempted to establish it.

43. It is necessary to add that this story rests only on the apparent authority of the great-grandson of Robert Uvedale who printed it in 1799 as part of his father's obituary (*Gentleman's Magazine* [Supplement for 1799], p. 1186). In the light of Newton's subsequent pursuit of a dispensation, the story is eminently plausible.

44. In 1661, Trinity expelled two fellows, Price and Smith, for failing to be ordained (Trinity College, *Master's Old Conclusion Book, 1607-1673*, p. 269). In 1666 James Palmer was expelled for the same reason (Trinity College, *Conclusion Book 1646-1811*, p. 106).

45. In 1669, Daniel Scargell of Corpus Christi was expelled for "asserting impious and atheistical tenets"; in the end he was restored to his fellowship but only after a humiliating public recantation (Cooper, *Annals,* 3:532). When Samuel Rolls was admitted doctor of physic in 1675, he issued a statement that if in a certain named book, which he did not own unless it should be proved that he was the author [*sic*], there were anything contrary to the doctrine of the Church of England, he disowned, disavowed, and abhorred it (ibid., p. 570).

46. The issue had a way of refusing not to come up. Years later Archbishop Tenison pressed him very hard to accept ordination; "why will not you? — you know more than all of us put together — Why then said S^r I, I shall be able to do you the more service by not being in orders" (King's College, Keynes MS 130.6, bk. 2). Evidently he had picked up a few tricks to deflect embarrassing inquiries. What the silence and evasions cost him can perhaps be measured by the case of William Whiston, who probably learned his heresy from Newton. Whiston, Newton's successor as Lucasian Professor, decided to meet head on the hypocrisy of a system maintained by the pursuit of patronage. He made every effort to affront the establishment once he began to publish his views about 1708. He sent copies of his books to the Heads. In 1709, he reprinted a number of sermons in a volume. One of the sermons ended with a prayer to Christ "To whom with the Father and the Holy Ghost, three Persons and one God, be all honour and glory..." At the end of the volume was a single erratum: "P. 123. 1. 23, 24. *r*[read] in the Holy Ghost, *and dele* Three Persons and One God" (Whiston, *Sermons and Essays upon Several Subjects* [London, 1709]). Whiston was a flamboyant personality. One gets the impression that he saw himself as a new Luther who would lead a new reformation. He was sorely and quickly disabused. No one was waiting to be led. He was summarily dismissed from both his fellowship and his professorship, and he spent the rest of his life vainly trying to gain an audience to listen to his take of injustice. Before 1687, Newton was much less prominent than Whiston was in 1710. He survived by keeping his distance and his silence.

47. It is true that Wickins's son reported that Newton distributed Bibles among Wickins's parishioners. Nevertheless, the son could not find any letters between Newton and his father after his father left Cambridge, and those from the earlier period merely transmitted dividends and rent to Wickins, who was mostly nonresident after 1675.

48. On 9 February 1685, James was proclaimed king in eight places throughout the city of Cambridge. One of them was in front of the great gate of Trinity and hence immediately outside Newton's window. He may have looked up from his revision of *De motu.*

49. Trinity College, O. 11a. 1^1. In contrast, Newton had never contributed to one of the sycophantic commemorative volumes of verse which the university frequently produced.

50. *The Cambridge Case, Being an Exact Narrative of All the Proceedings against the Vice-Chancellor and Delegates of that University* (London, 1689). The account in Howell's *State Trials* is merely a reprint

of the pamphlet. Its partisan origin has been forgotten, and it has come
to be accepted as the authentic record of the incident. Newton had a
draft of it, in the hand of his amanuensis, Humphrey Newton, among
his papers (King's College, Keynes, MS 113). He also had a fair copy, in
Humphrey Newton's hand, of the vice-chancellor's reply to the charges,
a part of the pamphlet (Keynes MS 115). He had five drafts, some with
corrections in his hand, of an answer to the questions propounded by
the lord chancellor at the hearing on 7 May (Keynes MS 116). The
pamphlet summarized the content of this paper without printing it in
full. Conduitt also recorded one story by Newton in which, at a crucial
point in the university's deliberations, his intervention forestalled a virtual surrender to the king (Keynes MS 130.10, ff. 3^V-4).

51. After 1696, he was not even present in Cambridge. Finally in January 1701, he appointed Whiston as his deputy with all the income of
the chair and in December of that year he resigned in Whiston's favor.
He resigned his fellowship in Trinity at about the same time.

VII
IN SEARCH OF BARON SOMERS

Robert M. Adams

When I first set off in search of Baron Somers, it was out of a conviction that he'd been missing for some time; and this in fact was true. Men of his own day knew very well where to find him, but he dropped steadily from view after the first few years of the eighteenth century. Born in 1651, he was eminent in the public affairs of England from his early thirties; by his mid-forties he had been ennobled and promoted to lord chancellor. Even after he had been removed from that office by the threat of impeachment, in 1701, he remained a man of distinction and reputation; but somehow he was starting to become remote, and with years his impression grew fainter. The death of Lord Somers in 1716 evoked an anonymous biography (probably by John Oldmixon)[1] and a lofty if somewhat suspect tribute from Joseph Addison, whom Somers had patronized generously, and who retained that reverence for his correct and distant patron that an ice cube may be supposed to feel for its fostering Frigidaire.[2] In the century after his death, two modest biographical studies appeared, one by Somers's kinsman Richard Cooksey (1791), one by Henry Maddock (1812).[3] In the course of "doing" the lord chancellors, Lord Campbell did Somers; and Lord Macaulay added the last coat of varnish by canonizing Somers as a Whig saint in the *History of England*.[4] In this state of preservation he endured till just recently, sitting on a shelf—the highest of all shelves, but just for that reason the least visible—and gathering dust.

One reason he slid so easily into dignified obsolescence was no doubt that disastrous fire in the law offices of the Honorable Charles Yorke (the place was Lincoln's Inn Square, the time 27 January 1752); it destroyed a vast mass of Somers's surviving private papers.[5] But other elements pointing him toward eminent oblivion were the formal reserve of his character and the extremely bad state of his health, especially over the last fifteen years of his life. Perhaps for these reasons, his last years contain no actions comparable in importance to those of his late thirties and forties. Yet he was a great and interesting man; everyone of his age agreed on this point. Before I had gone very far in the search for Somers, I found that Professor William Sachse of the University of Wisconsin had recognized the same vacancy I had, had taken up the search for Somers before me, and had in fact produced, just as I was setting out on the chase, a "political portrait," based on truly impressive quantities of research and much careful detail.[6] But on inspection, it turned out he hadn't found the Somers I was looking for—at least the Somers he found did not provide very good solutions to the anomalies I saw in the record. This is not an assault on Sachse's book, which I have plundered unscrupulously wherever I could, and to which I here pay tribute as a painstaking piece of work, very useful indeed within its chosen sphere. But Somers the political carpenter is its primary focus, Somers the legal workman its secondary concern. Of its more than three hundred pages, fewer than ten are devoted to Somers's early life and education; the social meaning of his involvement with the New Whigs is hardly glanced at; and his curious personal life is discreetly muffled in confusion. His patronage of the arts is indeed handled at greater length, but I think the record here means something different from what Sachse declares. And finally, on the matter of Somers's relations with that prickly fellow Jonathan Swift, I am quite sure that many things remain to be clarified.

These are the main heads of my paper, but the premise underlying them ought to be made explicit. I am interested in Somers, not as a politico, a lawyer, or even a specific historical actor, but as a human type. I think revolutions create not only new institutions but new human types. Baron Somers, who grew out of one revolution and personally engineered another, seems to me a perfect type of what these revolutions were striving to produce. Looking backward, we can see many disparate elements coming together, despite really striking incongruities, in his person; looking forward, we can see that the mold in which he cast them lasted, substantially unchanged, for a good long time. He was a combiner and then a shaper; these two sides of his being make for an active, intricate character.

Let us begin at the beginning, where the ground is surprisingly firm underfoot. John Somers was born 4 March 1650/51, in or near Worcester City—if we want to dispute, it must be over the specific house.[7] He was the son of John Somers who was the son of Richard Somers who was the son of John Somers, all of White Ladies in Claines in the near Worcester suburbs. As a local historian might guess, the White Ladies was originally a Cistercian nunnery, taken from the church by Henry VIII and bestowed—most likely in a quid pro quo involving lots of quid—on an early Somers. (But we shall have to note some oddities of its tenure.) It was a capacious stone structure, estimated during the civil wars to be capable of housing 500 soldiers; and it was not far from the parish town of Kidderminster where for nearly twenty years, starting in 1641, Richard Baxter was exercising a dynamic spiritual vocation. The Somers family, including as it did some members who had been born in Kidderminster, was drawn in many respects more forcibly by the magnetism of Baxter than by the nearer cathedral city of Worcester.[8]

Before settling down to his career as a country attorney, John Somers, father of the future chancellor, was a staunch parliamentarian in the civil wars. He probably fought with the new model, certainly against the king. What exactly he did, we do not know, but as the Restoration he took some pains to get himself a general pardon for whatever it was—whether rape, murder, felony, or any other malfeasance whatever.[9] The city of Worcester, royalist like many other episcopal seats, took the king's side in the wars, and was severely battered by a parliamentary siege. But the house at White Ladies was spared, and its owner emerged from the various scrimmages undamaged in person or estate, or, for that matter, in his convictions. A story is told that when a preacher at

Severn Stoke dwelt a little too pressingly on those themes of divine right and passive obedience which were dear to some tactless Restoration parsons, John Somers rose in his pew and fired a horse pistol into a beam over the preacher's head, as a way of conveying to him that that was enough of that.[10]

As a family long resident in the county, the Somerses were intricately interconnected with the squirearchy of Worcestershire: Lord Somers's Aunt Mary married a Blurton, who was connected with the enormously wealthy and flourishing family of Foley; the only daughter of that Blurton-Somers connection married a Cooksey, which family was connected with the active and numerous family of Windsor. The county studbook in Worcestershire was quite as intricately entangled as these volume usually are with Foleys and Winningtons, Cookseys and Blurtons, Salways and Seabrights interlaced in happy profusion. And this network of interconnections centered with particular intensity upon the Somers family because of a peculiar institution, the house known as White Ladies. Though it had been technically the house of the Somers family, it was not in fact the exclusive property of anyone. Richard Cooksey, Lord Somers's kinsman, provides an account of the establishment, dimmed a bit by nostalgia no doubt, but not really subject to question. After emphasizing the importance of Baxter in the life of the household, and the moral authority he exercised over its members, Cooksey proceeds to details:

That mansion was the occasional residence of three or four families. . . . They lived together in a style of which, in these times, it is difficult to form or give an idea.

Their mornings were employed by each in their respective occupations; the culture of a large farm; the cloathing-trade, then in a flourishing state; the producing and manufacturing teasels, woad, madder, and all dying materials; the making bricks and tiles, in immense quantities, to supply the demand, occasioned by rebuilding the ruined city and suburbs; (from this circumstance, in some of the abusive ballads of those times, Lord Somers was stiled the "brick-maker's son;"[11] and superintending the operations of above twenty families, who earned their subsistence under them, and dwelt in cottages regularly constructed for their comfortable accommodation. The labours of the day over, they repaired to one common table, in the great hall of the old nunnery, where seldom fewer than twenty or thirty relations and friends of the families assembled daily, and spent their evenings in the utmost cheerfulness and conviviality. — The products of the farm, the supplies of fish and game, and viands of every kind, received constantly from their country connexions, furnished their table with abundant plenty, and entitled such contributors to a place at it without ceremony or reserve. The annual slaughter of two brawns marked the festivity of Christmas; and a custom much better known to the Romans than to our countrymen, of having a large gilt salt-seller in the midst of the table, and a collar of brawn constantly exhibited thereon during Winter, was here retained within this century.[12]

The White Ladies, in a word, was a kind of bourgeois coop-commune, with an aroma of manorial elegance; it was also, as Cooksey hastens to assure us, a headquarters of political activity where the county families got together for long, leisurely conversations, in which they settled their local and parliamentary affairs. This curious background does something to explain how John Somers could be vilified as a man of no family, risen from the very dregs of society, and yet treated with respect and given immediate entree into the very highest circles of the realm. Rooted in a large, loose, cooperative group where everyone made money and just about everyone shared power or access to it, he also developed a wide range of social sympathies — how wide is suggested by the names of two men well known at White Ladies: Andrew Yarranton and Charles Talbot.

Like Somers's father, Captain Andrew Yarranton had trooped for Cromwell; hunted for his life after the Restoration, he retained for many years the name of a violent man; Aubrey tells us he died "of a beating and [being] thrown into a tub of water."[13] But he was hired by a number of gentlemen, including several who can be definitely identified with the White Ladies set, and sent abroad to look into practical projects and improvements under way in Germany and Holland. His book, *England's Improvement by Sea and Land* (two parts; 1677, 1681)[14] sets forth many practical proposals for better-yielding breeds of clover, ironworks, canals, toll roads and the like. But he has, in addition, social schemes like corn banks and credit unions, which he proposes in a language that beautifully mingles paternal affection with military severity:

And now all you poor Men in *England,* that work or labour in Mechanick Arts, you are mine: I know now I shall have many questions asked me, and amongst the rest, what will you do with all these poor People which you say shall be yours? My answer is, I will make them all rich and happy, and their Families also.

I will now begin to show them the way; but when they are Reading my Project, as most will call it, I order them to act like Soldiers, and command Silence; Suffer not your Wives to use any Twit-twat, nor ask questions by the way; but Read it over again and again, and then lay all your Heads together, Wife, Children, and Servants, and it's possible the younger Fry may live to see it Crown'd with a beautiful Blazing-head, as the Monument near *London-Bridge* is with the Urn.

Now my Children: for so I must call you, for I now will take care for you all (I will begin) Art thou for Revenge? I know thou art; for thou knowest where thy Shoo hath pinch'd thee long: Well, in this case, I think Revenge is lawful, because I know what thou wilt be at; but I ask thee this question, What is the Revenge that will best fit thy temper, and by thee is most desired? Sir, I desire to be revenged of some of the great Men of our Trade; but it is no further, than I may have some part of the benefit of the Trade as well as they; for it is not fit that some should have so much, and others so little, for it is we poor Men that have most Fingers. My Child, thou shalt have thy desire, if it be not thy own Fault; I know you and such as you, with your Families, are the Persons that work, labour, and toyl to make others Rich: Now let me intreat thee to do the same for thy self, as thou didst for others; then believe me the work is done.

Now follows the specific proposal for the corn bank, in which a family can build up a little credit, render themselves independent of employers and middlemen, and with the help of bank credit set up an independent operation of their own. Bank credit for the working man is the key to the operation, and a collectively owned bank enterprise is the first necessary step. By way of rendering the whole operation self-sufficient, Yarranton enjoins all his daughters,

whose Husbands work in Mechanick Arts, That they force their Husbands to eat good Wheaten-Bread, made of Corn that is taken out of the Bank-Granary; and also that they force them to drink good Ale and Beer, that is made out of Malt taken out of the Bank-Granaries.

It is good not only for their health but also for their credit rating to drink ale made of their own malt. And so Captain Yarranton proceeds to draw up the form of a bill to be presented in Parlia-

ment, authorizing the formation of a corn bank by the Clothiers
of Worcester, the Cap-makers of Bewdley, and the Stuff-Weavers
of Kidderminster, to be set up at New Brunswick near the Bridge
at Stratford upon Avon. Finally, he concludes like a man who
knows that for a worker words in print are not real words, but the
judgment of his mates is a serious thing:

> Now my Loving Countrymen I must leave you, and at *Christmas*
> when you have time to Chat by the Fire with your Wives, then let *Nic.
> Baker* at Worcester, *Sim. Wood* at Bewdley, and *Ned Momford* at *Kid-
> derminster* be your Oracles, and discourse of this Affair of Corn in Gra-
> nary. And in the mean time I will fetch a March up *Avon* and so up
> *Stower* to *Shopson,* and from thence to *Banbury,* and so down the *Shar-
> wel* to *Oxford,* and so down *Thames* to *London,* and I will see whether
> *Thames* River may be so perfected as Trade by a Water Carriage may
> be made Communicable and Easy, and I will do my utmost Endeavour
> to find out some convenient place upon the *Sharwel* to build Gra-
> naries.[15]

This sinewy, practical, radical argument for a corn bank was
clearly not addressed to the gentry at White Ladies; it is a working-class argument that proposes to give the working folk of
England a chance in the new money economy that is making and
breaking them. So blunt and frank an appeal to the principles of
class warfare, made in the very dialect of the tribe, we are not
likely to see again till the Chartist movement. But this was a man
whom Baxter and the White Ladies people knew well. The latter
had directly employed him; with their many technical enterprises, they had a direct interest in his technical knowledge; and
they were certainly sympathetic with some of his social ideals —
since, in effect, he was only proposing for the workers of England
what they had already put in practice themselves. Yarranton was,
admittedly, the most radical fringe on which White Ladies society touched, the infrared end of a political spectrum familiar to
John Somers from early childhood. But the touch was not remote,
nor the connection casual. Swift described Somers, in the opening section of "The Four Last Years of the Queen" as imbued
with "the old Republican Spirit,"[16] and it was a polemical com-
monplace among those attacking "the present set of Whigs" as
late as 1711, that if the latter couldn't reduce the nation to complete chaos, the only thing that would satisfy them was a repub-

lic.[17] A leader among the "present set of Whigs" was Lord Somers, and the charge against him, so often repeated, was not altogether wrong. He wasn't by any means a wild-eyed regicide, he had just reached Selden's old, practical conclusion, that a king was something created by men for convenience' sake. The more convenient he made himself, the better Lord Somers was prepared to like him.

The other range of social option available to Somers during his growing up is represented by Charles Talbot, duke of Shrewsbury, who also frequented the White Ladies.[18] He had good reason to do so, for despite his ancient lineage and enormous wealth, the young man was practically an orphan. When he was only eight, his father had been killed in a duel with the duke of Buckingham; the occasion of the duel was Buckingham's affair with Shrewsbury's wife. Whether or not the story is true that the lady, disguised as a page, held her lover's horse while he killed her husband, she was notoriously Buckingham's mistress after the fatal duel as well as before. Thus the young duke was in effect left homeless; and Somers's father was one of the guardians appointed to watch over his minority. There were some years between the boys, in Somers's favor, but they grew up together and remained friendly if not intimate all their lives. One potentially divisive issue had to be overcome. By family tradition and upbringing, young Shrewsbury was a Catholic, and he was also close to the court, Charles II himself having been his godfather. The inevitable tug of war over his soul ended in 1679 when he converted to the English church, under the reasonable ministrations of Archbishop Tillotson, and thereupon took his place amid the grandees of the Whig party, and in opposition to the court. No doubt his connection with Somers and the White Ladies establishment was partly responsible for his turn—however vacillating and uncertain—toward the popular party. But there is no reason to exaggerate either the degree of this turn, or the measure in which Somers and the Worcester society influenced it. For us, the important influence went the other way. As a friend of Shrewsbury, even if not an intimate one, Somers had access from boyhood to the polished manners and deft badinage of the higher nobility. The principles of Yarranton and Baxter led him to acquaintance in the "country" party, they kept him interested in local politics and the representational problems of towns like

Bewdley;[19] social intimacy with Shrewsbury led to acquaintance with men like the earls of Shaftesbury, Sir William Temple, the earl of Halifax and the earl of Wharton. The "New Whigs" whom Somers headed up in his political prime were distinguished among their enemies by this exact combination of old puritans with new skeptics — deists working hand in glove with presbyterians, the strictest of the strict with the loosest of the loose.[20] And the court leaders of the movement had polished their manners to such a high gloss of gentlemanliness that it was impossible to tell whether they were of one class or the other. Somers was prototypical, in this respect, and his father was quick to notice it. While his son was reading law at the Middle Temple, John Somers the father used to frequent the terms at London, and on the way from Worcester would leave his horse at the George in Acton, where he often spoke of his wonderful son. Cobbet, who kept the inn, said, "Why won't you let us see him, sir?" and Somers accordingly brought his son to the inn. But the first thing he did was to take the landlord aside and say, "I have brought him, Cobbet; but you must not talk to him as you do to me; he will not suffer such fellows as you in his company."[21] It's a story many fathers will understand.

The formal education of a young man so richly educated by social circumstance was curiously, and perhaps deliberately, desultory. He attended for a few years each the Worcester Cathedral School, then perhaps the private academy run by John Woodhouse at Sheriffhales, Shropshire, and then Queen Mary's Grammar School at Walsall in Staffs. The key to this oddly peripatetic academic career may be the elusive figure of Simon Barfoot, a Puritan divine who taught in the Worcester School till he was ejected in 1660, who disappears from public view for four years while the Woodhouse Academy was being established in Sheriffhales, and who then in 1664 turns up with his pupil Somers at Walsall.[22] In any event, the most interesting of these several schools is the one with which Somers is connected least clearly. Woodhouse's school at Sheriffhales was famous for the quality of its curriculum, the distinction of its graduates, and the radicalism of its puritan teaching. Baxter had a sizeable hand in its curriculum, which for sheer rigor compares with that outlined by Milton in *Of Education*.[23] But even if Somers never actually went there (Barfoot may well have been his private tutor during those empty years from 1660 to 1664), this was evidently the sort of education he got. The point is mildly important because he spent a relatively short period of less than two years at Oxford, before enrolling at the Middle Temple,[24] yet his intellectual training was formidable. In later life he corresponded in flawless Tuscan with Filicaja and Magalotti; he kept up with a wide range of philosophic speculation on the continent; he not only patronized but took part in antiquarian research. In a public ode, Filicaja assures us that Somers knew no fewer than seven languages in addition to English.[25] The books he collected, a few of which form the collection known as the *Somers Tracts,* he had to a very large extent read, not only read but also understood. Very few lawyers in the England of his day knew or were required to know anything of the civil law; Somers owned, and had personally annotated, over three hundred volumes on that rather arcane topic, as appeared when his library came to be sold.[26] Yet it was an important part of his style that he made no great display of learning or of industry. He translated for Tonson epistles by Ovid, biographies by Plutarch, and orations by Demosthenes, but always anonymously, and when he published legal arguments bearing on political matters of the day, he never failed to obscure his part in the transaction. Books, including some important ones, are attributed to him,[27] but never because he claimed authorship: he has to be practically convicted of writing anything.

Yet from the beginning, his friendship with Tonson,[28] his membership in the Kit-Cat Club, and his own inherent powers of discrimination enabled him, along with his considerable wealth and political influence, to exercise important literary directives. Sometimes this literary power took semicomic forms. When created lord chancellor, he was granted for his support the manors of Reigate and Howlegh in Surrey: possession of the estates entailed political power in the borough. Previously, Sir John Parsons, a London brewer, had been MP for the district; Somers, entering on his estates, let it be known that henceforth Stephen Harvey, Esq., would be the man. Harvey was one of Tonson's minor poets; his claim was to have translated Juvenal's seventh satire for a collection.[29] Disgruntled Parsonites objected to this carpetbagger from Parnassus; but Somers simply imported some more scribblers into the district, flooding it with Kit-Cat riffraff on the order of William Congreve, and so enabled Harvey to hold his seat.

More serious in its implications, and somehow hard to reconcile with this Restoration scalawaggery, is Somers's part in building the literary reputation of John Milton and Edmund Spenser. He it was who encouraged Tonson to bring out the important 1688 folio edition of *Paradise Lost,* the first posthumous edition of the poem and a major element in reviving its sunken popularity. Whether it was he or Tonson who decided to use the device of subscription to finance publication of a big book with limited appeal, is moot;[30] as a risk-sharing device it was far from an absolute novelty,[31] but its success with *Paradise Lost* led Tonson to use it again and again; without its revival in the 1688 Milton, the publishing history of the early eighteenth century would have been very different. John Hughes's 1715 edition of Spenser, in six volumes with a capacious glossary, was simply dedicated to Somers — there is no evidence that he inspired it as he definitely did the Milton edition of twenty-seven years before. But it marked an important step in the rehabilitation of Milton's great predecessor, and remained standard for over a hundred years.

Whoever thought of it, the new technique of financing book publication through subscription was symptomatic of deep and important changes. With a sovereign who spoke little English, had no interest in the arts, and spent more than a third of his reign out of the country, patronage of literature devolved on the general public, indoctrinated by booksellers like Tonson and concerned gentry or officials like Somers.[32] National pride entered in, too, so that when Somers was made lord keeper in 1693 (the chancellorship itself came in 1697), Edmund Gibson hailed his new dignity by dedicating to him a magnificent folio translation-edition of Camden's *Britannia,* with the observation that England now had its own equivalent to Richelieu and Colbert.[33]

I relegate to a footnote the many poems and books dedicated to Somers in the years after 1688,[34] and proceed merely to mention some of his more interesting intellectual contacts among what might be called the international freemasonry of deists and free-thinkers. Whether he knew Locke through Shaftesbury or Shaftesbury through Locke (he was on good terms with both, and with Newton as well), either could have opened the door for him to a large philosophical acquaintance on the continent. Jean LeClerc, for example, was a learned and laborious Huguenot theologian who had settled in Amsterdam: Somers knew him well, and corresponded with him from time to time.[35] His special interest was forbidding—the critical analysis of Biblical texts; but he was no narrow specialist. LeClerc was so liberal in his thinking that he was never allowed to hold a chair in theology, and thus became one of the great free-ranging critical scholars of his time, a man in touch with the farthest reaches of European thought in many different fields. Less powerful as an original thinker, but more skilled as a publicist, was Pierre Bayle, another Huguenot refugee in Holland. Bayle had quarreled with William of Orange and therefore declined the pension that Somers tried to arrange for him.[36] Touchy as Doctor Johnson with Lord Chesterfield, he worked on in his independent refuge at Rotterdam, creating the immense *Philosophical and Critical Dictionary* which foreshadows in so many ways the *Grande Encyclopédie* of the later century. In Italy, Somers's primary acquaintance was Count Lorenzo Magalotti, best known for his deistic *Lettres sur les Athées;*[37] at Somers's instance, he was made a member of the Royal Society, and their correspondence, parts of which survive,[38] was not simply an exercise in the use of the Della Crusca dictionary—they discussed authentic topics. In England, Somers patronized (among others, for his tastes were liberal) Matthew Tindal, for whom he is said to have written a preface to *The Rights of the Christian Church*[39] and John Toland, whose notorious "Life of Milton" was prefixed to a 1698 edition of Milton's *Prose Works* published, inevitably, by Tonson. Toland and Tindal, however provocative in their writings, were lesser minds than most of Somers's other acquaintances, but they were bugbears of the established church, and energetic exponents of that freethinking to which Somers, behind his polished facade, was evidently committed.[40] His friendship with them is one more element making toward a major explosion when the top blows off his relation with a passionate churchman like Swift later on.

I've mentioned Somers's connection with the Royal Society and simply note here that from 1698 to 1704 he was president of that organization. Though it brought him into contact with interesting people and may suggest a mildly positive side to his freethinking, I don't think Somers's connection with the society will bear much emphasis. The heroic days of the organization, chronicled by Bishop Sprat, were over, and Somers had no Baconian ideas or aspirations. He was not an experimenter, but a random collector at best, a virtuoso. As president, he allowed the laboratories and collections in Gresham College to deteriorate and did little to stimulate intellectual life in the society.[41] The one object associated with his tenure was apparently a curious chair formed out of a single piece of root.

But outside the Royal Society, Somers took his collecting very seriously indeed, buying in his chosen categories systematically, in quantity, and with great discrimination. He was particularly interested in books and manuscripts, most of all when they related to England's historic past;[42] but he also collected coins, medals, woodcuts, paintings, prints, and drawings, maintaining agents on the continent who bought for him at the great centers. Two things are remarkable about this taste of Lord Somers for collecting art. It had traditionally been the activity of aristocrats with ancestors to recollect and stately 'omes to decorate — or else of kings. In England, Somers's chief predecessors in the practice were noblemen like the second earl of Arundel and King Charles I. Paintings by the old masters and objects of virtù were thought to belong in ancient castles and royal palaces; they were not the normal perquisites of men whose fathers had been provincial attorneys — men who might choose to hang a Guido Reni or a Francesco Albano on the wall of a comfortable country house in Herts.[43] Even more striking is the fact that a man whose backgrounds were strongly Puritan was now an art collector. Puritan iconoclasm, Puritan suspicion of the old masters as Papist idolaters, was still strong; as late as the mid-nineteenth century, it would be deeply ingrained among the nonconformist classes. Within Somers's own lifetime, it was Cromwell's men (and among them, quite possibly, Somers's own father) who had broken up the glorious royal collections — to England's everlasting shame and loss — and scattered them abroad. When we find the son of a Cromwell trooper buying fine art, and the son of that wily popular agitator, the second earl of Shaftesbury, writing seriously and intelligently on the topic, there's no mistaking that a major change in taste has occurred.

It occurred, in very large part because Somers did not try to challenge the crowned heads and great lords directly in their chosen field, the auction room. As so often in his life, he opened a new path by compromising. To be sure, he collected works of art by the great masters, and at the very highest level; but what he collected were not, as a rule, full-scale oil paintings. He bought a

few of those, but mostly prints and drawings—four thousand of
the latter and "a much greater number" of the former.[44] Among
the artists represented in his collections were Raphael, Michel-
angelo, da Vinci, Titian, Correggio, Veronese, Giorgione, Tin-
toretto, Rubens, Van Dyke—not to pursue the list to the end.[45] A
catalog of his holdings was printed for use at the sale that followed Lord Somers's death; it doesn't list the paintings or the coin
collection, it doesn't list the magnificent library of over nine
thousand volumes with its collection of rare books and important
manuscripts, but it does give us reason to think that in the history
of collecting and of taste, he broke a kind of new, if middle,
ground.

Finally, though collectors of old masters have been known to
neglect modern artists, Somers also patronized those of his contemporaries who were within reach. He gets few points for his
portrait by Kneller, for this was a famous man and a fellow Kit-
Cat.[46] But he also went out of his way to patronize native-born
British artists, when he could find them. Jonathan Richardson
père, who went outside his craft to write an early book of Milton
criticism, painted Somers's portrait; so did Simon Dubois, a
Dutch painter who had emigrated to London. And the career of
George Vertue, engraver and antiquarian, got its primary
impulse from Somers's patronage.[47] It was an engraved copy of
Kneller's portrait of Tillotson, commissioned by Somers, that
gave young Vertue his start; he went on to catalog and reproduce
the great English collections, both those still in existence and
those that had been broken up. I don't argue that Vertue's work
represents any pinnacle in the history of art; a history of engraving, referring specifically to Vertue, describes his achievement
concisely:

a capital engraver, a valuable antiquary, a faithful student of the arts, if
not in the true creative sense an artist. But such a man was just what was
needed, at this particular epoch; he preserved the traditions, he marked
time, and he loyally kept the art of line-engraving before the public at
as high a level as the times could appreciate.[48]

Engraving, an art form inherently more democratic than painting, would be a primary path of access for the eighteenth-century
English gentleman to the world of art: one thinks of the vogues
for Hogarth and for Piranesi. Thus Vertue performed a service of

popularization which combined precisely Somers's concern for the arts, his awareness of the past, and his willingness to operate within a liberal but not imperial budget — a very specific fulfillment of Somers's tastes, extending almost forty years after he had ceased to be available for comment.

In all these social details, apart from the facts themselves, we can see grounds for contrasting judgments being formed about Somers. His collections, his portraits, his social intimacies, his several houses and manors, his patronage, his polished, unemphatic style — these things impressed some observers and enraged others, depending on how much they thought his ancestry mattered and what they believed about it. In a number of respects, it's evident that even Somers's virtues could be held against him. For example, his influence with King William was remarkable because, among other things, he could speak fluent French, if not Dutch.[49] This gave him, not an unfair advantage perhaps, but a real one; and it didn't endear him to lords with vast acres who happened to be tongue-tied outside of English. Above all, it's fair to suspect that Somers was mistrusted because he wielded a sort of power unfamiliar to Englishmen, and mysterious because almost invisible.

Landed estates and hereditary titles were (as they still are) the oldest and most respected forms of social power in England; Somers had neither. He was not the avowed leader of a faction, a cause, or a sect; he was not a merchant prince, though he outdid many of them in the splendor of his establishment. Where did his power — limited but real — come from? This brings us to the question of the New or Modern Whigs, and the massive mobilization of credit.

In laboring the point that the core of the New or Modern Whigs consisted of money men and credit men, supported and amplified by a coalition of family interests and by attracting intermittent support from other groups on individual issues, I'm not sure how far I labor without an opponent. But to present a proper image of Somers, who worked at the very heart of this coalition, it seems useful at a minimum to introduce two modern Whigs as illustrations of the class of man with whom he was importantly associated for his entire active career. Professor Sachse barely alludes to them in the footnote-fringes of his political portrait; yet they seem to me more important, because more novel, than any number of the ministers with whom he transacted the traditional formalities of public business. With Sir Thomas Abney and Sir Robert Clayton, he was into essential stuff, at least under one definition. They were both City figures — longtime aldermen, Fathers of the City even, sheriffs, members of Parliament, and in their time (or a little out of it, as we shall see) lord mayors. Both were up to their ears in money and credit, and both had intimate dealings, financial as well as political, with Lord Somers.

Abney, though descended of good Derbyshire stock, had the particular misfortune to be born a fourth and youngest son; looking misfortune in the eye, he moved to London and entered the ranks of trade. We first hear of him, on the occasion of his marriage in the 1660s, as a citizen, a fishmonger, and a nonconformist.[50] When he came to hold public office, his trials and tribulations over the problems of occasional conformity are touchingly described by Jeremiah Smith, the preacher of his funeral sermon. However, this earnest and pathetic discourse, beyond assuring us that "he sought no gain but with a good conscience; nor made haste to be rich; yet did God own and bless his fair and righteous methods with considerable increase,"[51] makes no mention of what his vocation actually was. The word *fishmonger* is not pronounced, nor does the word *banker* occur. In fact Abney, though he began as a fishmonger, always remained of the company, and was immortalized on his election as mayor by a choir of melodious fishmongers who produced a poetical pamphlet entitled *The Triumphs of London*,[52] quickly advanced to higher forms of finance. We hear of him repeatedly in connection with real-estate deals, and also as a banker. He was an early and vigorous promoter of the Bank of England, served on its original board of directors, and subscribed £4,000 to its capital stock — which, in those days, represented a lot of herrings. He became enormously wealthy and famous for his philanthropies. Between them, he and his widow supported Doctor Watts the hymnologist for the last thirty-six years of his life; they left their house and magnificent grounds in Stoke Newington to become a public park. But their country seat was Theobald's in Herts, the seat of kings and in the intimate neighborhood of Brookmans, where Lord Somers resided.

As a matter of fact, Sir Thomas's promotion to the very lucrative and honorable office of lord mayor of London took place rather outside of normal chronological order and in a very tight election where the swing vote was controlled by John, Lord Somers. As part of his arrangement with Sir John Parsons over the borough of Reigate, Somers engaged Sir John the brewer to vote for Sir Thomas the fishmonger instead of for the Tory candidate, Sir Charles Duncomb the usurer.[53] It's not hard to figure the obligations for which this political leverage of Somers was the payoff; the Bank of England and the money men involved in its formation had been repeatedly approached by Somers to lend William's government large sums to support the war against France. Somers was the specific individual who arranged these deals: Macky says that "very few Ministers in any Reign ever had so many friends in the House of Commons [as Somers] or could go to the City, and, on their bare word gain so much Credit of the Publick."[54] Sir Thomas Abney and Sir Robert Clayton were among the biggest moneymen of the City, on whom the junto government called again and again for loans of a size that absolutely staggered the minds of Englishmen unused to modern financial calculations. After the crushing defeat of Neerwinden in the summer of 1693, it was John Somers who went to the Guildhall and quickly raised a loan of £300,000 to put William's forces back on their feet; when the Bank of England was founded just a year later, its first undertaking was to make another loan to the government, this time of £1,200,000. No wonder Somers felt grateful to his friend and neighbor Sir Thomas Abney.

To suggest some details and gesture at the scope of these financial relations is even easier in the case of Sir Robert Clayton than for his colleague Abney. Clayton was an orphan, adopted by an uncle, and brought up to the trade of a scrivener: this was the code name of the day for a usurer, and it was perfectly well understood at the time that Clayton was a moneylender, who commonly lent against estates or the prospect of them, and wasn't always above foreclosing on them. Evelyn, who knew him well and liked him, phrases his judgment with great reserve. "Some believed him guilty of dealing, especially with the Duke of Buckingham, much of whose estate he had swallow'd, but I never saw any ill by him considering the trade he was of."[55] In October, 1697, after the Peace of Ryswick, he personally loaned King William £30,000 to pay off his troops; as a director of the Bank of England, he had a hand in passing many other loans. In his day, he was just about the richest man in England. All those who attended them were awed by the lavishness of his entertainments in London, and visitors marveled at the elegance of the country house at Bletchingly in Surrey, which he picked up "for the discharge of Lord Peterborough's debts."[56] The manor was in the near neighborhood of Lord Somers's estate at Reigate, and carried with it control of a borough for which Sir Robert himself regularly sat. He also possessed much property in the City, in Bucks, Dorset, Kent, Middlesex, Norfolk, Northamptonshire, and Ireland—not to mention his profitable iron and copperworks, or his shares in the Hudson's Bay and Royal African Companies. Nor did all this business enterprise preclude a meritorious quantity of philanthropic benevolence. Among other things, Abney and Clayton were both members of the board, successive presidents of, and generous donors to, St. Thomas's hospital in Southwark, where a statue of Clayton still stands.

The exact relation between Somers and men of the Abney-Clayton kidney isn't clearly spelled out in the records, and couldn't be believed if it were. The New Whigs, who defined themselves only partially as they went along, were a peculiar combination of city, court, and family interests. Merchants who had acquired new land and its accompanying political appurtenances made up one important element of the interest; Williamite peers and comprehensive churchmen like Burnet and Tillotson (both intimates of Somers) made up another part, especially important in the Upper House. And there were those, no small number of them, who rallied to the New Whig interest under the primary influence of patronage; pensions and places were forthcoming to stout Whig supporters, and even to less stout supporters who could now and then throw a vote in the right direction. When we combine Mr. Robert Walcott's estimate that in 1701 there were forty representatives of the London bourgeoisie in the Lower House (though the City of London was entitled to only four seats)[57] with Dennis Rubini's calculation of the number of "placemen,"[58] who at the same period amounted to at least a hundred and maybe much more—when we add to this a specific example like that of Dr. Charles Davenant, where we can visibly see secret service money being used to corrupt a man to write against his convictions and conscience[59]—then it becomes clear that parliamentary democracy is taking a new shape. The secret currents of money enabled men to wear several different hats, and to act today, under one hat, in a way that would turn to their own profit tomorrow, under another. As M.P.s they voted to borrow money, which as bankers they proceeded to loan to the government; with the interest (formerly usury) which it earned, they purchased estates from which they or their creatures were elected in increasing numbers to parliamentary seats; a parliamentary seat was an ideal base from which to arrange further pensions and places for themselves, or for the purpose of silencing inconvenient critics.

It was a splendid merry-go-round, and so long as the junto held together, while the country party remained divided and amateurish, Lord Somers stood at the very center of it, binding together the relatively unstable units of which his party was composed by the liberal use, among other expedients, of a particularly useful all-purpose glue, the name of which was money.

In any event, Somers, though he dealt constantly in big money, wasn't driven by it,[60] and never acquired—like the duke of Marlborough, for instance—a reputation for greed. He made plenty of money, and spent it where his interests lay, but not on broad acres or pillared residences. For Somers was not a family man, either in the vulgar domestic sense, or in the aristocratic sense of coming from, and feeling responsible toward, an extended family. He never married[61] and never cultivated any particular intimacy with cousins or nephews, such as he had. Founding a line, putting up a public structure, establishing a foundation, a library, or a fellowship—deeds of philanthropy which would have carried his name down to posterity—never appealed to him. He had no taste for the conventional solidities, or for the conventional pieties either.

His private life has, in fact, been the subject of amazingly contradictory reports. Bishop Burnet, who knew him for years, characterizes him as

very learned in his own profession, with a great deal more learning in other professions, in divinity, philosophy and history. He had a great capacity for business, with an extraordinary temper: for he was fair and gentle, perhaps to a fault, considering his post. So that he had all the patience and softness, as well as the justice and equity, becoming a great magistrate.[62]

With the addition of some Victorian unction and emphasis, this is the same picture that is painted by Macaulay.[63] It is reinforced by the utter silence of Archbishop Tillotson regarding anything odd in Somers's private life, and by the labored flattery of Addison. There is even a story in Oldmixon's 1716 *Life*, of a certain clergyman who came calling in search of patronage: Somers tipped him £100 but gave him to understand that return visits would not be welcome — the reverend gentleman's private life leaving something to be desired.[64] By the end of the eighteenth century, Hannah More was including Lord Somers in her *Religion of the Fashionable World* as one who "was not only remarkable for a strict attendance on the public duties of religion, but for maintaining them with equal exactness in his family."[65]

When you have a bishop and an archbishop in your moral corner, along with Mr. Addison and a story that you don't even associate with parsons on whom the breath of scandal has fallen, it seems odd that one's reputation should be touched by a tough and in no way finicky duchess. But so it is with Somers. The duchess of Marlborough concedes very readily, and in spite of obvious personal dislike, that Somers was a man of good talents. "But," she continues, "there was one thing that appeared to be a great blemish to a Lord Chancellor, that he lived as publicly with another man's wife as if she had been his own."[66] The same story is repeated, with a great deal of romantic and pseudo-pornographic detail, in Mrs. Manley's scandalous *Atalantis*.[67] An extra feature of the story is that Somers made sure of the lady (her name was Mrs. Elizabeth Fanshawe Blount) by keeping her husband, Christopher Blount, in jail for debt. Refutations of this story generally take the form of conceding its main outlines and changing its coloring.[68] Blount was in jail through his own improvidence, it is said. Somers as a way of helping out the abandoned and penniless wife, took her on as a housekeeper. But "housekeeper" is a notorious euphemism, that doesn't always mean what it means to an icy, self-bound figure like Swift, and in any case the charge against "Madam Blount" — the common, public word for her — was not that she slept with Somers, but that she pimped for him.[69] A housekeeper, indeed! Even a sharp, shady man like John Macky, who met Somers only casually in the way of business, saw something that the bishops either missed or suppressed: "He is of a grave deportment, easy, and free in conversation; something of a libertine, of middle stature, brown complexion, near fifty years old."[70] The last phrase dates the observation around 1700. It wasn't altogether scandal, or if it was scandal, it was very widespread scandal, that the bad health that haunted Somers after the 1690s, was basically syphilitic. His kinsman Cooksey concedes that "he was by no means nice, or in the least degree delicate" in his amours, and Birch reports his "indulgences" were "ravenous and eager, and without much care of choice."[71]

What's curious here is that the people who can see the libertine in Somers are those who don't seem to be particularly scandalized by it; those who would or ought to be shocked don't seem to see the quality in the first place. Addison was of course a loyal henchman; Burnet and Tillotson followed well-known episcopal precedent in keeping their eyes, ears, and mouths shut in the presence of a wealthy, influential lord. In a word, Somers managed his private life with perfect and open disregard of the official morality; and he was perfectly right in doing so. The official morality never penetrated, or even tried to penetrate, the glossy veneer of his manner. Indeed, the moralists went out of their way to cooperate and thus made the cover-up so successful that by the end of the eighteenth century, Lord Somers had been converted to a Sir Charles Grandison *avant la lettre*. His political enemies didn't shrink from talking scandal, but he simply disregarded them, and with brilliant success, even though they included one of his former familiars and admirers, a clergyman named Swift.

Dates start to get important here. Elizabeth Fanshawe was born in 1662 and married Christopher Blount in 1684; her arrangement with Lord Somers dates from the period when he was lord chancellor, that is, 1694-1700. The affair was notorious, to the extent of being mentioned in the public prints, by 1694.[72] Swift was in the household of Sir William Temple from 1689 to 1694 and again from 1696 to 1699; it was surely during these periods that he became acquainted with Somers, who was a regular visitor at Moor Park. Unless he was extraordinarily obtuse, Swift must therefore have known about Somers's private life for at least fifteen years before he said the unequivocal things about it that appeared in *Examiner* no. 26.[73] But there were several obvious, if not especially creditable reasons for his long silence. Somers was a powerful political ally of Temple, Swift a mere private chaplain. Somers had money, access to power; the way of the world was behind him. He also had livings to bestow on aspiring young clergymen, and literary patronage to bestow on talented writers.

He had given Addison a pension; he had granted the living of Puttenham to Swift's cousin Thomas (January 1693/4). But on Swift himself, who had many expectations, he bestowed nothing. We do know he commended Swift in 1708 or 1709 to be chaplain to Lord Wharton. About the episode there is a wonderful and terrible, if perhaps apocryphal, anecdote, which goes back to Samuel Salter:

> Lord Somers recommended Swift at his very own [i.e., Swift's] earnest request to Lord Wharton, but without success; and the answer Wharton is said to have given, which was never forgotten or forgiven by Swift, laid the foundation of that peculiar rancour with which he always mentions his Lordship. The answer was to this purpose: "Oh, my Lord, we must not prefer or countenance those fellows: we have not character enough ourselves."[74]

What would gall Swift to the very marrow is the implication that "we" rakes and libertines cannot afford to associate with "those fellows" — the moral element of the community, but particularly the clergy. Swift would recognize the freemasonry of the cynical, to which (as he must have shown) Somers was as much committed as Wharton. Though it was many years later when he said of Somers that he had every qualification for office except virtue,[75] the seeds of that judgment must have been laid thus early.

His public view of Somers changed very abruptly. As late as "The Contests and Dissensions among the Greeks and Romans" (September 1701) he was an explicit supporter, equating Somers with Aristides, whose only fault lay in being too just.[76] But the Bookseller's Dedication to Somers of *A Tale of a Tub* which, as I will argue, is pervasively if subtly hostile, had to be written between the death of King William (March 1702) — an event to which it alludes — [77]and early 1704. If Swift began changing his mind about Somers in 1703, that would be almost immediately after the coldness of Anne had made it evident that Somers was not going to get back any of his old jobs. But Swift maintained a show of good relations till the deep wound of 1708 or 1709, which led to the savage assault of *Examiner* 26, 1 February 1710 — based on facts that had been public knowledge since at least 1694.

I need only run swiftly over the reasons for seeing covert hostility in the Bookseller's Dedication. Throughout, the *Tale* is uniformly contemptuous of the Royal Society, of which Somers at the time was president. In the dedication proper there can be no question about the allusions to Somers's distinguished ancestry, military prowess, and talents for dress and dancing. They are absurdities "in character" of course, the Bookseller's character, but they are also cruel sarcasms at the expense of a fifty-year-old chronic invalid, to whom Swift, in *The Four Last Years of the Queen,* would attribute a bitter "consciousness of his humble Original."[78] The very idea of the Bookseller usurping over the author and dedicating to Somers for profit what the author intended for Prince Posterity and fame, is sardonic;[79] it may include a hit at Tonson as the type of the new busybody tastemaking publisher.[80] In any case, Somers figures in the dedication as the sort of money man whom everybody flatters with compliments he does not deserve—and Swift is particularly bitter about this flattery, because for years he had been a partner to it, actively in the *Dissensions* pamphlet, passively in suppressing what he cannot have failed to know about Somers. Shall we then read sardonically that passage of the dedication which says, "there is no virtue either of a public or private life, which some Circumstances of your own, have not often produced upon the stage of the world"?[81] The stage of the world carries with it the sense of putting on a show; the idea of producing on a public stage the virtues of a private life is incongruous or worse. Again, when Swift speaks of Somers's "undaunted courage in mounting a Breach, or scaling a Wall," is he making a rather blunt, if underhanded, erotic joke?[82] Ordinarily one wouldn't think of this sort of thing, but when irony and sarcasm start to be perceived in a text (and here they're perfectly unmistakable), it's not easy to know where to stop them. For example, what lies behind all that play with the motto, "those to whom everybody allows the second place have an undoubted title to the first"?[83]

One thing it could mean in context is the second place awarded to Jonathan in Lord Somers's distribution of patronage to the two cousins Swift. In December of 1693 the two cousins were still on excellent terms with one another; there had been, after all, good reason to assign the first bit of patronage to Thomas, the elder by a year and the one who was anxious to get married. But as the years piled up toward a decade, and it became apparent that nothing was going to be done for him, nothing at all, Jonathan unquestionably became jealous and resentful. Perhaps he was the one to whom second place had been allotted, but who was quite sure he deserved the first.

Another innuendo implicit in the maxim has to do with Lord Somers's relation to the *Tale* itself. At the time of publication, and recurrently during the eighteenth century, a story was heard that Somers himself had written at least part of the *Tale*—that he, the earl of Shrewsbury, and the third earl of Shaftesbury had cooked up something like a primitive version of the *Tale* between them.[84] They had done it as a jest, being all men around town together, and had given the only MS of their *jeu d'ésprit* to Sir William Temple, with whom they were all acquainted. One or other of the Swift cousins then found the MS in Sir William's library and edited and updated it; Jonathan added the digressions, and after Sir William's death, published it, with the tacit complicity of the original authors.

Now there are several things against this story, on the face of it. All three of the supposed original authors were alive and articulate in 1704, when the *Tale* was published. None of them said anything about it, one way or another, in public or in private. Their collaboration, if any, would have had to be before 1697, when many of the distinctively Swiftian trappings began to be added to the *Tale;* but that makes Shaftesbury, who was born in 1671, a very youthful fellow indeed to be collaborating with the lord chancellor and the secretary of state, born respectively in 1651 and 1660. None of these three "authors" showed much satiric flair or bite elsewhere in their writings; none of them showed even so much interest in narrative allegory as is displayed by Thomas Swift's sermon, "Noah's Dove." To say nothing of the digressions, which were far beyond them, the basic story of the *Tale* was not particularly in their vein. All this, combined with the apparent lack of hard evidence *for* their involvement, might seem decisive; yet the possibility cannot be quite foreclosed that there's something to the story.

In that extraordinary "Apology for the &c" which Jonathan Swift (speaking almost but not quite in his own person) prefixed to the fifth edition of the *Tale* in 1710, he undertakes to explain the process by which the *Tale* came to be printed originally in 1704. And throughout, he makes a good deal of mystifying play with various figures denominated "the author," "the editors," and "those in whose power the papers then were." As long as we

suppose Jonathan Swift is the author and somebody else is the editor, we are involved in one absurdity after another. For example,
we are told that the author had not been "master of his papers for
a year or two before their publication."[85] But we have seen that
the Bookseller's Dedication to Somers was written after the death
of King William (March 1702), and we know that the Dedication
to Prince Posterity had to be written after the appearance, in
1699, of Bentley's enlarged *Dissertation*. We know that Swift was
publishing with John Nutt, in 1701, the "Contests and Dissensions"; and Nutt was the original publisher of the *Tale*. So long as
Jonathan Swift is identified with "the author," it is ridiculous to
speak of his not being "master of his papers"; he was adding to
them right up to the moment of publication. But if he is the "editor" (an editor, no doubt, who assumed pretty large control over
his basic materials) then the generic title author may refer to
somebody else. And we are encouraged to look further by a curious passage in the "Apology for the &c" where Swift discusses elements of the *Tale* "which prejudiced or ignorant readers have
drawn by great Force to hint at ill meanings, as if they glanced at
some Tenets in Religion."[86] Foremost among these elements is the
passage on the number *three* in the introduction; it is a number
that the Hack says he was determined to have at any cost as the
number of his oratorical machines, because three is his favorite
mystical number. Some readers, among them William Wotton,
had seen in this numerological byplay a jesting with the Holy
Trinity; but Jonathan Swift now, in the "Apology" hastens to
assure them they are wholly mistaken:

In the Original Manuscript there was a description of a Fourth [ma-
chine], which those who had the Papers in their Power, blotted out, as
having something in it of Satyr, that I suppose they thought was too particular, and therefore they were forced to change it to the Number
Three, from whence some have endeavor'd to squeeze out a dangerous
Meaning that was never thought on. And indeed the Conceit was half
spoiled by changing the Numbers; that of *Four* being much more
Cabalistick, and therefore better exposing the pretended Virtue of
Numbers, a Superstition there intended to be ridicul'd.[87]

All sorts of red herrings and false scents distinguish this statement. Four is not a more cabalistic number than three. The
figure "I" seems to know both the inmost thoughts of "those who

had the Papers in their Power" and the contents of the manuscript before they got hold of it. How could they possibly have
trimmed and altered the manuscript in the short period between
March 1702 and publication date, without making themselves
known to an author who nonetheless knew their inmost intentions?[88] Finally, there's that puzzling fourth machine. As a
defence against blasphemy, it's altogether useless, since a couple
of extra machines remain in the passage itself, which the Hack
has felt impelled to disqualify, in order to get his favorite number
three. They are the bar and the bench. Swift could easily have
used this extra pair to duck the charge of blasphemy. If then he
specified still another machine "in the Original Manuscript," the
only conceivable reason for doing so is that there *was* an original
manuscript and that it had this feature in it. So that what we are
looking for is this: a fourth (but really a sixth) wooden machine
for oratorical elevation—in addition to the gallows, the stage, the
tub-pulpit, the bench and the bar—a sixth machine, which is
indissolubly linked to an indiscreet, indeed, a shocking satiric
reference.

It's a bit of a teaser.

Fortunately there's an eighteenth century solution to the
puzzle.

Richard Cooksey, whose "biography" of Lord Somers we've
already cited, touches on this very criticism of Wotton's concerning the play on the number three. Swift, as the ostensible author
of the *Tale,* says Cooksey, had to bear all sorts of bitter criticism,
for "the tertuffes of the church, in those times, could not brook
the introduction of ridicule, though for the best purposes and
with the purest intention, in a matter they styled of divinity."
And, he continues, these "tertuffes" (whom I take to be Tartuffes
with a dash of Worcestershire) went still further:

They charged him with a crime of which he was perfectly innocent —
that, in descanting on the number three, to which he confines the
modes of a man being elevated among the vulgar, —the stage, the gallows, and the pulpit, he alluded to the holy trinity. Whereas the original
author had made the number four, and added a *throne* as another species of exaltation; but, for obvious reasons, had struck out this and other
passages that savoured strongly of republicanism, though sufficient still
remains to convince the reader, that the real writer had some tincture
and principle of that sort; to which Swift, if he had any, which is doubtful, was ever diametrically opposite and averse.[89]

The throne as final machine clearly answers the needs of the problem as no other could. The sting that it carries in this context is not to be mitigated, because the symbol is inseparable from the single, specific person whom it designates. It is well within the range of Lord Somers, who had worked to set William on his wooden machine and even harder to keep him from falling off it. I don't necessarily mean that he personally wrote the original passage; he may have found it or copied it or developed it as a joke with some of his urbane and disabused friends. We shouldn't in any case forget that the largest category of books in his very spacious library consisted of volumes of theology, to which the allegory of the three brothers was very germane.

Let me dwell a moment on the dilemma. If, against all probability, Jonathan Swift was the author of the "Original Manuscript" with its jeer at the throne, then somebody else, unnamed, ill defined, with no existence whatever outside this specific circumstance, must have been the "editor." But the editor is so hazy that he is sometimes singular, sometimes plural. At one moment, he is "a judicious Friend" of the Bookseller, who is very cautious and responsible about making changes in the manuscript;[90] on other occasions, he is someone over whom the author had no control at all, who proceeded altogether on his own, made alterations quite incomprehensible to the author, and did not scruple to take "a good Sum of Money for the Copy" of a work he had not written.[91] Well, if he's so flimsy, let us dismiss him with the customary critical cliché: he is a persona, a disguise for Jonathan Swift, who was clearly his own editor and just pretended that somebody else was. But then when he talks of an original manuscript, and attributes to it an element of which we see he was himself incapable, it seems to me we are bound to take him seriously.

I have made elsewhere, and have yet to see confuted, an argument that Thomas Swift had a hand in the original *Tale* and the "Discourse on the Mechanical Operation of the Spirit"—which the printer obligingly tells us was written, when it reached him, in a different hand than the *Tale* proper.[92] Here now I am reaching into one of the very last elements added to the book, and giving some credit to an "Original Manuscript" about which Jonathan Swift was kind enough to inform me. Perhaps it would seem that I am out to strip Swift altogether bare of his greatest, if not his most popular book. Not at all. The *Tale of a Tub* is a volume of shreds and patches, a ragged and tattered volume built up out of

scraps and tags and loose verbal flitters from the great paper-
storms of the seventeenth century. It grew around a center, the
Tale proper, the importance of which lies precisely in its triviality
and worthlessness — the qualities that make it a prototype of modern authorship. Festooned about it are the satiric apparatus of
dedications, prefaces, introductions, and digressions which make
it a volume in bulk but not in structural coherence. The more
miscellaneous its materials, the funnier the book's character as a
burlesque of modern scholarship, the more grotesque its gigantic
pretensions and its capering, ridiculous, journalistic performances. The book borrows liberally from the likes of Doctor John
Eachard and Mr. Tom Brown of facetious memory;[93] there is no
reason at all why it shouldn't also have laid under contribution
one or several "original manuscripts." Though I don't want to
put too much weight on a metaphor, it seems to be that the basic
structure of the *Tale* is that of a pearl: at its center is the alien
grain of common sand, an irritant but without any particular
character of its own; around it, the fancy and the rage of Swift,
working against the hostile element, built up layer after layer of
protective wit, of irridescent satiric display.

We may seem to have wandered away from Lord Somers. I
think not. For I think Somers represented everything against
which Jonathan Swift stood most furiously opposed, and nothing
would delight me more than to find him at the heart of the book
in which the entire seventeenth-century enterprise is summarized,
between loathing and fascination. It wasn't any simple process, as
I see it, by which he got to the heart of the book; he had to be
swallowed first and rejected afterwards. For the hungry, half-
insane Hack who is the ostensible author of the *Tale,* represents
an ultimate outcast. He is a distracted and degenerate heir of a
great tradition, forced to exist in a world of money-grubbing
booksellers, pretentious pretenders to learning, and patrons
demanding flattery. The world of honor is gone, as Sir William
Temple said,[94] the world of money is on us. Somers, as the quin-
tessential money man, with his secret connections, his casual
morals, his easy superiority, and his suave adjustments to this
pragmatical preposterous pig of a world, represented the compromise of the future. In his tastes, his manners, his religious
indifference, his practical ideas on government, he carved a path
which had only to be widened a bit to serve the ruling oligarchy

for more than a century. Swift was imbued with a lost-cause, last-ditch mentality; that is why he was such a great satirist, and why, speaking always for the common forms and traditional values of community, he became such an individual eccentric. Lord Somers, rooted more deeply in the way of the world, camouflaged himself into a near anonymity from which it's high time he be rescued; not just for the sake of what he was, interesting as that is, but for what he provoked.

NOTES

1. Pat Rogers, "The Memoirs of Wharton and Somers," in *Bulletin of the New York Public Library* 77 (1974), 224-235.

2. *Freeholder*, no. 39, 4 May 1716.

3. Cooksey's *Essay on the Life and Character* was published in Worcester and sold in London (1791); Maddock's *Account of the Life and Writings* (a thoroughly dreary piece of labor) is London, 1812. Unless otherwise indicated, the place of publication of all books cited in this paper is London.

4. John Campbell, *Lives of the Chancellors* (New York, 1874), IV, 457 ff.; Thomas Macaulay, *History of England* (New York: American Book Exchange, n.d.), IV, 503-504.

5. Yorke was a collateral descendant of Somers; he had just taken over Somers's papers, amounting to more than sixty folio volumes, from Joseph Jekyll, Somers's brother-in-law, when the fire occurred. The only fortunate thing about the whole episode was that the *Somers Tracts* had already been singled out of the surrounding materials; the first volume of that collection was published the very year of the fire.

6. W. L. Sachse, *Lord Somers* (Madison: University of Wisconsin Press, 1975).

7. Some say he was born in the White Ladies itself, others that he was born in a house in College Churchyard, near St. Michael Bedwardine, where his birth was recorded; see John Noake, *Notes and Queries for Worcestershire* (1856), pp. 1-2.

8. Somers's grandfather, Richard, not only married a Kidderminster girl but, as Cooksey tells us, spent his last days with Baxter and wanted to be buried in Kidderminster churchyard; Cooksey, *Essay*, p. 19.

9. Any smart lawyer who like Somers had been involved in a civil war would get himself a pardon for these and any other imaginable malfeasances, whether or not he had actually committed them. We can't judge directly from the precautions a man takes, to the deeds he has performed.

10. John Noake, *Guide to Worcestershire* (1868), p. 316, gives the minister's name as Wybrough and the time as the Interregnum — a date

that speaks well for the courage of the preacher, if not of Somers. The father, Kidderminster-loving Richard Somers, didn't settle Severn Stoke on John, father of the future lord chancellor, till after his marriage with Katherine Ceavern, November, 1648.

11. See the ballad "Father's Nown Child," in *Poems on Affairs of State,* ed. W. J. Cameron (New Haven, Conn.: Yale University Press, 1971), V, 422-428.

12. Cooksey, *Essay,* pp. 13-15.

13. John Aubrey, *Brief Lives,* ed. Clark, II, 316. See also Yarranton's *Full Discovery of the First Presbyterian Sham-Plot, or a Letter from One in London to a Person of Quality in the Country* (1681), where Yarranton's vivid story illustrates the intimate connection thought to exist between him and Baxter in the nervous days of 1681.

14. *The Improvement Improved,* also by Yarranton, sounds like a defence of the 1677 book, but its date is 1663.

15. Yarranton, *England's Improvement by Sea and Land,* pp. 170-171, 173, 177.

16. *The Four Last Years of the Queen,* in *Prose Works,* ed. Temple Scott (Bohn, 1897-1908, X, 22-23). In *Faction Display'd* (1709), William Shippen summarized Somers in three not inaccurate words (line 246), as "Deist, Republican, Adulterer." Dennis Rubini reports that as late as July, 1700, after the death of Queen Anne's son, the duke of Gloucester, the junto and the great financial interests were actually planning a commonwealth; *Court and Country 1688-1702* (1967), p. 169, citing among the evidence Hist. MSS. Comm. Portland MSS, IV, 3, which specifically names Somers and Montague.

17. See for typical comments Joseph Trapp, *The Character and Principles of the Present Set of Whigs* (1711) and my "Mood of the Church and the *Tale of a Tub*," in *England in the Restoration and Early 18th Century,* ed. H. T. Swedenberg (Berkeley, Los Angeles, London: University of California Press, 1972), pp. 71-91. An anonymous pamphleteer on the Sacheverell controversy nutshelled the whole outlook in a title: *The New Association of those Called Moderate Church-men with the Modern Whigs and Fanaticks to Under-mine and Blow-up the present Church and Government* (1702).

18. Modern biographies of the duke of Shrewsbury are those of T. C. Nicholson and A. S. Turberville, *Charles Talbot* (Cambridge, 1930) and Dorothy Somerville, *The King of Hearts* (London, 1962).

19. He was honorary recorder for both London and Worcester, and remained so long after his other and higher offices had been stripped from him. At the height of his struggles against impeachment we see him involved in complex questions regarding the charter of Bewdley: see Rebecca Warner, *Epistolary Curiosities,* 2d series (Bath, 1818), pp. 1-3.

20. "The Triumph of the Great L-S-" (1701), impersonating Somers, brags that

We've made a League, much stronger than the Fashion
With all the honest Atheists of the Nation,

and represents it as a successful swindle on the Prigs, who are simply
"Bigots metamorphos'd into Whigs."

21. John Oldmixon, *Life* (1716), p. 11.

22. On Sheriffhales academy see Joshua Toulmin, *Historical View of the State of the Protestant Dissenters in England* (Bath, 1814), pp. 225-230; and H. McLachlan, *English Education under the Test Acts* (Manchester: Manchester University Press, 1931), pp. 45-49. On the Walsall school, D. P. J. Fink, *Queen Mary's School 1554-1954* (Walsall, 1954), pp. 199-209.

23. McLachlan, *English Education.*

24. He matriculated at Trinity College 23 May 1667, and enrolled in the Middle Temple 24 May 1669.

25. *Opere de Vincenzio de Filicaja* (Venice, 1755), II, 50.

26. Sachse, *Lord Somers,* p. 13. The largest category of books in his library of nine thousand printed volumes (in addition to MSS) consisted of theological works, ibid., pp. 192-193.

27. Publications attributed to Somers:

1. *The Memorable Case of Denzil Onslow* (1681). Sachse calls it doubtful.

2. *A Brief History of the Succession of the Crown of England* (1681). Unchallenged.

3. *A Just and Modest Vindication of the Proceedings of the Two Last Parliaments* (1681). A composite production with which the names of William Jones, Robert Ferguson, John Somers, and Algernon Sidney have been associated; only the last is dubious.

4. *The Security of Englishmen's Lives* (1681). Partly perhaps by Lord Essex but the greater part pretty surely by Somers.

5. "Ariadne to Theseus" and "Dido to Aeneas," in *Ovid's Epistles by Several Hands* (1680 and repeatedly reprinted).

6. "Life of Alcibiades," in *Plutarch's Lives by Several Hands* (1683-86).

7. *Jus Regium* (1701). Perhaps by Somers, perhaps by Defoe.

8. *Jura Populi Anglicani or the Subject's Right of Petitioning* (1701). Perhaps.

9. *Several Orations of Demosthenes... to encourage the Athenians to oppose the exorbitant power of Philip of Macedon* (1702). Somers was general editor.

10. *Vox Populi Vox Dei* (1709) reprinted as *The Judgment of Whole Kingdoms and Nations Concerning the Rights, Powers, and Prerogatives of Kings* (1710). Attributed to Defoe and others; no specific evidence for Somers.

Dryden's Satire to his Muse, which appeared in the early 1680s, is by

Thomas Shadwell, not Somers. *A Discourse concerning Generosity* (1693) has been associated with Somers's name, but there's no specific evidence for it. *Anguis in Herba* (1701) is by Henry Maxwell. *King William's Affection to the Church of England Examin'd* (1703) is probably by Defoe. There's nothing specific to identify as Somers's *A Letter, Balancing the Necessity of Keeping a Land force in Times of Peace: with the Dangers that May Follow On It* (1697). Some of his speeches at trials, decisions in law cases, defenses at his impeachment, etc., were printed, but are not considered here.

28. Tonson too has found a rash of biographers in Harry M. Geduld, *Prince of Publishers* (Bloomington: Indiana University Press, 1969), Kathleen Lynch, *Jacob Tonson* (Knoxville: University of Tennessee Press, 1971), and G. F. Papall, *Jacob Tonson, Publisher* (New Zealand: Tonson Publishing House, 1968); Appendix 2 lists all the books appearing under Tonson's imprint.

29. In addition to his literary attainments, Harvey had attended the Middle Temple, was a barrister, and served as steward for Somers in the management of Reigate.

30. Tonson said it was Somers's idea, but under the circumstances Tonson could always be counted on for a bit of deferential inaccuracy.

31. Sarah Clapp, "Subscription Publishers Prior to Jacob Tonson," in *The Library*, 4th series, XIII (1933), 158-183.

32. Cf. Blackmore's regretful remarks on William's neglect of the arts:

> He shun'd the Acclamations of the Throng
> And always coldly heard the Poet's Song.
> Hence the great King the Muses did neglect,
> And the meer Poet met with small Respect.
> But tho' the Muses and their tuneful Train
> In this fam'd Monarch's Military Reign
> Had of the Royal Favour little Share,
> Still they were kinder *Bocai's* tender care.   (Bocai = Iacob Tonson)
> He still caress'd the unregarded Tribe,
> And did to all their various Tasks prescribe.
> *A Collection of Poems on Various Subjects* (1718), p. 105.
> (The poem was first printed in 1708.)

33. Edmund Gibson, trans. and ed., Camden's *Britannia* (1695), the dedication.

34. Among the dedications to Somers were (a provisional list):
1. John Locke, *A Consideration of Lowering of Interest* (1692).
2. John Bowler, *A Sermon on the Death of Queen Mary* (December 1694).
3. Joseph Addison, *A Poem to His Majesty, Presented to the Lord Keeper* (1695).

4. Edmund Gibson, trans. and ed., Camden's *Britannia* (1695).
5. John Locke, *A Further Consideration of Lowering of Interest* (1695).
6. John Cary, *A Vindication of the Parliament of England* (1698).
7. Guy Miege, *New State of England* (3d edition), 1699.
8. Thomas Madox, *Formulare Englicanum* (1702).
9. Thomas Rymer, *Foedera* (1704).
10. Joseph Addison, *Remarks on Several Parts of Italy* (1705).
11. John Phillips, *The Vision of M. Chamillard Concerning the Battle of Ramillies* (1705).
12. John Evelyn, *Acetaria, a Discourse of Sallets* (1706).
13. Shaftesbury, *The Letter Concerning Enthusiasm* (1708) and others.
14. Henry Newton, *Epistolae, Orationes, et Carmina* (Lucca, 1710).
15. Thomas Madox, *History and Antiquities of the Exchequer* (1711).
16. Jacob Tonson, ed., *Paradise Lost* adorned with sculptures (1711).
17. Richard Steele, *Spectator* 1 (8 January 1712).
18. John Ayliffe, *Ancient and Present State of the University of Oxford* (1714).
19. John Hughes, ed., *Works* of Spenser (1715). Kneller's Kit-Cat portrait shows Somers holding a volume of this set.

Samuel Garth's *Dispensary* concludes with a lofty and flattering address to "matchless Atticus" who is clearly identified as Somers, but I discount this, as also, for different reasons, the "Bookseller's Dedication" before *A Tale of a Tub*.

35. The only biography of LeClerc is a brief one by Annie Barnes, *Jean LeClerc* (Paris: Droz, 1938).

36. The dissertation of L. P. Courtines, *Bayle's Relations with England and the English* (New York: Columbia University Press, 1938), makes no mention at all of Somers or the proposed pension, though *Biographia Britannia*, p. 3749, which is the source of the story, actually cites the words of a letter offering 150 guineas.

37. On Magalotti, see an account in the *Nouvelle Biographie Generale* (Paris, 1860), pp. 666-667. His letters on atheism are a polite variety of raillery masquerading as argumentation, but they display a very cosmopolitan spirit. He was elected a fellow of the Royal Society in 1709.

38. Originals of the correspondence in the Bodleian; exact references not available.

39. Tindal, *The Rights of the Christian Church* (1706). The jealousy of Swift over Somers's conversation with "inferior" minds of liberal tendency comes out in *Examiner* 26; describing Rochester but alluding to

Somers, his predecessor, Swift says, "he has never conversed with Toland, to open and enlarge his thoughts, and dispel the prejudices of education."

40. In the discussion on the coronation oath which became important after 1688, the question to be asked of the sovereign was, "Will you maintain the true profession of the gospel and the Protestant reformed religion established according to the laws for the time being"; but this was voted down. Campbell, *Lord Chancellors,* IV, 100.

41. Z. C. von Uffenbach, visiting London from Germany in 1710, found the quarters of the Royal Society a shambles: see *London in 1710,* trans. and ed. W. H. Quarrell and Margaret Mare (London: Faber and Faber, 1934), pp. 98-101.

42. He encouraged Rymer's work in the compilation of the giant *Foedera,* and the two antiquarian volumes of Thomas Madox, *Formulare Anglicanum* (1702) and *History and Antiquities of the Exchequer* (1711).

43. Brookmans, now the site of a BBC transmitter, was standing about as Somers left it, as late as 1891. The big country house of the district was Theobald's, owned by Sir Thomas Abney; Brookmans was recognized by Somers's enemies as well as his friends to be a relatively modest residence.

44. *A Collection of Prints, Drawings, &c... of the late Rt. Hon. John Lord Somers* (1717), cited by Sachse, *Lord Somers,* pp. 196 ff.

45. For the spirit of Somers's collecting, see his letter to Shrewsbury in Italy dated 25 June 1703, Hist. MSS Comm. (Buccleuch MSS, II, pt. 2), p. 662: "The prints you chose are very fine and I shall not be a little proud of a room where I am setting them up.... I have still an appetite to a good picture, and, whatever you please to say, I can completely rely upon your taste and judgment, but I ought to think a great while of parting with so much money. I think as well of Guido (Reni) as of any master. The doubt I have of that particular picture is if it be not too large for my little house, as you are pleased to describe it. I should be out of countenance in putting your Grace to any trouble upon an occasion so little necessary; but I persuade myself the considering a picture may be a kind of diversion."

46. Engravings by Mr. Faber from the Kit-Cat portraits were published by Tonson in 1735; there is a chronological catalog of Kneller's works by baron Killanin (New York: Batsford, 1948).

47. Horace Walpole, *A Catalogue of Engravers Who Have Been Born or Resided in England* (Strawberry Hill, 1763), pp. 2-3.

48. M. C. Salaman, *The Old Engravers of England* (Philadelphia, 1907), p. 178.

49. We can be sure that Somers's languages included French, even if his library didn't include many French volumes (Sachse, *Lord Somers,* p. 194)—witness his easy converse with LeClerc and Bayle. On the point of Dutch there seems to be no information.

50. The relatively perfunctory account of Abney in *D.N.B.* is taken almost word for word from Jeremiah Smith's "Memoirs of Sir Thomas Abney" published as a supplement to his sanctimonious funeral oration titled *The Magistrate and the Christian* (1722).

51. Smith, "Memoirs," p. 47.

52. It was customary for the company to which a new lord mayor belonged to celebrate their colleague's advancement in a ceremonial pamphlet of this nature; the drapers had done the same thing for Sir Robert Clayton when he became mayor in 1680 (*London in Luster*).

53. In the popular vote, Sir Thomas Abney had been decisively beaten, but the election was passed on to the aldermen who by a vote of 14 to 12, with Sir John Parsons providing the swing vote, elected Abney. Duncomb was handicapped by a previous conviction for forgery; but he later got his mayoralty anyhow.

54. John Macky, *Memoirs of the Secret Services of John Macky, esq.* (1733), p. 49.

55. Evelyn, *Diary*, 18 November 1679.

56. Ibid., 3 July 1676.

57. *English Politics in the Early 18th Century* (Cambridge, Mass., 1956), p. 26.

58. *Court and Country*, pp. 31 ff.

59. See my "Mood of the Church and the *Tale of a Tub.*"

60. Swift in the *Four Last Years of the Queen*, says flatly of Somers, "Avarice he hath none," p. 23; and Swift, who prided himself on his superiority to money, was a severe judge in these matters.

61. Oldmixon's *Life* (p. 25) tells of Somers's courting in 1690-91 a Mrs. Anne Bawden, daughter of a wealthy city alderman, but says the matter broke off in disagreement over the proposed marriage portion. Since the Bawdens were kinsmen of Oldmixon, the story has been made grounds for assigning to him authorship of the 1716 *Life;* Pat Rogers, "The Memoirs of Wharton and Somers," *Bulletin of the New York Public Library* 77 (1974), 229. If true, it also defines the onset of Somers's affair with Mrs. Blount, which would be unlikely to have begun before 1691 and was public knowledge by 1694.

62. Gilbert Burnet, *History of his Own Time* (Oxford, 1823), IV, 187-188.

63. See above, n. 4. Lord Campbell says of Somers, flatly if a bit innocently, that his "private life embellished by many virtues could not have been liable to any grave imputation, since it has received the un-qualified approbation of Addison," *Lives of the Chancellors*, IV, 457. Horace Walpole refers to Somers as "one of those divine men who, like a chapel in a palace, remain unprofaned while all the rest is tyranny, cor-ruption, and folly," *Catalogue of Royal and Noble Authors*, "Somers."

64. Oldmixon, *Life*, p. 116.

65. Hannah More, *Estimate of the Religion of the Fashionable World* (1791), ad init.; I note that an American edition of Hannah More is

Works (New York, 1935) changes the text to read "the Hales, and the Clarendons, and the Somer_sets_" (I, 275), but the intention is clearly Lord Somers.

66. Sarah, Lady Marlborough, *Private Correspondence* (1838), II, 148.

67. Mary Manley, *The New Atalantis* (1710), II, 492-493. Also in the same author's *Memoirs of Europe* (1710), I, 218-221, and of course Swift, *Examiner* 26, 1 February 1710, which is just catching up belatedly with the explicit though anonymous words of *A Letter from the Grecian Coffee House* (1701), p. 7: "His L——p's keeping Bl——t in Jayle, while he lay with his wife."

68. Cooksey, *Essay*, pp. 27-28.

69. *The New Atalantis* is particularly lurid on this theme.

70. John Macky, *Memoirs*, p. 49.

71. Cooksey, *Essay*, p. 46; Birch, in Sloane MSS 4223, f. 208v, cited by Sachse, *Lord Somers*, p. 82, nn. 47, 48.

72. "Father's Nown Child" has all the details straight in 1694:

> If any man doubt, there's one Madame Blount
> Who's witty and pretty and goes very sprunt
> Will tell you how often Jack Somers has don't,
> Which nobody can deny.
> *Poems on Affairs of State*, V, 247.

Of Madame Blount the modern editor says rather startlingly, "she has not been identified with any certainty." See also "Advice to a Painter" (1697:

> Here in polluted Robes just reeking, draw
> Th'Adulterous Moderator of the Law;
> Whose wrinkled Cheeks and sallow Looks proclaim
> The ill Effects of his distemper'd Flame.
> If more you'd know, consult his friend *Tom Hobbs.*
> Who vamps him up with his Mercuriall Jobs.
> *Poems on Affairs of State*, VI, 16.

See also "The Golden Age Revers'd" (1703), ibid., VI, 520, and "The Seven Wise Men" (1704), ibid., VI, 629.

73. *Examiner* 26, 1 February 1710, "to ruin and imprison the Husband, in order to keep the Wife without Disturbance."

74. James Caulfield, *Memoirs of the Celebrated Persons Composing the Kit-Cat Club* (1821), p. 78. Swift denied that he ever actively applied for the chaplain's post, but he was eager for preferment, still expected it from Somers, and was introduced by Somers to Wharton in the matter of the First Fruits, on which Wharton was cold and rude. A note from Addison to Somers of 7 May 1709 explicitly though errone-

ously says Wharton has made Dr. Swift one of his chaplains; *Letters of Addison,* ed. Graham (Oxford: Clarendon, 1941), p. 136. Whether the celebrated words between the two peers were actually spoken or not, Swift would be the last person to know and the first to suspect; his rage would turn against both. For their joking implied not only his contemptibility but their mutual identity; the man he had gone out of his way to flatter was suddenly made identical with one who openly despised him.

75. "Notes on the Characters of Macky," in *Prose Writings,* ed. Herbert Davis (Oxford: Blackwell, 1939-1959), V, 258.

76. Aristides is not only Swift's name for Somers in the "Dissensions" pamphlet, but one of the characters whose lives, the Bookseller tells us, were ransacked by his hireling scribes, to make up a panegyric of Somers, *Tale of a Tub,* ed. Guthkelch and Smith (Oxford: Clarendon, 1958), p. 24. Don't we here again (in the covert allusion to himself as an indiscriminate flatterer) strike the note of secret self-loathing that was a partial consequence, or cause, of Swift's despising authors as a servile breed?

77. "The history of a late reign," *Tale of a Tub,* p. 26. Against all probability and precedent, Ehrenpreis (*Swift* [Methuen, 1962] II, 122) takes the "late reign" to be that of James II. But Somers, as junior counsel in the bishops' case, has been but moderately influential, and only in *ending* that reign; all his major offices had been held under William. In 1704, when the *Tale* appeared, a "late reign" could only have meant that of William.

78. "Four Last Years of the Queen," in *Prose Works,* X, 23. See also the "Notes on the Characters of Macky," where Swift declares that Somers's father "was a noted Rogue," and *Examiner* 26, which is no less explicit that Somers descended "from the dregs of the people." In this constant hammering on the topic of "low birth" (though in fact Somers's people were respectable provincial gentry, altogether equatable with the Harley family, for instance), Swift may be evincing a certain sense of identification with Somers. The Swifts weren't any blue-blooded aristocrats themselves, their ruling passion was loyalty and subordination. In Somers, who should have respected his betters but presumed to equality with them, it's arguable that Swift saw that element of himself which his loyalty always had hard work to repress—the element that knew he was a better man than these rich, hollow, titled libertines before whom he had to practice a parson's deference.

79. Compare Tom Brown, ironically impersonating a City spokesman in his condemnation of wits: "Then, like a parcel of Sots, they write for Fame and Immortality; but this Gentleman [Blackmore] is above such trifles, and, as he prescribes, so he writes for the Good of Trade," Preface to *Commentary Verses* (1700).

80. Tonson wasn't of course the publisher of the *Tale;* that was John Nutt. But the close relation of Tonson and Somers, in and around the

Kit-Cat Club, was widespread public knowledge. A Tory like Shippen, in *Faction Display'd* (1709), makes Tonson an integral element of the plot he is denouncing, see p. 13.

81. *Tale of a Tub,* p. 26.

82. Ibid., p. 25. On mounting a breach and scaling a wall, compare John Dunton, *History of Living Men* (1702), p. 69, speaking of the duke of Ormond: he is not one of those "who never scal'd any Fort, but a Bawdy-house"; and Setter in Congreve's *Old Bachelor,* III, ii: "I often march in the rear of my master, and enter the breaches which he has made."

83. The original of the motto is in Herodotus VIII, 123-124.

84. Cooksey, *Essay,* pp. 22-24.

85. *Tale of a Tub,* p. 4. The "Bookseller to the Reader" before the *Mechanical Operation of the Spirit* confounds the confusion by saying that the MS has been in his possession for the last six years, i.e., since 1698; this is totally impossible, since the text refers to many events that occurred since 1698.

86. Ibid., p. 8.

87. Ibid.

88. In all the charade of characters connected with the *Tale,* the most amazing part is played by the Bookseller, whose story when we assemble it is full of insane improbabilities. He received the original MS of the *Tale* six years ago without apparently knowing who was the author (p. 28); he received the MS of the "Fragment" at a different time and in a different hand (p. 260), yet instinctively knew they belonged together, and duly added to them various pieces that could only have been written at a later date (The Bookseller's Dedication to Somers; The Author's Dedication to Prince Posterity). He promised a large sum of money to someone who represented himself as the author (p. 16), though he knew all the time who the real author was (p. 16), though elsewhere he didn't know who the author was (p. 28). He allowed various other people to modify and censor the material (pp. 17, 260-262). Learning that the real author was about to publish a proper text, he hurried his own version into print in 1704 (p. 17); but six years later, knowing who the real author was and standing on excellent terms with him (as evidenced by his prefixing the "Apology for the &c.,") he still didn't change perceptibly the surreptitious text he had printed in 1704.

89. Cooksey, *Essay,* pp. 21-22.

90. *Tale of a Tub,* p. 26.

91. Ibid., p. 17.

92. Ibid., p. 260.

93. Jonathan Swift was very touchy about his wit in the *Tale* being all his own; but his reading in works of controversial raillery and banter was very widespread, as I expect to show in a proper edition of the *Tale,* now in process; and a great deal of what he read stuck in his mind and came off on his pen.

94. Sir William Temple, "Of Ancient and Modern Learning," ad finem.

VIII

CHILDREN'S LITERATURE AND BOURGEOIS IDEOLOGY: OBSERVATIONS ON CULTURE AND INDUSTRIAL CAPITALISM IN THE LATER EIGHTEENTH CENTURY

Isaac Kramnick

"I think I can, I think I can, I think I can," says the smiling little engine. I'm not very big, but I'll do my best, and "I think I can, I think I can, I think I can." Lo and behold, the little engine can. It pushes the broken-down train loaded with toys and good things to eat across the mountain to where the little boys and girls eagerly wait. Some big and important engines had said they couldn't, but by working hard and repeating over and over again "I think I can," the little engine did the job and everyone is very happy, none the least of whom has been Mabel C. Bragg, whose book, *The Little Engine That Could,* has sold over five million copies since its first appearance in 1926.

In the success of that engine and of Mabel Bragg there is itself a story. Written just before the Depression, the book caught fire during the thirties, and it has succeeded in part because it has touched so deeply the wellspring of American ideology. The little engine was faced by a serious problem it met it head on, and proved what could be accomplished by hard work and the simple will to achieve, the will to do. The American individualist ethos, its heritage of self-reliance and optimistic problem solving, is enshrined here. No collective solution is offered, no sharing of troubles. The engines don't cooperate to solve the problem. Nor, it should be added, do they call on any outside solution, public or social. All that was needed was a resourceful and clever little engine that had faith and confidence in itself, an engine that knew that it, the individual engine, albeit little, could.

Few would dispute that much of contemporary children's literature has a high component of ideological content. A good deal of work has been done in recent years revealing the socioeconomic, racial, and sexist quality of the stories read to our children. The question posed here, however, is whether this is some new conspiracy thought up by the defenders of the status quo today, or whether children's literature has in fact always performed this service. My suggestion is that children's literature has always been highly ideological, and in this discussion I want to explore the origins of this literature in English and to offer the thesis that, indeed, from its very beginnings in the late eighteenth century, children's literature in English has been designed to serve ideological objectives.

This paper will have three parts. I want first to set the historical stage, to say something about the evolution of industrial capitalism in England during the eighteenth century and to sketch some of the general themes of the liberal bourgeois creed that emerged during this, the birth of bourgeois civilization as we now know it. In the second part I will turn to some comments on the changes that took place in society and the family under the impact of industrial capitalism. I will suggest that you couldn't have children's literature until you had a notion of childhood and also of motherhood which assumed that a mother at home read stories to children, children who were considered special kinds of human beings. The final and largest part of the paper involves looking at specific examples of English children's literature like *Goody Two-Shoes,* written in the late eighteenth century, in which I will try to describe the dimensions of bourgeois ideology disseminated and also how these works helped spread the new stereotypical roles of men and women, of boys and girls, which were emerging in the bourgeois family.

INDUSTRY, SCIENCE, AND PROTESTANTISM:
THE MAKING OF BOURGEOIS ENGLAND

Between 1760 and 1800 England was fundamentally transformed by the Industrial Revolution. All across England's "green and pleasant land" were rising "dark satanic mills." These mills did more than mar the aesthetic landscape, they brought in their wake a new set of values and a new ideology—the values of the middle-class factory owners and managers, bourgeois values. Ultimately in the nineteenth century this ideology would triumph; the bourgeoisie would topple the aristocracy, and traditional society would give way to liberal capitalist society. In the late eighteenth century the battle lines were formed. Middle-class ideology was the challenger. It was radical and progressive; it called for changes to liberate and unshackle the individual still bound by traditional restrictions.

The central tenet of the bourgeois ideology as it picked away at the old order was its conviction that status and power should be achieved and not ascribed. What was important was what one had done and accomplished, rather than who one was by dint of title or family connections. Merit, talent, and hard work should dictate social, economic, and political rewards, not privilege, rank, and birth. The individual stood alone. It was this individualist premise, the solitary individual responsible for his or her own fate, which was central in the new bourgeois ideology. It was the individual, not the heir of a family title, or member of a guild, the individual alone in the market place of merit and talent, who was self-reliant and determined for himself his success or failure. The three main battering rams used by the bourgeoisie in the late eighteenth century to destroy the aristocratic edifice that was still England were the machine, science, and the Protestant ethic. In all three the individualism basic to bourgeois ideology took on practical and concrete form.

A representative figure of the Industrial Revolution was the great potter Josiah Wedgwood, whose factories were some of the largest in all England and whose china still is the pride of English workmanship. In 1783 Wedgwood assembled his workers and told them that the great and wondrous changes that had occurred in their lifetime were the product of one thing—industry, a word pregnant with meaning for the Unitarian Wedgwood.

From where and from what cause did this happy change take place? The truth is clear to all. Industry and the machine have been the parent of this happy change. A well directed and long continued series of industrious exertions, has so changed, for the better, the face of our country, its buildings, lands, roads and the manners and deportment of its inhabitants, too.[1]

The last point is important. Industry had changed manners and deportment, according to Wedgwood. The new economic order required a new ethic—the bourgeois ethic. English men and women had a responsibility to properly order their lives. So Wedgwood continued in his lecture to the workmen:

If a married man can maintain a wife and four or five children with no more than you do, or may earn, who have only themselves to provide for; surely some small weekly saving may be made, which, I can promise you, you will afterwards find the comfort of, when you marry, and have a house to furnish, and other things to provide for a wife and a growing family. Most of you visit public houses, wakes, and other places where TIME and MONEY IS WASTED and where you acquire habits in your youth which entail poverty and distress on those who depend on you later.[2]

I want to return to this statement later, for it provides a revealing insight into how the family structure was fast changing under the impact of the Industrial Revolution, but for now let me simply point out that Wedgwood practiced what he preached. He was an important pioneer in developing factory discipline. Bourgeois values were drilled into his workers. Time was a new idol, together with care and regularity. He trained his workers to notions of time by inventing the first punching in clock. He also introduced a system of bells to summon them to work and to end the day. The bell stood in a central place in each floor next to the clock. In addition to methodically organizing the day, he banned drinking in his potteries and insisted upon cleanliness. There were penalties for workers who wasted clay, and he posted detailed regulations for washing the floors and keeping the benches clean. He told his workers "to lay up the clay with as much cleanliness as if it were intended for food."[3]

The greatest impact of inventions and new machinery was, of course, in the cotton and the steel industry with inventions like the spinning jenny and the steam engine. These two industries came to symbolize the Industrial Revolution, and with them there emerged two new social heroes—the entrepreneur and the engineer. Shortly behind them stood another new hero—the scientist. Science was seen by all as the source of endless improvement, and it was a bourgeois science that flourished, science as a practical ameliorative enterprise, science as useful. Science was applied physics, mechanics, electricity, and chemistry, all with useful and material applications. Not theoretical astronomy, but the empirical chemistry of Priestley was the ideal. It was a science that would serve industry and manufacture well. In Manchester, Birmingham, and Sheffield, philosophical societies sprang up where manufacturers and scientists read papers on the latest chemical breakthrough in dying, or on the principles of steam, or electricity. Out of this movement came the present day Royal Society of Arts, founded in 1754. The society signified the marriage of science and the bourgeois age. It held competitions "to embolden enterprise, to enlarge science, to refine art, to improve our manufactures and extend our commerce."[4]

Perhaps the most important writer on the social mission of science during the Industrial Revolution was Thomas Cooper, chemist, political radical, cotton manufacturer, and good friend of Joseph Priestley. His writings are fascinating, perhaps even more so in light of our contemporary concerns with the environment. Cooper's lectures on science make it quite clear that eighteenth-century bourgeois science was a science of domination, of material and physical domination.

Science is the knowledge that multiplies a thousandfold the physical force of a human being. Its concern is rendering every hour of existence more desirable. Science compels every object around us to contribute in some way or other, to our pleasure, to our profit, to our comfort, or to our convenience which multiplies not only human enjoyment, and alleviates human suffering, but multiplies also the human species, by providing more extensively the means of constant employment and comfortable subsistence.

Cooper has an even more immediate materialist tribute to pay to science.

It is to science, chemical and mechanical, that England is indebted for having made her island the storehouse of the world, for having compelled the nations of the earth to pour into her lap their superfluous wealth; for having acquired the undisputed command of the sea her merchants are as princes.[5]

Science makes profits, and science makes princes of middle-class merchants.

Wedgwood and Cooper are representative figures worthy of citation, not only because what they said about the machine, industry and science would become important themes in the first books written for children in these same years, but also because they were both Unitarians, followers of the dissenting Protestant theologian, scientist, and political radical, Joseph Priestley. Dissenting Protestants in eighteenth-century England were not simply Unitarians, to be sure. It was a term that also included Baptists, Congregationalists, Presbyterians, and Quakers. These dissenters made up only 7 percent of the population compared to the over 90 percent that were Anglicans. But it was this tiny 7 percent that was at the heart of the industrial and bourgeois revolution that was transforming England. Each of the new industries had a disproportionate number of Protestant dissenters at its helm, like Wedgwood, or Wilkinson in steel, Walker, Oldknow, Strutt in cotton. Watt the inventor was a Presbyterian. The scientific and inventive circles were headed by the like of Joseph Priestley or Richard Price who invented actuarial science, and thus that most bourgeois of industries, the life insurance industry. It was also from the ranks of these Protestant dissenters that the great bourgeois political radicals came — Priestley, Price, James Burgh, the dissenter William Godwin, the Quaker Tom Paine, the dissenter John Wilkes.[6] And as we shall see, it was from their ranks that many of the first writers of children's books came, with, as one might expect, all their ideological baggage intact.

Not only were the Protestant dissenters vital for the leadership role they played in science, industrialism, and political radicalism, but also they had another important contribution to make in the destruction of aristocratic England. They inserted into the new set of bourgeois ideals a heavy dose of the Protestant ethic so critical for the development of capitalism. Their writings praised thrift and self-denial. They attacked idleness and luxury while praising simplicity, productivity, and usefulness. The juxtaposition of these good and bad qualities became at the same time a symbolic contrast between the middle class and the aristocracy. The middle class was resourceful, hard working, frugal, productive, and useful. The aristocracy was lazy, idle, luxurious, and thoroughly unproductive and useless.

The Protestant dissenters, that incredibly creative 7 percent of the population which produced Priestley, Wedgwood, Cooper, Price, Paine, and Watt, were crucial, then, in the transformation of England because they combined, indeed epitomized, the economic and cultural expressions of the new bourgeois ideology.[7] They were also critical for the particular issue under discussion here, the transmission of values to children, because like most marginal minorities, they were preoccupied with educating children. Only in this way could their special traits be passed on from generation to generation. Thus it was that in eighteenth-century England the best schools were the dissenting academies.[8] Joseph Priestley was here once again the central figure. He was perhaps the greatest of the teachers in the dissenting academies from the 1760s into the 1780s, and he educated a whole generation of the sons of the middle class, complete with such new studies as bookkeeping and mechanics. A speech by Priestley in 1791 to a group of wealthy backers of one of these academies indicates how important the dissenters felt it was to pass on to children the values of this new age, when it was such bliss to be young.

Train our youth to the new light which is now almost everywhere bursting out in favor of the civil rights of men and the great objects and uses of civil government. While so favorable a wind is abroad, let every young mind expand itself, catch the rising gale, and partake of the glorious enthusiasm, the great objects of which are the flourishing state of science, arts, manufactures, and commerce, the extinctions of wars, with the calamities incident to mankind from them, the abolishing of all useless distinctions, which were an offspring of a barbarous age, producing an absurd haughtiness in some and a base servility in others, and a general release from all such taxes and burdens of every kind, as the public good does not require. In short, to make government as beneficial and as little expensive and burdensome as possible. Let them be taught that the chief objects of their instruction are the young, and expecially those in the middle classes of life, such as those of whom the converts to Christianity in the early ages generally consisted.[9]

Priestley's speech is a veritable catalog of the new bourgeois political and social values, and in their academies the Protestant dissenters set about passing them on to the young, especially those in the middle classes. Another vehicle for transmitting the values of the new bourgeois civilization to succeeding generations was children's literature. Central to the development of this new genre during these years were the dissenting school teachers and radical political figures in Priestley's circle.

FACTORIES, MOTHERS, AND CHILDREN:
THE FAMILY IN THE INDUSTRIAL REVOLUTION

One of the reasons that there was little or no specific literature for children written before this period is that until the industrial era, there was little or no notion of childhood as a special time of life that needed special things like literature. Phillippe Ariès revised traditional notions of the family and of children with his claim over a decade ago that at a definite period in time (the seventeenth and eighteenth centuries) the middle class withdrew from contact with the collective community and sought privacy and solitude far from the "pressure of the multitude or the contact of the lower classes."[10] In doing this it organized itself in its homes around the private and nuclear family. Parallel to this development, Ariès suggested, there evolved a new notion of childhood. Children no longer went from dependent infancy into the immediate fellowship of old and young alike where they mixed freely in work or play with the adult world. Childhood for the bourgeoisie, Ariès argued, came to be a special time of learning, of play, of transition from dependency to responsibility. It is this new notion of childhood that Rousseau codified in his *Émile*.

In the preindustrial era children died more often than lived. It was hard to invest emotional energy in an infant who probably would not live long. There was no separate world for children. They shared the games, toys, and fairy tales of the adult world. Their lives were lived together with older generations, not apart. They were not considered precious things requiring special clothes, entertainment, living areas, or immunity from the crudeness or exigencies of adult life.[11]

Ariès's thesis, to be sure, has been severely questioned in some quarters, but it has recently received an important restatement for England.[12] In their *Children in English Society,* Pinchbeck and Hewitt confirm the Ariès argument for eighteenth-century bourgeois England. In pre-Restoration England, they argue, families tended to extend to large numbers, including older relatives, cousins, in-laws, servants, apprentices, and the like. Increasing wealth of the middle classes in the eighteenth century encouraged a new, more comfortable mode of living. Servants' and apprentices' living quarters were separated from the family's, encouraging "more intimate family relationships and a degree of family self-consciousness in a way hitherto impossible." Commenting on these developments in eighteenth-century England, Pinchbeck and Hewitt conclude:

Just as the institutional development and acceptance of formal education in schools with the consequent isolation of the child from adult society, was a prerequisite of the emergence of modern sociological and psychological concepts of childhood, so also the gradual isolation and individualization of the family as a social and psychological entity ultimately contributed to the same end. The ties between parent and child were necessarily strengthened in a family reduced to parents and children, a family from which servants, clients and friends were excluded.... In the main these influences were far more observable among the middle classes of eighteenth-century England than among any other section of contemporary society.[13]

It is not possible or necessary to settle here the question of whether or not childhood was an invention or major contribution of the bourgeoisie to modern life. What is much less problematic, however, is that at least in England, there is the obviously relevant fact that the bourgeoisie does invent a specific genre of literature for children. Harvey Darton, the definitive historian of children's books in England, has written that "children's books did not stand out by themselves as a clear but subordinate branch of English literature until the middle of the eighteenth century."[14] Pinchbeck and Hewitt are even more specific. "Not until 1780," they write, "did professional authors turn their attention to writing juvenile literature."[15] Darton links the growth of this literature to the rise in the eighteenth century of the "large domesticated middle-class," literate and leisured, and freed from the passions of religious and civil strife. Like others, Ian Watt, for example, he sees the rise of children's literature related to the birth of the novel in general in England and thus as reflective of increased literacy and the "spread of the reading habit into middling social life."[16] But neither Darton nor Pinchbeck/Hewitt goes beyond this vague identification of children's literature with the increased size of a literate middle-class readership. What becomes apparent, however, from reading these books, as we shall see, is that this literature self-consciously expressed the values of that middle class and served as an important vehicle for the socialization of children to these values. The writers of these children's books were very much a part of the bourgeois progressive nexus outlined above. Their connections overlap extensively with those political, scientific, industrial, and religious circles; so, too, do their values.

Returning for a moment to the Ariès thesis, and assuming the jury is still out, there is no doubt that while his argument that the notion of childhood is a relatively modern one is extremely important, it fails to relate this in great detail to the equally important transformation within the family unit itself under industrialization, most particularly the changes in the life and role of the mother. Ariès and others have made the evolution of the private, nuclear, middle-class family, the family Wedgwood idealized in his talk to his workers, appear to be a self-conscious choice, whereas, in fact, it was a major structural consequence of industrial capitalism and beyond people's control.

In preindustrial England, there was little separation of domestic life and productive work, between home and work.[17] Before industrialization women played a central economic role. They controlled the dairy and all the spinning. They were the bakers and the brewers. In large numbers they were millers, butchers, fishwives, and they dominated shopkeeping. They were even occasionally smiths and ironmongers. Of critical importance, of course, is that most of these economic enterprises from the dairy to spinning took place at home. The woman's role at home was thus as a functioning productive unit, not simply the care of children. The preindustrial home attests to that. There were few divisions into rooms with particular functions, no separate cooking, eating, and sitting rooms. While the preindustrial mother worked in the dairy or at the wheel, her relationship to her children was quite different from that of the postindustrial middle-class mother. In addition, the high rate of infant mortality meant that the individual child seldom became the focus of any sentimental cult of parental interest.

Childhood was short. Children were little adults, themselves important economic units. Many children who survived left home at seven or eight to become servants or apprentices. The preindustrial mother did not see child care as her major role because she was busy doing economically productive work and children were not yet the object of a cult of innocence and protectiveness. More important, perhaps, is the subjective point. Less concern was given to child rearing when there was little time for it, and when it did not exclusively define a woman's usefulness. One might also note that the preindustrial father was around the home or farm more often, to lend a hand himself with the children.

What happened under the impact of industrialization, of course, was that the crucial unity of work and home was destroyed. Men and some women were separated from the intimate daily routine of the household. Many women in turn were increasingly separated from productive enterprise as more and more of their former work was mechanized or centralized in factories. Single women often worked in factories, to be sure, but where these dramatic changes really altered life styles was among married women. Formerly they were independent economically or at least partners, then they became increasingly dependent economically on men. Housework and child rearing in the increasingly more private home and nuclear family became their major concern and, with this, the role that has stereotyped most married middle-class women throughout the modern period. This transformation is already abundantly clear in the passage quoted from Wedgwood's speech to his male employees in 1783. The wives were home tending to their children, totally dependent economically on their husbands.

What I am suggesting is that this new role of women is also a critical variable in understanding the evolution of a peculiar literature intended for children. It is to industrialism, then, that we owe this, the man at work and the wife at home. And it is in this familial context that children's literature could develop. Having books to read to children became an important part of the new womanly role of child rearing.

To claim that this literature for children was new is by no means to suggest that it sprang out of nowhere with no antecedents. Behind the emergence of children's literature in this period lay the literary traditions of the fable, and the folk and fairy tale. In the late seventeenth century, English translations were made of Aesop's fables and Reynard the Fox.[18] Perrault's fairy tales (1628-1703) were translated from the French in the eighteenth century, and several of them, Cinderella, Sleeping Beauty, and Red Riding Hood would, of course, later become staple fare in the nursery. By and large, however, the fable and the fairy tale were not intended exclusively for children, and throughout the eighteenth century they were not regarded as suitable reading for children.[19] It would only be a later age that would see this as children's literature. Much the same can be said of the three books that would eventually become giants in the children's book trade. While *Pilgrim's Progress, Robinson Crusoe,* and *Gulliver's Travels* would become classics in the literature for children, and indeed they had begun so to emerge already by the end of the century, they were, of course, not written as children's books. That *Robinson Crusoe* and *Pilgrim's Progress,* at least, became children's books is in fact in part explained by their ideological affinity to the kind of literature that emerged in the latter part of the century specifically written for children, a literature concerned with and expressive of the values emerging in the new bourgeois civilization of England.

Another thread of influence on the development of a self-conscious children's literature was the didactic Puritan tract designed for children which flourished after the Act of Uniformity of 1662. These "good Godly books" preached of sin, hell, gloom, and doom. The Puritans were preeminently concerned with children and their stern moral training, echoes of which would be heard in the dissenters' books for children written in the late eighteenth century. Perhaps the most important link between the Puritan children's tract and the dissenting children's novel was the work of Dr. Isaac Watts (1674-1748), the great hymn writer and nonconformist divine. He wrote many volumes of hymns "for use of children" in easy-to-memorize rhymed verses, verses learned by heart to this day. His rhymes contain less fear than moral humility. They were, he wrote, "intended to deliver children from the temptation of learning idle, wanton, or profane songs."[20]

The commercial outlet for much of this early children's literature, the fable and fairy tale adapted for children, the Puritan moral and religious tract, was the chapbook. Quite literally cheapbooks, they were small and flimsy publications printed and sold by "running stationers," itinerant peddlers or chapmen at fairs or house to house. For a halfpenny or a penny these men hawked abbreviated and vulgar stories taken from popular folk or religious tales. Many were specifically designed for children, complete with illustrated woodcuts. By the middle of the eighteenth century, however, the fifteen to twenty page cheap and gaudy chapbook had ceased to be the major venue for children's literature.[21] There developed, instead, a fictional literature written specifically for children by respectable and well-known public figures and published by respectable men and women in the London publishing trade, a literature concerned with and expressive of the values emerging in the new bourgeois civilization that was England.

It is appropriate to note here that John Locke himself played a minor but not insignificant role in the evolution of this bourgeois children's literature. In *Some Thoughts Concerning Education* (1693), Locke applied the principles of his *Essay Concerning Human Understanding* to the education of children. Instead of losing themselves in abstract speculation and imaginative flight, children, he wrote, should use their powers of observation and experience in examining the world close at hand. They should be taught to read books that dealt with their world, not with imaginative other worlds. The child should not be given books, he wrote, "such as should fill his head with perfectly useless trumpery." In this category he placed fairies and fairy lore, superstition, books of "goblins and spirits." Avoiding useless trumpery meant eschewing enthusiasm and imagination for the sober world of common sense. Locke was even moved to comment on the scarcity of such books for children and to advice that such be written.[22] How well his advice would be taken! If nothing else, children's literature as it evolved after 1750 would be eminently practical and commonsensical. The fairies had fled, and what replaced them as the themes of children's books was by no means "useless trumpery." Goblins and spirits gave way to subjects that Locke the theorist of liberal capitalism would have found much more congenial.

Particularly instrumental in bringing together children and the world of bourgeois capitalism was the entrepreneurial wizardry of John Newberry. His *Little Pretty Pocket-Book* of 1741 was tremendously successful, as was his *Tom Telescope* in 1761 and his *Goody Two-Shoes* in 1765. Newberry was a commercial innovator who virtually invented the children's publishing trade. With his *Little Pretty Pocket-Book*, for example, he provided a ball or a pincushion for an extra twopence. In each of his stories he carried advertisements and previews of another he was publishing. He published his books cheaply and quickly, and he included delightful illustrations in them. The books often sold for a half penny like the chapbooks, easily in the range of even a working-class family.[23]

Newberry brilliantly sensed the potential for exploiting childhood in the capitalist market. The later years of the eighteenth century, indeed, saw a veritable explosion in consumer products directed at children, an interesting but seldom explored addendum to the Ariès thesis. Games — board games, card games — mechanical toys, scientific toys, doll houses, rocking horses, all flourished. In the early part of the century there was no such thing as a shop specializing in toys for children; by 1780 they were found everywhere. Perhaps the most spectacular success story in this area was the jigsaw puzzle, invented in 1762 by a young Englishman, John Spillsbury, who produced cut up maps for teaching geography. His creation became an instant sensation. Children were a new and large market, ripe for a capitalist economy geared to home demand. Parents spent money on them. Mothers, of course, were also spending on other elements of the bourgeois household. We know now that it was, in fact, the purchase of crockery, buckles, textiles, pins, and buttons that fueled the Industrial Revolution.[24] We also know that coincidentally women's journals developed and flourished in the 1760s. But while the purchase of children's books illustrates the new importance of children generally, as well as in the capitalist market, there is an important difference. Children's books differ from these other consumer goods because they were bought for motives more complex than mere comfort, entertainment, adornment, or amusement. They were bought for reasons other than their being useful or commodious. They were bought to instruct. It is thus that we must now finally turn to the actual content of this new literature.

ROBINS, ENGINEERS, AND HEROISM: THEMES FOR CHILDREN

The first truly important novel for children written in English was *The History of Little Goody Two-Shoes*, published in 1765 by John Newberry. Its author is to this day unknown (one of the leading candidates is Newberry the publisher). *Goody Two-Shoes* is as fine an introduction to the genre as one could hope for. Its basic theme will be repeated again and again in subsequent books —success comes to the self-reliant, hardworking, independent individual.

The story is about a young girl, Margery Meanwell, who, along with her brother, Tommy, is orphaned at the beginning of the book. Many of the characters in these early examples of children's literature are orphans (as they are in modern works, too). There are obviously several explanations for this, none the least important of which is that it deals with an obvious area of anxiety for young readers, the death or absence of parents. I would also add that at least in these early children's books orphanhood also involves an important and necessary ideological statement. Orphans allow a personalization of the basic bourgeois assumption that the individual is on his or her own, free from the weight of the past, from tradition, from family. It intensifies and dramatizes their responsibility for their own fate by dint of their own hard work, self-reliance, merit, and talent.

In this story Margery and Tommy are wretched like most orphans. Tommy has two shoes and Margery is even worse off for she has only one shoe when the reader first meets her. Their relatives have nothing to do with them, because they are so ragged and poor. A worthy clergyman, Mr. Smith, takes charge, however. He sends Tommy off to sea as a sailor and takes Margery into his family. The first thing he does for her is to buy her a pair of shoes. Margery is so thrilled at the novelty of having two shoes that she shows them to whomever she meets. The neighbors call her Goody Two-Shoes, as a result, and the name sticks.

We thus settle the mystery of her name. While Goody Two-Shoes has come down to our time as a familiar expression, it did not originate as a term for Margery because she was so good. It was merely a shortened locution of good dame two shoes, hence Goody Two-shoes. One can only speculate that the popularity of this, the first real children's book in English, spread the name of its heroine, who in the course of the book does become an almost sickening do-gooder, and thus it developed that her name aptly seemed to describe such an exemplary child.

As the story unfolds, Goody Two-shoes overcomes adversity, teaches herself to read, and becomes an itinerant teacher. She turns out to be a very popular and successful teacher, partly because she gives her pupils little rhymes and homilies with which to learn spelling and reading. The book is filled with these lessons, and they are of an interesting ideological nature.

he that will thrive
must rise by five

where pride goes . . . shame will follow

where vice enters the room . . . vengeance is near the door

industry is fortune's right hand, and frugality her left.

make much of three pence, or you ne'er will be worth a groat

abundance, like want, ruins many, contentment is the best fortune.[25]

Goody Two-shoes's success as a teacher leads to a promotion. She becomes the principal of the school. From this point on in the story she is called Margery Two-shoes. At her school she continues to give moral instructions to her pupils. Many of these are virtual prototypes for the themes developed in all these early children's books. One such example is the tale she tells her students of one Mr. Lovewell, an apprentice in London who became the servant to a city merchant. He spent his leisure not as servants usually do "in drinking and in schemes of pleasure, but in improving the mind." One of the things he did was to make himself a complete master of accounts. Needless to say, these achievements and his sobriety and honesty recommended him to his master. He was given an office of trust in the counting house. He became in time so useful to the merchant that he was given a share in the business. In addition, as one might suspect, Mr. Lovewell marries the niece of his former master. The moral is made as Margery Two-shoes tells her students:

See what honesty and industry will do for us. Half the great men in London, I have been told, have made themselves by this means; and who would not be honest and industrious, when it is so much our interest and our duty.[26]

As principal, Margery Two-shoes continues her good deeds. At night she teaches poor servants to read and write, for example. The only payment she asks is that they say their prayers and sing psalms. Even this philanthropy has a double payoff, spiritual and material. She comments: "By this means the people grew extremely regular. The servants were always at home, instead of being at the alehouse, and more work was done than ever."[27]

A well-to-do man, Mr. Jones, asks Margery to be his wife. With her marriage Goody Two-shoes becomes a lady, and, moreover, who should appear on her wedding day but her long lost brother. He arrives rich and successful from beyond the sea where he had made a large fortune. He is thus able to provide a large marriage settlement for her. Six years later Mr. Jones dies and Goody Two-shoes, now Lady Jones to everyone, is left with a large fortune. Unchanged by it, she continues to live a life of simplicity and noble philanthropy. One of her many achievements is to offer a free loaf of bread to all the poor who attend church. At the end of the story, however, Lady Jones does confess to her young readers that after she had married she had in fact been tempted to live a life of idle luxury with all her riches. She had resisted it, though. The book ends with a beautiful rendering of the peculiar tension at the heart of the bourgeois and Protestant ethic. The bourgeoisie and the ascetic Protestant must accumulate and acquire wealth, but they must also deny themselves. They cannot consume all; they must disdain show and luxury. They must plow some capital back; they must save. Self-denial is the cornerstone of capitalism, and this is in fact the final message of the book. Meanwhile, presiding over the whole process is the ever watchful Calvinist God. The book ends:

Ah said I, why did I long for riches. Having enough already why did I covet more? This is a lesson, a load of riches bring instead of felicity, a load of troubles; and the only source of happiness is contentment. Go therefore you that have too much and give it to those who are in want. ... This is a precept from The Almighty, a precept which much be regarded, for the lord is about your path and about your bed, and spieth out all our ways.[28]

God was not the only patient one in these early tales for children. Animals, too, were about the path and by the bed, and the greatest teller of animal tales in this formative period of children's literature was Sarah Trimmer (1741-1810). By no means new in folk or fable literature, the use of animals was new, however, in literature specifically written for children. Mrs. Trimmer is usually given credit for teaching the English to be kind to animals, which according to some becomes an important and long lasting middle-class trait, as opposed to the attitudes of both the lower and upper classes. It might be noted that in their infinite wisdom the librarians at Cornell University have put Trimmer's books in the College of Veterinarian Medicine library.

Trimmer's animal tales were, of course, thinly disguised vehicles for the transmission of bourgeois values. An example is her very successful *Fabulous Histories Designed for the Amusement and Instruction of Young People* written in 1786. The message is simple. We can learn a lot from animals. There is, for example,

The exact regularity with which they discharge the offices of cleanliness and economy. Idle persons, for instance, may be admonished by the bee, a thoughtless mother by a hen, an unfaithful servant by a dog and so on.[29]

When Sarah Trimmer tells a story about a bird family, it turns out to be a good bourgeois bird family. The little birds love and respect their parents; the parents dote on their offspring. The bird father is industrious, spending most of his day away from the nest gathering food while the mother sits home keeping the nest clean and tending to her loved ones. The father bird lectures his children about not associating with birds that do not respect the property of others. It is most important with whom you keep company, he states.

Mrs. Trimmer's message is that being kind to animals is not only good in itself but also pays off in the end. In the last chapter of her *Fabulous Histories* she has a reckoning of what happens to all the humans who have appeared in the story. The boys and girls who were good to animals did well in the world. They were respected by all. The young boy who beat his animals and cared only for himself was despised by all who knew him and, even worse, was finally killed by a horse he was beating. The good farmer Wilson, a neighbor to the bird family, always took good care of his cattle and

his prosperity increased with every succeeding year and he acquired a plentiful fortune, from which he gave portions to each of his children, as opportunities offered for settling them in the world.[30]

This theme is not unlike those stressed by another woman who wrote children's stories in the 1790s and the early 1800s, Maria Edgeworth (1767-1849). Edgeworth grew up among her father's friends in that hotbed of scientific and political excitement, the Lunar Society of Birmingham. She would later become an important Anglo-Irish novelist, author of *Castle Rackrent* (1800) and *Belinda* (1801). Edgeworth's stories for children are fine examples of the various motifs and themes of this early literature. One of her stories, for example, *The Purple Jar,* teaches the lesson of self-control and self-denial, or in more modern jargon, of the need to postpone immediate gratification.

Passing shops on a trip to buy a pair of shoes, seven-year-old Rosamund wants to buy everything she sees. What particularly strikes her fancy is a pretty purple jar. Her mother reminds her that she desperately needs shoes, that hers are falling apart. To no avail, Rosamund chooses the jar instead. No sooner does she get the jar home, however, when she realizes it is useless and not even purple. It seems to have been filled with a purple liquid. She soon despises the jar, but her parents drive home the lesson by requiring her to wear her old broken down shoes for a month.[31]

In another story, *The Little Merchants,* Edgeworth offered the classic format that much of children's literature took in those years and has kept, indeed, to this day. It is a tale of two boys and their differing paths to success or failure. The genre is full of contrasting sons, daughters, brothers, sisters, cousins, horses, dogs, or what have you. What is constant is that one member of the pair is always energetic and hardworking, the other lazy, idle, and profligate. The ideological message in these years was clear. One part of the contrast represents virtuous middle-class values, the other, usually despised aristocratic values or occasionally lower-class values, which, of course, to the middle class were often seen as the same. After all, both the upper and the lower classes drank, gambled, and were lazy, according to the sober hardworking bourgeoisie.

The Little Merchants contrasts two twelve-year-old street entrepreneurs in Naples, Piedro and Francisco. Piedro is the son of a less than honest fishmonger who is taught by his father to be sharp and cunning, to deceive customers on value and price, to take advantage of the customer's ignorance. Piedro is lazy and sleeps most of the day, habits he also learns from his father. Francisco, on the contrary, is the son of an honest gardener, who has taught him to be scrupulous and truthful when he sells fruit. He is taught that lying never pays, and that cheats and thieves end up to no good. "His industry was constant, his gains small but certain.... He realized his father's maxim that honesty is the best policy."[32]

Some English tourists in Naples, apparently cheated wherever they go, are very impressed by Francisco's honesty. They tender him the ultimate compliment an Englishman can bestow. "Bless you my good boy, I should have taken you for an Englishman by your ways of dealing."[33] Honest Francisco, it seems, had shown them the bruised half of a melon when they picked it out. Piedro on the contrary had tried to sell them old fish as fresh. All this honesty pays off in the end for hardworking Francisco. One of the English gentlemen to whom he had been so honest takes him back to England and makes him a famous artist. Piedro, however, lives a life of crime in Naples and suffers disdain from all his peers. One might note that nothing is said about Francisco's dear old father and how he took to his son being carted off. In the scheme of values of the readers that is irrelevant compared to the wondrous luck of being lifted from Naples and planted in the natural home of honest tradesmen, England.

By far the most important and enduring of Maria Edgeworth's children's books was her *Harry and Lucy,* a tale of brother and sister in which many of the ideological themes sketched at the outset of this paper are emphasized. It is a hymn to science and industry and the godlike figures who have made England what it was in the 1790s, the factory of the world. The family setting described in the book is also interesting. The father is a teacher, the mother a housewife, superintending the development of her children, a bright inquiring son, and, of course, a scatterbrained and ineffectual daughter.

As in many of these early stories the family is constantly performing scientific experiments, with thermometers, barometers, hygrometers, water pumps, and air pumps. Occasionally they experiment in the fields, with flowers and plants. The most exciting parts of the book, however, are the trips taken to various industrial sites around England. When holidays arrive, no trips to castles, cathedrals, battle sites, or great homes; that would enshrine the past. In the new bourgeois age the family visits industrial factories. The young reader is treated, for example, to a fifty-page description of the workings of cotton mills with the father lecturing on the spinning jenny. The particular factory was one of Arkwright's. His fortune was well deserved, lectures the father, unlike that of most in England. Arkwright was being paid for his inventiveness, his industry, and his perseverance. The father waxes rhapsodic about the romance of cotton. He informs Harry and Lucy that the machinery in these mills earns nearly £1,000 in a working hour and that in only three minutes 40,000 pounds weight of cotton wool is spun, which makes a length of thread that would more than circumscribe the whole earth.[34]

From the cotton mills the family moves on to Staffordshire for a visit to Wedgwood's potteries. Here the father teaches the children the various chemical processes involved and then delivers his social message.

It was by this attention to little as well as to great objects and by steadily adhering to one course of pursuits, that Wedgwood succeeded in accomplishing all that he began . . . the consequences of his success we all know, and we all rejoice in them. He made a large fortune for himself and his children, with a character, and reputation above all fortune. He increased amazingly the industry, wealth, and comforts of the poor in the neighborhood; raised at home and abroad the fame of the arts and manufacturers of his own country, extended her commerce, and spread her own name with his productions to the most remote regions of the civilized world.[35]

Some of these holiday outings elicit veritable poetic flights from Edgeworth. After the potteries, for example, the family visits a steel mill where they see:

half smoldering heaps of coal, clouds of smoke of all colors, from the chimneys and founderies and forges. The hands and faces of everyone were covered with soot. Lucy said it was the most frightful country she had ever beheld. Harry acknowledged that there was nothing beautiful here to be seen; but it was wonderful, it was a sort of sublime. He could not help feeling a great respect for the place, where steam engines seemed to abound, and in truth, to have the world almost to themselves.[36]

Even more typical is the praise of Watt and his steam engine. He is given godlike qualities. The father lectures:

Watt is the man whose genius discovered the means of multiplying our national resources, to a degree, perhaps even beyond his own stupendous powers of calculation and combination in bringing the treasures of the abyss to the summit of the earth. He has commanded manufactures to arise, as the rod of the prophet produced water in the desert, and thus afforded the means of dispensing with that time and tide which wait for no man, and of sailing without that wind, which defied the commands and threats of Xerxes himself. This potent commander of the elements, this abridger of time and space, this magician whose cloudy machinery has produced a change in the world, the effects of which, extraordinary as they are, perhaps are only now beginning to be felt, was not only the most refined man of science, the most successful combiner of powers, and calculator of numbers as adapted to practical purposes; but one of the best and kindest of human beings.[37]

Children's literature has always had as one of its functions providing heroes and models for young people, and here at its beginnings children's literature in English makes quite clear that replacing statesmen, clerics, chivalric knights, and warriors as fit heroes for children are new bourgeois heroes — engineers, scientists, and industrial entrepreneurs.

These books are never subtle about their idological message, the superiority of the bourgeois world to the aristocratic. A friend of Harry and Lucy's father tells the children of some foreigners who have recently visited England. They are used to make the obvious point. If the middle class is superior class, then surely the nation where the middle class looms so significant is a superior nation. Bourgeois ideology is joined to nationalism for the young readers. These foreigners were used to wealth, but Edgeworth notes:

They were surprised by the comfortableness of persons in the middle ranks of life, here. They were struck by the liberty enjoyed and the equal justice done to all, as far as they could see in England. They found that many of our most distinguished men have made their own fortunes, many risen by their own talents and exertions, from the lower ranks of life. They found that in this country though birth has great advantages, education does more, and industry and genius have the road to fame, and wealth, and honors open to them.[38]

At the end of this passage Maria Edgeworth adds, "Harry understood all this, though it might seem a little above his years." That Harry understood all this, as the author puts it, seems strange to the modern reader, that is, that any eight or ten year old would relate easily to this kind of language. But this speaks to the point made earlier. We live now in an age that assumes a specific language and conceptual ability distinctly appropriate for a stage of life called childhood. These books though written in an age when childhood was emerging as a separate time of life are still written as if this time of life does not come complete with its own level of language facility. The language is still for children as small adults. It is also worthwhile to note that Edgeworth singles out Harry as understanding. Lucy didn't. Harry, moreover, was awed by the sight of the steel mill, and was moved to compare it to the sublime, Lucy was merely frightened by it.

Harry and Lucy was an important vehicle in transmitting the sexual stereotypes emergent in the new notion of the family—the superiority and usefulness of men. It is the new family we see in the book. It is always the father who lectures, who knows about and deals with the world out there, outside the household, while the mother tends to the home. In a revealing incident the factory master takes Harry and Lucy by the home of one of his workers. They happen to arrive as the husband is beating his wife. Immediately thereafter they see the children and the wife waiting on the husband hand and foot. Harry and Lucy ask the master why he does not intervene in this family scene. He replies that he has "no right to do this. Every man has the liberty to do as he pleases in his own home and in his own affairs."[39] This is liberal freedom. It is crowning the new bourgeois home and family structure with the sanctity of laissez-faire ideology.

This factory master, Mr. Watson, is, indeed, a most significant symbolic figure in *Harry and Lucy*. He is the model bourgeois master, the new heroic model. He sets rigorous limits on his own pleasures and devotes his principal concern to business. Edgeworth describes a visit to his house.

The dinner was plentiful though plain and there were creams and sweet things in abundance, for the master loved them . . . and his wife and sisters were skilled in confectionary arts. . . . As soon as the cloth was removed, Mr. Watson swallowed a glass of wine and pushing the bottle to his guests, rose, saying . . . I must leave you now to take care of yourselves. . . . I must go to my business.[40]

On his rounds to the factory and to the workmen's homes, he takes Harry. He teaches him about "balance of accounts" and about the fascinating and mysterious world of debts, credit, and so forth. Several of the workmen, Harry is told, leave Mr. Watson part of their money to be put into the savings bank. "By so doing the men obtained a provision for the time when they might be sick, or must grow old."[41] On their walk, Mr. Watson and Harry come upon a worker dressed in rags. The master lectures the poor man. Edgeworth describes the scene.

You earn a great deal . . . if you would put less of your money into your cup you would have more on your back . . . the ragged man walked away ashamed, while his companions laughed at him. . . . Mr. Watson was steady as well as good-natured to the people. . . . The industrious and the frugal he encouraged, the idle and the drunken he reproved, and he took pains to see that justice was done to them all.[42]

Mr. Watson has taken over the varied social, political, and cultural roles of the traditional landed aristocrat. His visits to the workers' cottages, dispensing justice and bourgeois homilies as he goes, has replaced the paternal care of the gentry on their rounds of the cottages. Like the landed Justice of the Peace, the factory master is responsible for justice in his domain, for the well-being of his charges. Edgeworth herself notes this new and profound role of the factory master in bourgeois England. She does this through young Harry's report to his father about the trip with Mr. Watson to the factory and to the workers' homes.

Father, said Harry, after a long silence and looking very serious. I thought that a great mechanic was only a person who invented machines and kept them going to earn money and to make things cheaply. . . . But now I perceive that there is a great deal more to be done. . . . And if I ever grow up to be a man, and have to manage any great works, I hope I shall be as good to my workmen as Mr. Watson is. . . . I think I will be as just and as steady, too, if I can. . . . I see it is not so very easy to be just, as I should have thought it was. . . . There is a great deal to be considered. . . . I feel that I have much more than I knew of before to learn.[43]

Meanwhile, as Harry resolves on the noble mission of his glorious future, Lucy is told that she should have no such great expectations. She should simply listen to father and Harry as they teach her what is important for her to know.

By acquiring knowledge, women not only increase their power of being agreeable companions to their fathers, brothers, husbands or friends, if they are so happy as to be connected with sensible men, but they increase their own pleasure in reading and learning of scientific experiments and discoveries.[44]

If there were any doubt about the sex roles envisioned in the bourgeois ideal, Maria Edgeworth dispels them in her preface to the book. She apologizes to the reader for Harry appearing "too knowledgeable for his age," and for Lucy appearing "too childish and volatile" with "no respect for accuracy." But, she adds, these actions of Lucy provide the "nonsense and the action necessary to relieve the readers attention."[45]

The fundamental messages of *Harry and Lucy* were not lost on posterity. Decades later they would be invoked in Louisa May Alcott's *Little Men*. Father Baer criticizes his young boys for their lack of industry and self-denial, their fondness for cakes, candy, and fairy tales. They read too much in useless literature like the *Arabian Nights*, he charges. Better, he notes, that they read books like *Harry and Lucy* which are "not fairy books and are all full of barometers and bricks and shoeing horses and useful things."[46]

In the eighteenth century, children's literature was part of the political assault on aristocratic England. Some of the most important radicals wrote children's literature. The former dissenting minister and anarchist philosopher, William Godwin, did, for example. In his *Dramas for Children* (1808) he gives a moving speech to a middle-class character who had just been ridiculed by an idle and supercilious aristocrat. It is a fitting sentiment from Godwin, the friend of Thomas Holcroft, who was the English translator of Beaumarchais's *Marriage of Figaro*.

My ancestors were respectable heads of families, who filled each his station in the world with credit and with honor. They bequeathed to me, it is true, a condition in which I am called upon to labor; but I inherit also from them a love of independence, and an abhorence of every mean or dishonest action . . . the man who toils to gain an honorable subsistence is infinitely more entitled to the esteem of the virtuous than he whose greatest merit consists in a gaudy equipage and a costly expenditure.[47]

Mary Wollstonecraft also wrote children's stories. In her *Vindication* she would announce that she wrote for middle-class women against the "pestiferous purple" of aristocratic society, for the middle class where "talents thrive best." Her *Original Stories from Real Life,* written in 1791, emphasizes one particular bourgeois theme for young readers—time. Mrs. Mason, the governess-tutor whose towering, all-knowing presence dominates the book, continuously lectures Mary and Caroline, the little heroines of the book who are fourteen and twelve, on the importance of time. Mrs. Mason, Wollstonecraft tells the reader, "always regulated her own time and never loitered her hours resolutely away." She instructed her girls to read every day at a precise time, and she would become angry when "whole hours were lost in thoughtless idleness." To make her point, she relates to the girls the sad tale of the young man who lost his fortune because he never planned and organized his time. The moral is clear. One "must never loiter away in laborious idleness the precious moments." Mrs. Mason insists that girls be kept constantly busy in order to resist the assaults of Vice. She is also preoccupied with neatness and has contempt for luxurious ornaments. She notes that "economy and self-denial are necessary in every station." She cautions the girls not to give in to their caprices and appetites, nor to squander their money. "If you wish to be useful, govern your desires," she tells them; "do not spend money in indulging the vain wishes of idelenss and a childish fondness for pretty things."[48]

Next to Wollstonecraft, perhaps the most important woman radical in the 1790s was Anna Barbauld (1743-1825). The close friend of Priestley and Price, she, too, was a writer of children's stories, indeed, one of the most important figures in these early years of the genre. One of the most outspoken opponents of the Test and Corporation Acts, this fiery dissenter was a leading member of the Stoke Newington dissenting community. She wrote radical tracts, poetry, and with her brother, the physician John Aikin, she wrote one of the most famous early pieces of children's literature, *Evenings at Home: Or the Juvenile Budget Opened.*[49] Like most early examples of this genre, this work consists of a lengthy series of short moralistic tales to be read to young readers. The content of Barbauld's stories is also typical of the genre. They are full of science and antislavery, natural rights and anticolonialism. And, of course, they sing praises of the new industrial order and the heroic industrialist.

One such story depicts Richard Arkwright's rise to fame and fortune. His powers know no limits. The father in the story notes that "this is what manufacturers can do; here man is a kind of creator, and like the great Creator, he may please himself with his work and say it is good." When the father tells the children that he will take them to a real factory, he emphasizes the good middle-class fun of it all. There is, he notes, "more entertainment to a cultivated mind in seeing a pin made, than in many a fashionable diversion which young people half ruin themselves to attend."[50]

In another story, "The Female Choice," Barbauld repeats Wollstonecraft's new middle-class ideal of working women in contrast to useless and idle aristocratic women. Two visions appear to a sleeping girl: one, a beautifully dressed woman, offers the sleeping girl endless amusement and excitement; the other is plainly dressed and states:

I am the genie who has ever been the friend and companion of your mother. I have no allurements to tempt you with like those of my gay rival. Instead of spending all your time in amusements, if you enter yourself of my train, you must rise early, and pass the long day in a variety of employment, some of them difficult, some laborious, and all requiring some exaction of body or mind. You must dress plainly and aim at being useful rather than shining.[51]

Barbauld calls one vision "dissipation" the other "housewifery."

Things were much more exciting, however, for the young boy readers of Barbauld. Like Edgeworth, Barbauld was concerned with providing new heroes for the young male reader. She made this point rather dramatically in two of the stories in *Evenings at Home*, "True Heroism," and "Great Men." Great men, she informed her youthful readers, were no longer "kings, lords, generals, prime ministers" and other traditional figures of status. The new heroes whom children should look up to were

those that invent useful arts, or discover important truths which may promote the comfort and happiness of unborn generations in the distant parts of the world. They act still a more important part, and their claim to merit is generally more undoubted than that of the former, because what they do is more certainly their own.[52]

No surprise, then, that most of these true heroes were engineers. In this particular story Barbauld has the young son taken by his father to see the "Great Man," Brindley, the engineer responsible for the new canal system. The father speaks of Brindley just as Burke spoke of nobility or royalty. "I wish you to look upon him as one of those sublime and uncommon objects of nature which fill the mind with a certain awe and astonishment."[53] Another true hero and great man held up to the readers of *Evenings at Home* was Benjamin Franklin, a figure who persistently turns up in the classics of early children's literature.

Few wiser men have ever existed than the late Dr. Franklin. His favorite purpose was to turn everything to use, to extract some potential advantage from his speculations. He understood common life and all that conduces to its comfort. He left treasures of domestic wisdom that were superior to any of the boasted maxims of antiquity.[54]

We know, of course, that not everyone shared Mrs. Barbauld's conception of true heroism. All this moral and technical instruction was wasted on the purity and innocence of childhood, Lamb wrote in a famous exchange with Coleridge.

Mrs. Barbauld's stuff has banished all the old classics of the nursery.... Science has succeeded to poetry no less in the little walks of children than with men. Is there no possibility of averting this sore evil? Think what you would have been now, if instead of being fed with tales and old wives' fables in childhood, you had been crammed with geography and natural history!

"Damn them! I mean the cursed Barbauld crew, those blights and blasts of all that is human in man and child."

Wordsworth agreed. These stories filled young children with useless knowledge, far beyond their capacity to understand. He satirized these children's books in the well-known verse of is *Prelude*.

> A miracle of scientific lore,
> Ships he can guide across the pathless sea,
> And tell you all their cunning; he can read
> The inside of the earth, and spell the stars;
> He knows the policies of foreign lands;
> Can string you names of districts, cities, towns,
> The whole world over, tight as beads of dew
> Upon a gossamer thread; he sifts, he weighs;
> All things are put to question...[55]

TOMMY, HARRY, AND LITTLE JACK:
THOMAS DAY AND THE NEW GENRE

Thomas Day's *Sandford and Merton* is a book unknown to most people today. It has not lived on as a familiar expression like Goody Two-shoes, yet *Sandford and Merton* was one of the most widely read English books from the 1780s deep into the Victorian era. Published in the 1780s, it went through some forty-five editions in England, Ireland, and the United States. It was translated into French and German, and many an English literary figure like Dickens would later write about its importance in their youth.

Day (1748-1789) was a fascinating figure. A political radical, he championed America in the War of Independence, opposed slavery, and called for suffrage extension and reform of Parliament. He was also a leading English disciple of Jean Jacques Rousseau and, through Rousseau, an early pioneer in the development of what we would today call progressive education. Day was at the same time a close friend of Wedgwood, Wilkinson, Watt, Priestley, and Maria Edgeworth.[56] One might expect that a Rousseauean primitivist would have little to do with these apostles of industrialism and science. But this was not the case. The two tendencies could coexist side by side, and in Day, indeed, within the same person. Primitivism and industrialism could come together because there was a common enemy, the idle and unproductive aristocracy.

Sandford and Merton is a story of two boys, Tommy Merton, a rich boy of good family, and Harry Sandford, a son of an honest farmer. Like Rousseau's *Émile,* the central character of this novel, however, is a tutor, the Reverend Mr. Barlow. It is he who seeks to shape and mold Harry and Tommy into good and virtuous republican citizens. A vague plot runs through the book. It is the tale of poor Harry's education to life, his sojourn with the rich and elegant family of Tommy, and his repudiation of that family and its values. What is central to the book and what accounts for its importance and popularity is not this plot, however, but the hundreds of pages filled with stories and fables told by Mr. Barlow to educate the boys. It is in these tales that the morals are made and the ideological values proclaimed.

The stories and fables are always structured in the same way. As we noted earlier, they tell of the adventures of two men, dogs, horses, or what have you. One is invariably rich and lazy; the other is humble and hardworking. One rejects riches and luxury; the other wallows in them. Needless to say, the humble hardworking boy, dog, or horse always triumphs. One variation that recurs often in *Sandford and Merton* is for the pair of whatever to be deserted on an island, on the desert, or in a cave. The place may vary but what is constant is that the contrasting duo must resort to primitive and basic means to survive. This involves Day in a reworking of *Robinsoe Crusoe* and the ideological lesson is the same. The humble child, dog, or horse is always ingenious, resourceful, inventive, and self-reliant. He responds creatively to adversity by making tools, food, and shelter. The overly sophisticated and gentler of the pair, never having worked for himself and used to servants, is ineffectual. The humbler can cope and survive. He is usually rescued and returned to his home where, of course, he soon makes his fortune.

Like *Robinson Crusoe* itself, these tales told by Barlow in *Sandford and Merton* repeat the myth that informs liberal capitalist civilization. They depict man alone, independent of family, independent of the corporate ties of guild, church, and locality. He is free of history, free of tradition, free of association and society. He forges his own life through his merit and hard work. These tales also bear the imprint of Day's radical politics in the 1780s. On one hand they proclaim that if aristocratic men continue to govern, England will not cope and will decline. If, on the other hand, middle-class men of inventive ingenuity and cleverness were to govern, the island would prosper and thrive. Rousseau, one might also note, is by no means inappropriate here. Mr. Barlow, after all, reminds Harry and Tommy that when Émile's tutor tells him not to read any books because all books are worthless, he does exempt one book, *Robinson Crusoe*.

Sandford and Merton is a veritable catalog and summary of the values and concerns of the new bourgeois age. For its frontispiece it bears the quotation:

I don't know that there is upon the face of the earth a more useless, more contemptible, and more miserable animal than a wealthy, luxurious man without business or profession, arts, sciences, or exercises. [57]

Harry Sandford describes Tommy Merton's family as totally lacking in worthwhile traits.

As to all the common virtues of life, such as industry, economy and punctuality in discharging our obligations, or keeping our words, these were qualities which were treated there as fit for nothing but the vulgar. . . . Instead of there being brought up to produce anything useful, the great object of all their knowledge and education is only to waste, to consume, to destroy, to dissipate what was produced by others.[58]

The aristocracy are never on time; they don't keep promises, they waste, and they consume. They disgust the bourgeoisie.

Sandford and Merton even contains a lesson on property rights. In a moving scene the boys give their clothes and some of Mr. Barlow's bread to a poor urchin. Proud of themselves they appear before the good reverend for what they expect will be his praise. Instead, Mr. Barlow coldly answered, "You have done very well in giving the boy clothes, because they are your own; but what right have you to give away my loaf of bread without asking my consent." The boys answered that the beggar was hungry and poor. To this Mr. Barlow replied, "This is a very good reason why you should give away what belongs to yourself, but not why you should give away what is another's . . . here is a story you may read on that subject."[59]

In his attitude toward women, Thomas Day strikes a careful compromise between the feminism of Wollstonecraft and the apparent sexism of Rousseau's *Émile*. While, like Rousseau, he sees women as by nature dependent and in the service of men, he also sees them with an important role to play in the home as opposed to the useless role of the aristocratic lady. What Day in fact does is to show how both Wollstonecraft and Rousseau have assimilated the new postindustrial notion of the family. Like them he envisions women as the home-centered republican mother working hard within the home and raising good republican children. In *Sandford and Merton* Day has an old farmer reminisce about changes in the family. A great deal of the upheaval, confusion, and transformation of the role of women in the eighteenth century is touched by the farmer's comments:

When I was young we all did our duty and worked hard . . . this brought down a blessing upon our heads and made us thrive in all the worldly concerns. We were all at work by four, women then knew something about work. . . . The girls today all they want is finery, but scarcely one of them can milk a cow, or churn, or bake, or do anything that is necessary in a family. . . . Bring us a cargo of plain honest housewives, who have never been at boarding schools. They go to boarding schools and learn French, and music, and wriggling about the room. And when they come back who must boil the pot, or make the pudding, or sweep the house, or serve the pigs.[60]

In addition to *Sandford and Merton,* Day wrote one other children's book, *Little Jack,* published in 1786. This book is almost a perfect summing up of all that I have said about these books. It could be the mold out of which would come the Horatio Alger stories of the next century as the bearer of the mission to socialize children to bourgeois values. It has the additional noteworthy feature of having a plot that is developed throughout the book — the majestic rise and triumph of Little Jack.

Little Jack was an orphan (no surprise) raised by a poor and elderly soldier in the north of England. When the old man first finds Jack deserted on the moor, a note of predestination is struck. The old man exclaims, "who knows but providence which has preserved this child in so wonderful a manner may have destined it to something equally wonderful in his future life."[61] Right he was.

When Little Jack was twelve, the old man dies and he sets out to find work. His first job is in a small iron factory where he turns into "the most honest, sober, and industrious lad in the place." One unfortunate day, however, he got into a fight with another worker and is fired. As luck would have it (and luck is very important in all stories of this genre, including Horatio Alger), this was the day a group of elegant ladies and gentlemen were visiting the factory. They had come, as Day put it:

to view with astonishment the different methods by which that useful and necessary ore of iron is rendered fit for human use, to examine the furnaces where it is melted down, to disengage it from the dross, with which it is mixed in the bowels of the earth, and whence it runs down in liquid torrents like fire. They beheld with equal pleasure the prodigious hammers which moved by the force of the water mould it into massy bars, for the service of man.[62]

One of these visiting ladies is impressed with Little Jack's independence, and when he is dismissed for fighting she offers him a job as her stable boy.

In the lady's service Little Jack has a good deal of extra time which he used in studying mechanics and science. He was, we are told, "sober, temperate, hardy, active, and ingenious." This interlude of self-improvement continues for several years until trouble appears in the person of a relative of the gracious lady,

a young gentleman who having been educated in France and among genteel people in London, had a very great taste for finery, and a supreme distaste for the common. He constantly strutted, pranced, and dressed himself.[63]

Harry and Tommy are recreated and it should surprise no one that Little Jack can't stand him. Little Jack and the precious relative clash. After a nasty fight Jack loses his job and is picked up by a recruiting sergeant who immediately presses him into the navy.

The ship that Little Jack (unlike Goody Two-shoes, he never seems to acquire a more adult name as he grows up) is on, stops on an island. Jack becomes separated from the others and is left behind. There then ensues the liberal myth à la *Robinson Crusoe*. "Little Jack found himself now abandoned upon a strange country, without a single friend, acquaintance or even anyone who spoke the same language."[64] But Jack copes. He builds a house, eats fish and berries, and is generally as self-reliant and inventive as one could be. Finally, a boat going to India picks him up. In India he is put into the service of His Majesty's army, but unfortunately his regiment is captured by what Day calls the "Tartars." As a prisoner Jack has the good fortune to save the life of the chief's favorite horse which so endears him to the chief that he is put in charge of all the horses of the tribe.

Procuring some iron, Jack makes horseshoes, much to the astonishment of the Tartars (and to the reader, who never is told where the iron came from). Jack laments that "he could not help observing that it was a great pity that they had not learned to make a horseshoe instead of dancing and dressing hair."[65] Jack and the whole regiment are finally freed by the Tartars through the intervention of the English ambassador. The chief loves Jack and hates to see him go. As a parting gesture he gives him horses and skins as presents. Rather than cart them about, unsentimental Jack sells the chief's gifts and "found himself in the possession of a moderate sum of money."

Good Jack was above temptation. He did not squander his

money on buying useless trinkets in India like most of the other soldiers. He saved his windfall and took it back to England with him. In England, of course, he was too virtuous to sit and merely live off his new wealth. He was, as Day tells, "too active and too prudent to give himself up to idleness." Instead, he went into the iron and steel business. He returned north to his old master. In a few years he was a partner, and eventually he took over the whole business. "He improved the business so much as to gain a considerable fortune, and became one of the most respectable manufacturers in the country."[66]

But even with this great wealth, Little Jack had no taste for prideful and luxurious show. He remained simple and frugal. Most of his money went to improving the business. He built himself "a small but convenient house on the spot of his daddy's hut. Hither he would sometimes retire from business and cultivate his garden with his own hands, for he hated idleness."[67] And so with this final note of middle-class sentimentalism, the house on the site of daddy's hut, the story of Little Jack ends—except, that is, for Jack's final words. He has told this, his life story, to children everywhere "in order to prove that it is of very little consequence how a man comes into the world, provided he behaves well and discharges his duty when he is in it."[68] The ideological message is clear. Little Jack is a bourgeois and protestant model for all would-be successful young people, preferably, of course, boys.

There were, of course, other methods by which the middle class in late eighteenth-century England would socialize children to its new values. Children's literature was not the only way this could or would be done. Indeed, the role of children's literature was surely secondary to other more established institutions for socializing the young. Religion would be a very important force, as of course would be the school and the family itself. All that is suggested here is that at this time it also became apparent to some that this socialization could be assisted by writing literature for children.

And so it would continue to this day. Children's literature plays a critical role in transmitting social, political, cultural, and ethical values to the young. In the late eighteenth century, to be sure, these values were, by and large, critical of the dominant value system. In many ways they were radical and progressive. In the nineteenth century, these values became, and are still today, the dominant values—the values of the bourgeois class which succeeded in deposing the aristocracy. Children's literature thus became in the nineteenth century and is still today a major bulwark supporting the status quo. But even though the political thrust has shifted from progressive to regressive, the ideological continuity persists from Little Jack to the Little Engine. One can almost hear prideful, self-assured Little Jack repeating at various crises in his life on the way to the top—"I think I can, I think I can, I think I can."

NOTES

1. Josiah Wedgwood, *An Address to the Young Inhabitants of the Pottery* (New Castle, 1783), p. 22.

2. Ibid., p. 14.

3. Quoted in Neil McKendrick, "Josiah Wedgwood and Factory Discipline," *Historical Journal* IV, 1 (1961).

4. See D. G. C. Allen, *W. Shipley—Founder of the Royal Society of Arts* (London, 1968). See also Robert Schofield, *The Lunar Society of Birmingham* (Oxford, 1963); Eric Robinson, "The English Philosophers and the French Revolution," *History Today* VI, 2 (1956), and "The Derby Philosophical Society," *Annals of Science* IX (1953); J. Taylor, "The Sheffield Constitutional Society," *Transactions of the Hunter Archaeological Society* V (1943); L. S. Marshall, *The Development of Public Opinion in Manchester 1780-1820* (Syracuse, 1946).

5. Thomas Cooper, *Introductory Lectures on Chemistry* (Columbia, S.C., 1820), pp. 78, 96. Cooper was a Manchester cotton manufacturer who was active in the radicalism of the 1790s. He and James Watt Jr. visited Paris early on in the French Revolution. Burke attacked the two in a famous speech in the House of Commons. Cooper emigrated to America during Pitt's repression. In America he had a fascinating second career. For details see Dumas Malone, *The Public Life of Thomas Cooper* (Columbia, S.C., 1961).

6. See Everett E. Hagan, *On the Theory of Social Change* (Homewood, Ill., 1962), pp. 261-309. See also Witt Bowden, *Industrial Society in England Towards the End of the Eighteenth Century* (New York, 1925); T. S. Ashton, *Iron and Steel in the Industrial Revolution* (Manchester, 1924); G. Unwin, *Samuel Oldknow and the Arkwrights* (Manchester, 1924); A. E. Musson and Eric Robinson, *Science and Technology in the Industrial Revolution* (Manchester, 1969); D. G. C. Allen, *W. Shipley;* Raymond V. Holt, *The Unitarian Contribution to Social Progress in England* (London, 1938); Duncan Coomer, *English Dissent*

under the Early Hanoverians (London, 1946); Betsy Rodgers, *Georgian Chronicle: Mrs. Barbauld and Her Family* (London, 1958); C. M. Elliot, "The Political Economy of English Dissent 1780-1840," *The Industrial Revolution,* ed. R. M. Hartwell (Oxford, 1970); Neil McKendrick, "Josiah Wedgwood"; R. B. Rose, "The Priestly Riots of 1791," *Past and Present* 18 (1960); E. P. Thompson, "Time, Work—Discipline and Industrial Capitalism," *Past and Present* 38 (1967); Anthony Lincoln, *Some Political and Social Ideas of English Dissent 1763-1800* (Cambridge, 1938).

7. For further discussion of this theme see my *The Rage of Edmund Burke: Portrait of An Ambivalent Conservative* (New York, 1977) and "Religion and Radicalism: English Political Thought in the Age of Revolution," *Political Theory* V, 4 (1977).

8. Irene Parker, *Dissenting Academies in England* (Cambridge, 1914); Herbert McLachlan, *Warrington Academy, Its History and Influences* (Manchester, 1943), and *English Education Under the Test Acts* (Manchester, 1931).

9. Joseph Priestley, *Proper Objects of Education in the Present State of the World* (London, 1791), pp. 22, 39.

10. Phillippe Ariès, *Centuries of Childhood* (New York, 1962), pp. 411, 415.

11. See Peter Laslett, *The World We Have Lost* (London, 1965); J. H. Plumb, "The Great Change in Children," *Horizon* XIII, 1 (1971); "The First Flourishing of Children's Books," in *Early Children's Books and Their Illustrations* (Morgan Library, New York, 1975); *The History of Childhood,* ed. L. Demause (New York, 1975).

12. For a recent criticism, see David Hunt, *Parents and Children in History* (New York, 1970).

13. Ivy Pinchbeck and Margaret Hewitt, *Children in English Society,* 2 vols. (London, 1969) I, 306-307.

14. Harvey Darton, *Children's Books in England* (Cambridge, 1958), p. 1.

15. Pinchbeck and Hewitt, *Children in English Society,* I, 299.

16. H. Darton, *Children's Books in England,* p. 5; see also Ian Watt, *The Rise of the Novel* (Berkeley and Los Angeles, 1959).

17. See Eli Zaretsky, *Capitalism, The Family and Personal Life* (New York, 1976); Shiela Rowbotham, *Woman's Consciousness, Man's World* (London, 1974); *Hidden From History* (New York, 1975); Ann Oakley, *The Sociology of Housework* (New York, 1975).

18. See *Early Children's Books and Their Illustrations,* passim.

19. M. E. Thwaite, *From Primer to Pleasure* (London, 1963), p. 35.

20. Ibid., p. 53.

21. See Victor E. Neuberg, *The Penny Histories: A Study of Chapbooks for Young Readers over Two Centuries* (Oxford, 1968).

22. John Locke, *Some Thoughts Concerning Education* (1693), ed. R. H. Quick (London, 1899), pp. 149, 156.

23. William Noblet, "John Newberry, Publisher Extraordinary," *History Today* XXII (1972), 265-271.

24. See J. H. Plumb, *The Commercialization of Leisure in Eighteenth Century England* (Reading, 1973); Alison Adburgham, *Women in Print* (London, 1972); Linda Hannas, *The English Jig Saw Puzzle 1760-1890* (London, 1972); Neil McKendrick, "Home Demand and Economic Growth: A New View of the Role of Women and Children in the Industrial Revolution," in *Historical Perspectives: Studies in English Thought and Society,* ed. N. McKendrick (London, 1974).

25. *The History of Little Goody Two-Shoes* (London, 1965), pp. 36, 41, 67.

26. Ibid., pp. 67-68.

27. Ibid., p. 96.

28. Ibid., p. 127.

29. Sarah Trimmer, *Fabulous Histories Designed for the Amusement and Instruction of Young People* (Philadelphia, 1794), p. 69.

30. Ibid., p. 209.

31. Maria Edgeworth, *The Most Unfortunate Day of My Life and Other Stories* (London, 1931), pp. 40-45. For details of Edgeworth's life, see Marilyn Butler, *Maria Edgeworth* (Oxford, 1972).

32. Maria Edgeworth, *The Parents Assistant or Stories for Children* (New York, 1877), p. 325.

33. Ibid., 327.

34. Maria Edgeworth, *Harry and Lucy: Being the Last Part of Early Lessons,* 2 vols. (London, 1825), I, 229-230.

35. Ibid., II, 19-20.

36. Ibid., p. 162.

37. Ibid., p. 335.

38. Ibid., p. 77.

39. Ibid., p. 185.

40. Ibid., p. 173.

41. Ibid., p. 177.

42. Ibid., p. 179.

43. Ibid., p. 200.

44. Ibid., I, 10.

45. Ibid., p. xiii.

46. Louisa May Alcott, *Little Men* (New York, 1963), pp. 38-39.

47. William Godwin, *Dramas for Children* (London, 1808), p. 129. See also Thomas Percival's *A Father's Instructions: Consisting of Moral Tales, Fables, and Reflections, Designed to Promote the Love of Virtue, A Taste for Knowledge and An Early Acquaintance with the Work of Nature* (Manchester, 1775).

48. Mary Wollstonecraft, *Original Stories From Real Life with Considerations Calculated to Regulate the Affections and Form the Mind to Truth and Goodness* (London, 1791), pp. 78-97, 116.

49. Most of the book is Barbauld's. For details of Barbauld's fascinating career, see Betsy Rodgers, *Georgian Chronicle.* Her social and political writings are analyzed in my "Religion and Radicalism: English Political Thought in the Age of Revolution."

50. John Aiken and Anna Barbauld, *Evenings At Home: Or the*

Juvenile Budget Opened, 6 vols. (Philadelphia, 1792-96) II, 191.

51. Ibid., III, 329.

52. Ibid., VI, 223; see also V, 203.

53. Ibid., VI, 227.

54. Ibid., p. 250.

55. Lamb is quoted in Betsy Rodgers, *Georgian Chronicle,* p. 123; William Wordsworth, *The Prelude, or Growth of A Poet's Mind,* V, lines 315-323.

56. Michael Sadler, *Thomas Day—An English Disciple of Rousseau* (Cambridge, 1928); G. W. Gignilliat, Jr., *The Author of Sandford and Merton. A Life of Thomas Day Esq.* (New York, 1932); Robert Schofield, *Lunar Society.* For details on the impact and influence of Sandford and Merton, see William Stewart and William MacCaun, *The Educational Innovators,* 2 vols. (London, 1967), I, 23-26.

57. Thomas Day, *Sandford and Merton* (New York, n.d.).

58. Ibid., pp. 256-257.

59. Ibid., pp. 55-56.

60. Ibid., pp. 414-415.

61. Thomas Day, *The History of Little Jack* (London, 1797), p. 5.

62. Ibid., pp. 20-21.

63. Ibid., p. 27.

64. Ibid., p. 39.

65. Ibid., p. 50.

66. Ibid., p. 51.

67. Ibid., p. 53.

68. Ibid., p. 54.

IX

BURKE'S SUBLIME AND THE
REPRESENTATION OF REVOLUTION

Ronald Paulson

My subject is the way in which certain writers and artists represented the experience and idea of revolution. The problem to be
explored is how does a writer or artist represent something hitherto unknown and unexperienced? Presumably he can only define
or redefine it in terms of the known, in terms of models already to
hand.

I refer to the French Revolution, but I do not mean the art produced *by* the French Revolution (from the pivotal case of David's
Brutus onward). Rather I am interested in the representation of
the fact or phenomenon of revolution as seen from a little distance, from a counterrevolutionary situation. England was genuinely antirevolutionary, repressive in appearance if not in reality,
and yet it could look back to a revolution of its own and, more
recently, to a revolution of its American colonies, with both of
which some Englishmen at first wanted to connect the French
Revolution. France itself is less revealing because an artist like
David, the actual revolutionary, was too close to the phenomenon, immersed in problems of "selling" it, to represent it with the
degree of admiring or horrified detachment of a Blake or a
Burke.[1]

For an anonymous writer of the London *Times* in July 1789, the first sense of "revolution" which emerged was, simply, a release of the repressed. There was the city of Paris, the center of the civilized world, out of which suddenly erupted a crowd of the lowest classes. What an Englishman, with the model of the Gordon Riots still in his mind, saw was the lid blown off and the exposure and liberation of subconscious drives.[2]

The sequence, outlined in the 20 July issue of the *Times,* begins with the mob breaking down tollgates, destroying the barriers and the books of the excise officers, "by which very large entries of goods passed without paying the revenue." Then they attack the Bastille and release all the state prisoners. They take the governor and the commandant of the garrison to a place of public execution, "where they beheaded them, stuck their heads on tent poles, and carried them in triumph to the Palais Royal, and through the streets of Paris." Next they attack the "Hotel de Ville, or Mansion-house," and take "the Prévot de Marchand, or Lord Mayor" (the *Times* insists on the English parallels), who are beheaded and their heads exhibited.

The images that first come out of France, then, are of the destruction of prisons and state buildings, the beheading and exhibiting of officials' heads on tent poles, followed by the report that offers are being made of up to five million livres for the queen's head and by the even worse imaginings of the *Times* correspondents: "one man tearing from the mangled body of another pieces of flesh, and dipping the same into a cup, which was eagerly drained by the executioners."

Another version of the release of the repressed came from a supporter of the Revolution, Thomas Paine. The most famous metaphor in his *Rights of Man* (1791) appears at the very end of the second part (1792):

It is now towards the middle of February. Were I to take a turn in the country, the trees would present a leafless winterly appearance. As people are apt to pluck twigs as they walk along, I perhaps might do the same, and by chance might observe, that a *single bud* on that twig had begun to swell. I should reason very unnaturally, or rather not reason at all, to suppose *this* was the *only* bud in England which had this appearance. Instead of deciding thus, I should instantly conclude, that the same appearance was beginning, or about to begin, everywhere; and though the vegetable sleep will continue longer on some trees and plants than on others, and though some of them may not *blossom* for two or three years, all will be in leaf in the summer, except those which are *rotten*. What pace the political summer may keep with the natural, no human foresight can determine. It is, however, not difficult to perceive that the spring is begun.[3]

Paine's metaphor of natural process is, among other things, a response to Edmund Burke's organic metaphor for the state in his *Reflections on the Revolution in France* (1790). Paine refers to "the vegetable sleep" out of which man is just emerging, and even notes, thinking of Burke's British Oak, that some trees may *not* blossom — "those which are *rotten*."[4] The natural, and so irresistible, process of nature is his point — the first of the old connotations of the word *revolution* to be developed as its meaning changed from the rotation of celestial bodies to the fundamental transformation of society.[5] But also present are the connotations of spring, warmth, love, rebirth, youth, and happiness. One looks ahead to the images of Russian revolutionary films in which the crowds of workers converging on the prison or factory or palace are related by montage to the bursting buds of spring, the melting ice, the opening of the water flow, which becomes a raging torrent sweeping away all the locked, cold, and dead barriers.

The burgeoning of plants in spring is also a final metaphorical statement of the individual Frenchman rising as "the people," as a great crowd, leading to the central historical fact, whose symbolism escaped no one, the destruction of the Bastille. Paine links the crowd to "the burnings and devastations" of the Gordon Riots, which also destroyed a prison and the property of the ruling class, employed violence, and administered summary justice to officials of the state. Thus he brings the crowd as disorder, fire, and energy into conjunction with the Bastille, "the high altar and castle of despotism" (p. 78).

But if his primary images are of natural rebirth and the irresistible force of a crowd breaking down a prison, behind the contrast of energy and constraint is a larger one between youth and age, between circumstances and what Paine calls contracts (and Blake calls "charters"). There was, of course, nothing new about applying the imagery of rebirth to a new beginning, so-called, and Paine shares with a great many predecessors the old topos of life versus (and being constricted by) the written or printed word of the past, with its "power of binding and controlling posterity to the 'end of time'" (pp. 62-63).[6] The words "control" and "bind" are repeated again and again, connected with those men of the past, "who existed a hundred years ago" and made "laws" that now resist the "continually changing" circumstances of the living (p. 65). The past are the "dead," embodied in "musty records and mouldy parchments" and now in Burke's writings, and in his sources ("How dry, barren, and obscure" [p. 68]). Paine even notes, as he approaches the storming of the Bastille, that the archbishop of Vienne, at the time president of the Assembly, was "a person too old to undergo the scene" that was about to unfold, while the actor called for by the circumstances was "a man of more activity, and greater fortitude," the young Lafayette (p. 75). Indeed, the "living" are embodied in Lafayette, "a young man scarcely then twenty years of age" when he assisted in the American Revolution, which itself was part of the larger opposition between the old moribund governments of Europe and the young one in America.

By contrast, what one notices when reading Burke's writings on the French Revolution, is the point of view of the old man (which Paine of course recognized) defending his wife and daughters from the energetic young man. What in Paine is merely fertility and plant imagery, joined to the youth of Lafayette, is specifically sexual in Burke's counterattacks on the revolutionaries. Burke's strategy is to build up image patterns connecting plants and organic growth with the countryside, the country house, the estate, the great oak trees, the family, its generations, and the concept of patrilineal succession. By a process of analogy like the one he recommends in government, he moves from the plant to the family with its generations, the inviolability of inheritance, and his famous argument for "chivalry." "We wished," he says at the heart of his argument, ". . . to derive all we possess as an inheritance from our forefathers. Upon that body and stock of inheritance we have taken care not to inoculate any syon alien to the nature of the original plant."[7]

These image patterns build and merge to a point where they erupt in the double scene of the king being led in triumph by his rebellious subjects and the queen attacked in her bedroom as the mob cuts down her guard:

A band of cruel ruffians and assassins, reeking with his blood, rushed into the chamber of the queen, and pierced with an hundred strokes of bayonets and poniards the bed, from whence this persecuted woman had but just time to fly almost naked, and through ways unknown to the murderers had escaped to seek refuge at the feet of a king and husband, not secure of his own life for a moment. [P. 86]

There is, it needs to be said first, no evidence of Marie Antoinette's fleeing "almost naked." Imagery of clothing, adumbrated earlier, emerges at this point, and when Burke tells how "All the decent drapery of life is to be rudely torn off," all those religious customs and illusions of the past stripped away, revealing "our naked shivering nature," he is thinking of the queen: "On this scheme of things, a king is but a man; a queen is but a woman; a woman is but an animal; and an animal not of the highest order" (pp. 92-93).[8] In this scene at the very heart of the *Reflections*, the metaphorical stripping of society has become the literal stripping of the queen.

When you strip the queen (as when you lead the king in triumph), you discover the principle of equality, but you also prove your masculinity in relation to the king (the "father" of his people).[9] You pierce the queen's bed "with an hundred strokes of bayonets and poniards" as a surrogate for the queen herself, and, as Burke intimates, were she captured she would best play "the Roman matron" (Lucrece) and "save herself from the last disgrace by taking her own life" (p. 91).

Of course, one thing Burke is doing is to connect the French revolutionaries with Muntzer, the Anabaptists, and the sexual license traditionally associated with the radical Protestant sects.[10] But his own concatenation of the natural, genetic, and inherited with the revolutionary's sexual license is distinct; and as he refines upon the image of a queen's rape, what emerges is rather an insinuating seduction, for which his particular model—and, he believes, the revolutionaries'—is Rousseau's *Confessions,* with its young parvenus, "dancing-masters, fiddlers, pattern-drawers, friseurs, and valets de chambre," who enter the sacred family circle, seduce the wife or daughter, and undermine the authority, indeed take the place of the father-husband. Burke develops the model in the sequel to his *Reflections, A Letter to a Member of the National Assembly* (1791), where he argues that Rousseau has become for the revolutionaries a figure "next in sanctity to that of a father," and following his example, they encourage tutors "who betray the most awful family trusts and vitiate their female pupils" and they "teach the people that the debauchers of virgins, almost in the arms of their parents, may be safe inmates in their house." The National Assembly, he believes, hope that "the females of the first families of France may become an easy prey" to these dancing masters and valets, "and other active citizens of that description, who have the entry into your houses, and being half domesticated by their situation, may be blended with you by regular and irregular relations,"[11] for it is precisely the object of the revolutionaries "to destroy the gentleman of France." Thus, Burke concludes,

> by the false sympathies of this *Nouvelle Éloise* they endeavor to subvert those principles of domestic trust and fidelity which form the discipline of social life. They propagate principles by which every servant may think it, if not his duty, at least his privilege, to betray his master. By these principles, every considerable father of a family loses the sanctuary of his house. [P. 33]

If we place these passages back in the context of Burke's *Reflections* and the well-known passages idealizing Marie Antoinette, we see Burke opposing a vigorous ("active"), unprincipled, rootless, masculine sexuality, unleased and irrepressible, against a gentle aristocratic family, patriarchal and based on bonds of love. His point of departure, I should suppose, was Rousseau's well-known assertion in the *Confessions* that "seamstresses, chambermaids, and shop girls hardly tempted me; I needed young ladies. Everyone has his fancies, and that has always been mine."[12] Rousseau is much concerned with the "servant's intimacy with his mistress" (p. 172), for which end in fact he used his own musical and pedagogical talents, and he refers to cases of servants who enter a household and seduce the wife or daughter under the father-husband's nose. Burke is probably recalling Rousseau's account of M. de Tavel, Mme. de Warens's philosopher-teacher, who slipped into her affections and first drew her away from "her husband and her duties" by inculcating her with philosophical sophistries ("He succeeded in persuading her that adultery was nothing" [p. 190]).

But the most striking facts about Rousseau's own affairs with ladies at first seem at odds with Burke's model. (These are facts, incidentally, which do not apply to his long affair with the working-class Thérèse.) One fact is his passivity, and the other is that they are husbandless women. What Burke may have seen, or sensed, however, was the way Rousseau insinuated himself into this passive role to become an irresistible combination of both son and lover to the widow, for a third striking aspect of Rousseau's affairs, beginning with Mme. de Warens, is the oedipal dimension. She is "Maman"—"By calling her Mama and treating her with the familiarity of a son," says Rousseau, "I felt as if I had committed incest" (p. 189). He tends to choose his ladies from among widows and otherwise husbandless women, after the rival has already been disposed of (and they are, of course, older women—after Mme. de Warens, Mme. de Larnage is forty-four and the mother of ten). But in Mme. de Warens's case, the servant Anet fills the role of husband, and (although Burke cannot have known this) his death may well have been suicide in response to Rousseau's superseding him in his mistress' affections. Anet "died in our arms," Rousseau tells us, unruffled by the bizarre scene, "with no other spiritual exhortations than my own; and these I lavished on him amidst transports of such heartfelt grief that if he had been in the state to understand me, he should have received some consolation." And this is followed by Rousseau's "vile and unworthy thought . . . that I should inherit his clothes, and particularly a fine black coat which had caught my fancy" (p. 197), which he promptly puts into words. The pattern is completed by his taking over Anet's duties in Mme. de Warens's household, and finally by his being superseded himself by another young servant (a journeyman wigmaker who "succeeded in making himself all important in the house," he says): "In short I found my place filled" (pp. 250-251). Rousseau does, in perhaps ways that Burke sensed, all too well fit his model.

There remains throughout Rousseau's relations with Mme. de Warens and other ladies a distinct ambivalence. He can say, in a personal context (a sentence that would have been significant to Burke), "that it is not only in the case of husbands and lovers that the owner and the possessor are so often two very different persons" (p. 215). Then in *La Nouvelle Héloïse,* his novel about such a triangle, there is his praise of the young woman who has an affair before marriage but can regain her virtue as a wife, and in the second part of the *Confessions* there is his scathing opinion of the unfaithful wife: "morality and marital fidelity... are at the root of all social order" (p. 405). And yet, as he tells us, the success of *La Nouvelle Héloïse* made possible for him the conquest of any woman, "even of the highest rank" (p. 504).[13] And finally, as was all too evident in the *Confessions,* an actual seduction and an affair were not necessary to bring about the disruption of a family (recall the effect of his friendship with Mme. d'Houdetot on the d'Épinay household).

In psychological terms, then, Burke offers a rationale for repression: avarice, ambition, and sexuality are passions in men which must be controlled and restrained by the state; but Rousseau and his followers, in both private life and public, would outlaw all repression.[14] Sheer energy, the energy of ability without property, Burke believes to be the most dangerous threat to ordered society; for "ability is a vigorous and active principle, and... property is sluggish, inert and timid" (*Reflections,* p. 140). The *Letter to a Member of the National Assembly* ends with a peroration about the energy of the revolutionaries: "You are naturally more intense in your application," he says, than relaxed and detached Englishmen. "This continued, unremitted effort of the members of your Assembly I take to be one of the causes of the mischief they have done."[15] What Burke finds appalling is that this energy or unchecked id, which at its most elemental merely excretes filth and casts it on the aristocrats, on women, and on the ideal of chivalry, can be directed with such fearful intensity toward finding ways to possess the master's wife or daughter and to overthrow the king (and lead him in triumph).

All of this makes a fairly complicated model, with ramifications less corresponding to Rousseau's *Confessions* than suggesting that Burke fitted Rousseau into a prior model of his own. The peculiar obsession with sexuality and scatology in Burke's attacks on the revolutionaries can be explained, as they have been by Isaac Kramnick, in terms of Burke's psyche, especially his childhood experiences.[16] He was himself, after all, a parvenu, like Rousseau the music teacher or philosopher who uses his talents to insinuate himself into the lives of the great, toward whom his feelings were ambivalent. Long before reaching Burke's psyche, however, we have to explain the extremely conventional literary elements of his attack which derive from the polemics of the English Civil War and its aftermath, most powerfully expressed by Dryden, Swift, and Pope, in which religious enthusiasm leads to the

unleashing of sexual drives and/or the overthrowing of governments. In Swift's terms, we recall, the errant vapor rises from
semen adust to seek an outlet in orgasm or, when this is impracti-
cable, it rises to the brain, overturns it, and causes the individual
to overturn society as well. There is, in short, a high degree of the
conventional in Burke's vocabulary and imagery.

Kramnick tends to go straight to the archetype, over the head,
so to speak, of the literary text. He associates, quite properly, the
scatology, the anality, the darkness, and dirt of the Jacobins with
Satan, a black, sulfurous figure whose anus is saluted in the ceremony of the Sabbath. But the basis of such imagery is to be found
in Swift's Grub Street hacks and Pope's dunces, and, in so far as it
involves Satan, in the central paradigm of *Paradise Lost,* upon
which Burke as well as Dryden, Swift, and Pope built their satiric
fictions. For Burke, Paris is hell, and the story is of the troops of
God opposing the Jacobin fallen angels, with all the old associations of pride, impiety, and overthrown order.

The best clue to what Burke makes of Satan appears in a
speech he delivered in the Commons on 11 April 1794 in which he
describes the Jacobin hell:

The condition of France at this moment was so frightful and horrible,
that if a painter wished to pourtray a description of hell, he could not
find so terrible a model, or a subject so pregnant with horror, and fit for
his purpose. Milton, with all that genius which enabled him to excel in
descriptions of this nature, would have been ashamed to have presented
to his readers such a hell as France now has, or such a devil as a modern
Jacobin; he would have thought his design revolting to the most unlim-
ited imagination, and his colouring overcharged beyond all allowance
for the license even of poetical painting.[17]

This passage, with its reference to the "terrible" and to painting,
recalls Burke's own *Philosophical Enquiry into the Sublime and
Beautiful* (1757), in terms of which he is now saying that the true
sublime in government is a mixture of fear and awe or admira-
tion; whereas the false sublime, a perversion of this, generates
only fear and a grotesque energy. It is not surprising that Burke's
formulation in the *Philosophical Enquiry* is couched in terms
of a family:

The authority of a father, so useful to our well-being, and so justly venerable upon all accounts [i.e., sublime], hinders us from having that
entire love for him that we have for our mothers, where the parental

authority is almost melted down into the mother's fondness and indulgence [i.e., beauty].[18]

More interesting is Burke's allusion to Milton's hell, seen in the light of the two examples he offers in the *Philosophical Enquiry* of the terrible as the defining feature of sublimity. One of the prime qualities that evoke the terrible (which we might associate with anality) is obscurity, and Burke illustrates this, at the same time arguing for the greater suggestive power of the poet's words over the painter's images, with Milton's description of Satan amid his fallen angels, "above the rest / In shape and gesture proudly eminent / Stood like a tower. . . ." About the passage Burke says:

Here is a very noble picture; and in what does this poetical picture consist? In images of a tower, an archangel, the sun rising through mists, or in an eclipse, the ruin of monarchs, and the revolutions of kingdoms. [P. 62]

I think we can begin to see where Burke's imagery of revolution in fact came from and what it meant to him: it was the terrible of the sublime, with precisely the aesthetic distancing implied in his formulation that pain and danger "are simply painful when their causes immediately effect us [i.e., if we were in France]; they are delightful when we have an idea of pain and danger, without being actually in such circumstances" (p. 51). Burke could describe and come to terms with the revolution as a sublime experience, even while denying its sublimity.

But the description he quotes of Satan (from *Paradise Lost,* Book I) is preceded, two pages earlier in the *Enquiry* (illustrating the same concept, "obscurity"), by the description of Death in the second book, confronting Satan at the Gate of Hell, shaking at him "a deadly dart," *as seen by* Satan.[19] Our sensation derives from viewing not a static figure, however powerful, but an aggressive action; not just Satan or Death but the two confronting each other, and not just a confrontation but consecutively Burke himself facing Death and then facing Satan confronting Death. Between Satan and Death in this scene (though not mentioned by Burke) is the figure of Sin, the daughter-lover of Satan, who is himself seen rising above his fallen angels in Pandemonium, making a single powerful image of the son who challenges his father for the person of his mother. The deep ambivalence of the emotions is patent in the fact that it is Satan, the arch rebel, who himself has become the father figure, and each insists on *his* being a king and father, the other a son and rebel.[20]

What I wish to suggest is that one solution to the confrontation with this unthinkable phenomenon, the French Revolution, was to fit it into the framework of aesthetic categories. Burke is not unaware of that other category, the beautiful, associated by him with sentimental comfort and soft curving lines. But beauty, "that quality or those qualities in bodies in which they cause love, or some passion similar to it," he associates with the mother, the queen, and the chivalry that surrounds her, while it is desire or lust to which "we must attribute those violent and tempestuous passions" of the sublime. "We admire what is large and submit to it; we love what is small enough to submit to us" (pp. 91, 113), for if Burke sees revolution as the sublime, Rousseau and Paine presumably see it as the beautiful, emotions centering on the mother's breast and a future pastoral state with gently rolling hills and blooming flowers.[21] Later, in his *Third Letter on a Regicide Peace* (1797), Burke put it this way: "All the little quiet rivulets, that watered an humble, a contracted, but not an unfruitful field, are to be lost in the waste expanse, and boundless, barren ocean of the homicide philanthropy of France."[22] He is witness to the beautiful being transformed into the sublime (which he *tells* himself is a pseudosublime).

The accepted definition of the sublime experience before Burke wrote and redefined it was transfiguration in the presence of some great and unknowable power such as mountain scenery. In *Spectator* 411 and 421 Addison defined it as a sense of immensity or abundance which cannot be contained; as a desire or need to go beyond confines and controls; and as the reaching for what is "too big for its capacity," implying the wish to extend oneself beyond what is rational, possible, or prescribed. For Burke then, as his examples imply, to turn from the beautiful to the sublime is to turn from the comfort of the mother to the threat and incomprehensibility of the father. Its experience is of the son's revolt, with its implications of sexual release, followed by his feelings of guilt, and the accommodation by which he comes to terms with the father, internalizes him as superego, and becomes himself the father. It is first the feeling of the son Death as he challenges, and then of his towering father Satan as they confront each other, held apart by Sin the mother-lover. The ambivalence of the rebel toward the act of revolt is both because it is an aggressive act and because the object remains beyond comprehension.

Thomas Weiskel, in his brilliant Freudian analysis of the sublime, has drawn attention to the example Burke adduces, earlier in the *Enquiry,* of the "delight" of the sublime, which is in "escaping some imminent danger, or on being released from the severity of some cruel pain."[23] Burke's example (p. 34) is the simile Homer gives Achilles when he stands before Priam, who, in order to persuade Achilles to return the body of his son Hector, reminds Achilles of his own father Peleus. The mixed terror and surprise (and, of course, acquiescence on Achilles's part) are the result of a confrontation between a person who has wronged a second person, who is playing to him the role of his father (when, interestingly, the wrong itself was the killing of a son). "Priam," writes Weiskel, "has cleverly assumed the role of the father in Achilles' mind—thereby engaging in his interest powerful prohibitions against anger and parricide."[24]

On the next page of the *Enquiry* following the account of Satan, Sin, and Death, Burke brings together Job and God, another son and father, and contrasts the wild ass with work animals who serve the will of a master: the wild ass "is worked up into no small sublimity," he says, "merely by insisting on his freedom, and his setting mankind at defiance" (p. 66, referring to Job 39:5b-8a). The animals cited—the horse, wild ass, tiger, unicorn, leviathan—are examples of the power of God over man. And this congeries of allusions is followed a page later (p. 68) by the contemplation of God Himself, from which "we shrink into the minuteness of our own nature, and are, in a manner, annihilated before him." Job also, we recall, capitulates; he does not curse God and die but internalizes the father.

The oedipal formation is superimposed upon an original ambivalence (to authority—or to the idea of freedom) and so there is a rapid alternation of attraction and repulsion, evident in Burke's explanation of the initial effect the French Revolution had on him, of "gazing with astonishment . . . and not knowing whether to blame or to applaud":[25]

In viewing this monstrous tragi-comic scene, the most opposite passions necessarily succeed, and sometimes mix with each other in the mind; alternate contempt and indignation; alternate laughter and tears; alternate scorn and horror.[26]

Revolution is a theatrical performance (a metaphor Paine picked up and turned against him), just as hell is out of Milton's poem and painted representations of it, and the whole is a strange aesthetic experience, one important element of which is the inevitable distance of the Englishman from the immediate danger.[27] The acute Tom Paine saw to the bottom of Burke's sublime when he connected the towering oak with "the despotic principles of the government" which are centuries old and "too deeply rooted to be removed . . . by anything short of a complete and universal revolution." "Lay then the axe to the root," he says, completing the phallic dimension of the metaphor and projecting another version of what Burke sees the "cruel ruffians and assassins" doing to their king, the Rousseauean valets de chambre doing to their master.[28]

Long before Burke wrote his *Reflections on the Revolution in France,* his theory of the sublime as terror had already helped to launch the Gothic novel, which itself became part of the tradition of the sublime he drew upon in his formulation of revolution.[29] In Walpole's *Castle of Otranto* (1764) the terror (and the supernatural intervention) followed from domestic perversion—from Manfred's defiance of the lawful inheritance, manifested in the huge image of Alfonso the Good, and then from his implicit rivalry with his own son and his attempt to take his place, marry his intended, and propagate his own heirs ("Instead of a sickly boy," he tells Matilda, "you shall have a husband in the prime of his age"). In short, Manfred is both rebellious son and tyrannic father. With the advent of the French Revolution, and Burke's own imagery in his *Reflections,* the situation intensifies into the confrontation of servant and master, Caleb Williams and Falkland, in Godwin's novel called *Things as They Are* (1794), over the trunk containing evidence that Falkland is a murderer: Death faces Satan over Sin, in a scene remarkable for its sexual overtones.[30] Out of this scene grows the ambiguous pursuit in which Caleb and Falkland become both pursuer and pursued, virtually interchangeable figures by the time they reach the end, which is not an end but a cyclic exchange of roles: Caleb is now the murderer himself. A year after *Caleb Williams,* in 1795, M. G. Lewis's *The Monk* was published, and the alternation of attraction and repulsion we have noticed in Burke's account of revolution appears as Ambrosio's revolt from the monastic life in which he has been confined from childhood, into a sexual explosion, which leads to his own assumption of pious hypocrisy, compulsion, rape, incest, and murder.

The model of the sublime as it emerges in "Monk" Lewis does in fact correspond to one version of the general pattern Burke at once detected in the French Revolution: first destroy the father and then of necessity become more repressive than he was.[31] In Burke's horrified response they may at first appear as one, a single ambivalence, not entirely recognized, within himself. In the revolution proper they followed in sequence, and in the response of the monk Ambrosio they appear as stages of a cycle expressed first by an explosion of liberation-energy-sexuality, and then by countercompulsion, in which the rebel Satan first attacks and then becomes himself the God-the-Father he rebelled against.

The Marquis de Sade said of The Monk: "'twas the inevitable result of the revolutionary shocks which all of Europe had suffered."[32] He saw Lewis as someone "familiar with the full range of misfortunes wherewith evildoers can beset mankind" and he refers to all the "misfortunes" of the early 1790s. This may explain Godwin; it hardly explains Lewis, for whom The Monk was largely an aesthetic expression. The Bastille had to fall again, repressed desires be released, incest committed, but basically it was the aesthetic of sublimity Lewis was playing with—and it was play, because while the mixed tones of The Monk are usually explained in terms of Jacobean tragicomedy, they also perfectly fit Burke's explanation of the effect the French Revolution had on him as "this strange chaos of levity and ferocity, and of all sorts of crimes jumbled together with all sorts of follies."[33]

But if Sade's words do not apply to Lewis, they do describe William Blake, an advocate of revolution whose illuminated poem America (1793) opens with a chained youth being fed by the daughter of his captor, when he snaps the chain and rapes her (or rather she allows him to rape her, not unlike Ambrosio's Matilda):

> The hairy shoulders rend the links. free are the wrists of fire;
> Round the terrific loins he seizd the panting struggling womb;
> It joy'd: she put aside her clouds & smiled her first-born smile.

In fact, "Soon as she saw the terrible boy then burst the virgin cry," and her cry connects him with "the image of God who

dwells in darkness of Africa" and who has succeeded "on my
American plains."[34] The illustration (plate 1) shows this youth,
"fiery Orc" as he is called, chained down in the presence of a
lamenting Adam-Eve pair of parents, pity being one of the chains
binding Blake's downtrodden; he is involved in a complicated system of lines that make him appear entangled in the roots of a
great tree, which as well as Burke's ancient tree evokes the Tree of
Knowledge. Then in the second illustration (plate 2), he pushes
his way up out of the earth and the root tangle. "Blasphemous
Demon, Antichrist, hater of Dignities, Lover of wild rebellion,
and Transgressor of God's Law"—a little later "devourer of thy
Parent": these are the names Orc is called by Albion's Angel, the
spirit of English Toryism, whose name could as well be Burke.

Blake's plot resembles Burke's, seen of course from the other
side. Blake was no lover of Burke's theories: he was thinking of
Burke when he annotated Reynolds's *Discourses* with the remark,
"Obscurity is Neither the Source of the sublime nor of any thing
Else." He read the *Philosophical Enquiry* "when very young" and
hated it,[35] and when he drew his own of *Satan, Sin and Death* he
made Satan the young challenger and Death the old, bearded
Urizenic figure.[36] His contrary version of Burke is based on his
personal reading of Milton, together with the image of the young
American Revolution with which he grew up, and his awareness
(to which he also refers in the passage in *America*) of the "God
who dwells in darkness of Africa." David Erdman has pointed out
the connection between the rape in Blake's *Visions of the Daughters of Albion* (1793) and the atrocity stories in J. G. Stedman's
*Narrative of a Five Years' Expedition against the Revolted
Negroes of Surinam*, which Blake illustrated:[37] the situation is of
the triangle of the female slave, her slave-lover, and the master
who owns her and has her, which in this case leads not to the
slave-lover's rebellion (as it should) but only to stasis, recrimina-
tions, and feelings of guilt. It is possible that the extreme situation of black slave and white master, more patently than Burke's
submerged model of the sublime, lies behind Blake's fiction. The
agitation against slavery arose in England in the 1770s and 1780s;
the Society for the Abolition of the Slave Trade was founded in
1787; and in the next year the question was first raised before
Parliament. Supported by the oratory of Burke and Pitt as well as
Fox, the slavery model was at hand before the French Revolution

commenced. Behind Blake's triangle of Orc-Urizen-Enitharmon is the rebellion, which consists of the slave changing places with the master and taking his wife-daughter. But Blake was also, of course, aware of the basic issue in the minds of most commentators on the French Revolution: the closed aristocratic family with its hereditary rights and principle of primogeniture, which (as Paine was arguing) had to be broken open.

Paradoxically, however, Blake's revolutionary spirit operates in much the same way as both Burke's and Lewis's. The repressed id, released into a static domestic situation, disrupts it and then internalizes the master, becoming another, equally repressive version of the same. In history Robespierre was a regrettable example (*Book of Ahania,* 1795) and Napoleon a definitive one (*Four Zoas,* 1796-1807?), but the inevitability of the transformation is already understood pictorially in plates 8 and 10 of *America* (plates 3, 4), where Blake places Urizen and Orc in the same posture, rendering them, in a sense, as interchangeable as Falkland and Caleb Williams.

The comic equivalent of Blake's romantic triangle appeared at about the same time in Thomas Rowlandson's drawings and prints. Of course Rowlandson was not putting together a narrative series, as Blake was, but one subject he obsessively repeated from the 1780s onward shows a repressive father, an energetic young man, and often a pretty young girl. Blake calls the old man Urizen, showing him surrounded with books and tables of the law, immobile and almost engulfed in a long white beard like the Old Testament Jehovah's. Rowlandson's old men are simply horribly ugly, decrepit, wealthy, powerful, and possessive. His concern is with what Blake calls "the fiery joy, that Urizen perverted to ten commands," and the authority figure is a clergyman, a schoolmaster, a father, a husband, a physician, a lawyer —but always old and trying to suppress youthful high spirits. Then (it is difficult to be precise about dates with Rowlandson, but it would appear to begin in the 1790s)[38] the young man takes to subverting the old man, usually in terms of his young wife, daughter, niece, or servant-girl (plate 5). The house is a prison to be broken into, its walls scaled, doors unlocked, its windows penetrated; and the final result, for Rowlandson, is his exuberant pornographic drawings, in which the young lover carries out his Orc-like intentions over the discomfited, sleeping, or dead body of the old man.[39]

A drawing that is in most ways typical (plate 6) shows a young man making love to the old man's wife, daughter, or more probably servant-girl. Nature itself is erupting against the old man in the form of his boiling tea kettle, his violent cat, and the reflexes of his own gouty leg. But in one way the drawing is atypical: I refer to the fact that the handsome young man is a black servant. This is perhaps the closest Rowlandson ever comes to duplicating both the Rousseau-Burke model of the young servant-seducer and Blake's slavery model, and it presents us with the difference in a nutshell. Ordinarily, Rowlandson never gives much indication that his young man is anything but a younger son or at the least a gentleman. We have to distinguish between a revolutionary like Blake, whose concern begins with human slavery, and one like Rowlandson, the common man who wants to throw bricks at policemen, when both use the same situation.

Rowlandson embodies the pseudo-revolutionary imagery of Charles James Fox, Richard Brinsley Sheridan, the prince of Wales, and their circle. He emerged just as Fox was creating his ethos, by opposition to the British role in the American Revolution, to the Marriage Act (which had been imposed on rakes like his father, Henry Fox, to keep them from marrying young heiresses), and to the talk of a London police force.[40] The paradigm for the Fox circle was the conflict between the prince of Wales (their patron) and that great father-figure of a king, George III.[41] Every one of Rowlandson's drawings dealing with the subject of the old authority figure being discomfited or outwitted by his son — preferably with a young woman — would have had some personal application for this circle.

Fox summed himself up for his mistress, Mrs. Armistead, when he remarked, in a letter about his reactions to the French Revolution: "you know I have a natural partiality to what some people call rebels."[42] His revolutionary stance meant primarily that by gifts and temperament he was better suited to opposition than to office. He never understood the French Revolution and hated Paine's *Rights of Man*. Defending the French Revolution was, first, "defending his own version of what it had meant in its early days, those distant summer days of humanitarian sentiment and expansive benevolence" when it resembled the American Revolution, and second, defining a viable Whig position against Pitt.[43] The ambivalence he felt for the Revolution, hearing of the execution of Marie Antoinette, recalls Burke's: "What a pity that a people capable of such incredible energy should be guilty or rather be governed by those who are guilty of such unheard-of crimes and cruelties."[44] As with all the writers and artists we have discussed, "energy" is a key word.

The essential dynamic of both Blake and Rowlandson is energy, which is contained in and vitalizes the human form. In Blake this takes the form of the tension and release of thrusting and leaping figures. Energy is either constrained in contorted, agonized creatures, or it is released in flying or leaping forms;[45] its essence, associated with flames, flight, vortices, and serpents, is both awesome and threatening, wonderful and sinister in potential. In *America* 10 (plate 4) the ambiguity of human energy is embodied in the flames in which Orc (in a Urizenic pose) is either emergent or engulfed. He can be a transcendent expression of revolution, release, and creativity, or he can be an invitation to destruction.

The energy of Rowlandson's youths does not, like Blake's, transfigure the sexual encounter, and its most violent effect is on their elders. We might simply call the Rowlandsonian mode a parody sublime of overturning and collapse which reduces the eruption of volcanoes to the accidents of the aged as seen by youth. But I take Rowlandson's real emphasis to be on novelty, movement, and change, and it would be my opinion that if Blake needs the rationale of the sublime, Rowlandson needs an intermediate state, something like the picturesque. For Uvedale Price, writing in 1794, the picturesque is good because it depends on "variety" and "intricacy," "two of the most fruitful sources of human pleasure," and their consequences of "curiosity" and "irritation."[46] The beautiful *and* the sublime produce only stasis, either "insipidity and monotony" or the "iron bonds" of terror, while the picturesque fulfills man's basic need to overcome both of these. Rowlandson would have agreed with Price that the highest aesthetic pleasure is not familiarity but the perception of movement and that the basic characteristic of art is the portrayal and inducement of energy.

Rowlandson is perhaps only a context in which to understand Blake's genuine attempt to represent the experience of the French Revolution. But both were exploring a *kind* of revolution, and at times they occupy almost the same territory. In *Songs of Experience* (1794), Blake's most sublimated representation of revolu-

tion, the fiery youths are children imprisoned in the houses of
their parents, in the black coffins of chimneys, sometimes in their
black bodies (of slaves), and in the cages of schools. A typical
"Song of Experience" is "The School Boy" in which Blake opines,
"How can the bird that is born for joy, / Sit in a cage and sing?"[47]
At this point he is very close to Rowlandson and a drawing called
A Milk Sop (plate 7). A capped and gowned young man leans
from a window to steal a kiss from a passing milkmaid, while his
angry and horrified old tutor looks on aghast. The schoolboy is
clearly "born for joy" and unlike the trapped bird above him is
bursting out of the imprisoning cage of the window. The tutor is
a mild form of all the repressive fathers and aged husbands in
Rowlandson's triangles, but there is also a faint reminder that (as
Blake's schoolboy knows) inevitably "the blasts of winter appear":
the two infants in the milkmaid's pail, overweighed by the dog
stealing her milk from the other pail, indicate the consequences
and responsibilities that accompany the world of experience.
With joy comes potential grief and with love parenthood: "Joys
impregnate. Sorrows bring forth."[48]

Rowlandson's young men remain at about the level of Blake's
children. Looking back on all the cases we have dealt with, we
can accept a pair of generalizations. First, any discussion of revolution must begin with Condorcet's assumption that "The word
'revolutionary' can be applied only to revolutions whose aim is
freedom," in that that aim is paramount over either justice or
greatness.[49] But then, in practice, as Hannah Arendt has insisted,
there is first liberation, and this is not necessarily followed by
freedom, a quality much more difficult to achieve: "the notion of
liberty implied in liberation can only be negative, and hence . . .
even the intention of liberating is not identical with the desire for
freedom."[50] Rowlandson's people never progress beyond liberation; like Casanova, his young Orc could as well represent survival in the ancien régime, and his plots could be interpreted as a
symptom rather than a response. But in so far as they are parallel
to the apocalypse of the 1790s they continue to represent (along
with the Fox circle) the Enlightenment liberation of the 1780s.[51]

Blake, however, is very aware that the liberation of a constricted individual has to be followed by the creation of a new
order from the bottom up — a true revolution in every sense of the
word. The French Revolution summed up the phenomenon itself

by establishing a new calendar with Year One beginning with the execution of the king and the proclamation of the republic. Blake admits the inevitability of a 9 Thermidor and 18 Brumaire but proceeds to build his own New Jerusalem of the imagination over the facts of a smoky, chartered London. He abandons the political reality with the Napoleonic wars, seeing on this level only the cyclic return of Urizen.

The literary precedents out of which Blake put together his revolution allowed for the further stage beyond liberty to an attempt "to build a new house where freedom can dwell."[52] These were Milton's *Paradise Lost,* the *Book of Revelation,* the texts of Boehme and Swedenborg, and other works that explore the meaning of freedom in apocalypse. In Rowlandson's case, the literary and graphic precedents were memories of Restoration comedies, picaresque narratives like those of Smollett, and images of sexual libertinage out of Boucher and Fragonard.[53] But sources hardly matter: his plot is simply that most elemental of all comic structures in which the old society blocks the new, in the form of old fathers and masters keeping apart young lovers, with the consequent explosion of energy in which the new society overthrows —but then incorporates—the old. This is a comic equivalent of the sacrifice of the father by the son who then, having cannibalized him, *becomes* the father. Both, as Burke may have recognized, were elemental structures of literary and human experience by which people could understand the phenomenon of the French Revolution.

Perhaps my conclusion, that people understood the revolution by assimilating it to what they knew, will be clear if I quote from a final response, written by the naturalist Gilbert White in his journal at the beginning of 1793:

Jan. 21. Thrush sings, the song-thrush: the missle-thrush has not been heard. On this day Louis 16th late king of France, was beheaded at Paris, & his body flung into a deep grave without any coffin, or funeral service performed.

Jan. 28. Bees come out, & gather on the snowdrops.

Feb. 1. The Republic of France declares war against England & Holland.

Feb. 3. A strong gust in the night blew down the raingage, which, by the appearance in the tubs, must have contained a considerable quantity of water.[54]

With supreme detachment White relates the violent revolution of a nation's government to the usual process of the seasons. Though the king of France is beheaded, the thrush, the bees, and the springtime return as usual. We are back to Paine's metaphor at the end of his *Rights of Man* and to the movement, discerned by both Blake and Rowlandson, which reflects the cycle of the seasons and the old (but not forgotten) sense of the word *revolution* itself.

NOTES

1. I am, of course, thinking of the celebrated passage that opens Karl Marx's *Eighteenth Brumaire* and its reference to the French revolutionaries who "performed the task of their time in Roman costume and with Roman phrases." See James A. Leith, *The Idea of Art as Propaganda in France* (Toronto, 1965), and *Media and Revolution: Moulding a New Citizenry in France during the Terror* (Toronto, 1968), esp. pp. 43-52. See also Ernest F. Henderson, *Symbol and Satire in the French Revolution* (New York and London, 1912), and for a general account of the responses in England, America, and other countries, see R. R. Palmer, *The World of the French Revolution* (New York, 1971).

2. London *Times*, 20 July 1789: "we have all seen and felt the sad effects of an unlicensed populace in our own country, at the time of that dreadful conflagration in London during the riots of 1780." See *The Times Reports the French Revolution* (London, 1975), which prints selections from the papers of these years.

3. *Rights of Man*, ed., Henry Collins, Pelican Classics (1969), pp. 294-295. (The subsequent references in the text are to this edition.) Dr. Richard Price had already set the metaphor going in his notorious sermon of 4 November 1789 to the Society for the Commemoration of the Glorious Revolution, published and widely distributed as *A Discourse on the Love of our Country*, where he says that philosophers since Milton had planted the seeds of the ideas that were now growing to a "glorious harvest" in France. Burke would have seen this metaphor as a starting point for his own imagery, which Paine then accepted in its original sense. Price's ultimate metaphor, however, was of fire: "I see the ardor for liberty catching and spreading. . . . Behold, the light you have struck out, after setting America free, reflected to France, and there kindled into a blaze that lays despotism in ashes, and warms and illuminates Europe!"

4. The metaphor runs throughout Burke's works, surfacing as the "British Oak" in *Reflections on the Revolution in France*, ed. W. B. Todd (New York, 1959), p. 103. See his letter to the duke of Richmond,

17 November 1772: "You, if you are what you ought to be, are in my eye the great oaks that shade a country, and perpetuate your benefits from generation to generation" (*Correspondence,* II, ed. Lucy S. Sutherland [Cambridge, 1960], p. 377). As Yeats put it, Burke "proved the State a tree" ("Blood and the Moon"). For a good discussion of the changing senses of the organic metaphor in the seventeenth century, see Michael Walzer, *The Revolution of the Saints: A Study in the Origins of Radical Politics* (Cambridge, Mass., 1965), pp. 171-177.

5. See, e.g., Hannah Arendt, *On Revolution* (New York, 1963), pp. 35-36, 40-43; Perez Zagorin, *The Court and the Country: The Beginning of the English Revolution* (New York, 1969), pp. 10-14.

6. As Jean Starobinski has shown, there were all sorts of proleptic (accidentally so) images of rebirth as France approached 1789 (*1789, les emblemes de la raison* [Milan, 1973], pp. 31, 33). Although in one sense Paine is drawing on topoi used by the satiric tradition of Dryden and Swift and more recently extended by Fielding and Sterne into areas very close to those explored in *Rights of Man,* he is also responding immediately to Burke's "custom," which blocks the way, the "succession of barriers, or sort of turnpike gates . . . set up between man and his Maker" — i.e., kings, parliaments, magistrates, priests, and nobility (p. 89).

7. Burke, *Reflections,* p. 35. An "inheritable crown; the inheritable peerage; and an house of commons and a people inheriting privileges, franchises, and liberties, far from a long line of ancestors," says Burke, "is the happy effect of following nature," which means the principle of genetic and sexual inheritance.

8. Burke sets the clothing metaphor afloat on page 3 with the French society "as it stands stripped of every relation, in all the nakedness and solitude of metaphysical abstraction," then makes it literal in the "stripping" of the queen, and elaborates it on pages 92-93, 110, and 113. On the imagery of clothes and covering, probably deriving from Rousseau's assertion, "I demolished the petty lies of mankind; I dared to strip man's nature naked," see Isaac Kramnick, *Edmund Burke: Great Lives Observed* (Englewood Cliffs, N.J., 1974), p. 8.

9. On the traditional imagery of king as father, his subjects as his family, see Walzer, *Revolution of the Saints,* pp. 183-198. Burke makes striking use of the topos in his allusion to Medea, like the French, cutting up her father and boiling him to "regenerate the paternal constitution" (pp. 116-117; cf. Ovid, *Metamorphoses,* Bk. VII, and Hobbes's reference, which Burke is recalling, in *Leviathan,* chap. 30). The topos had already been broached by Paine in *Common Sense* (1776), where references to heredity and posterity lead into references to parent country, mother country, "separation," "independence," and the sundering of the family: "Wherefore, since nothing but blows will do, for God's sake, let us come to a final separation, and not leave the next generation to be cutting throats, under the violated unmeaning names of parent and child." After the "Massacre at Lexington" he refers to George III as "the wretch, that with the pretended title of FATHER OF

HIS PEOPLE can unfeelingly hear of their slaughter, and composedly sleep with their blood upon his soul" (ed. Thomas Wendel [New York, 1975], p. 90). For a treatment of the subject, see Winthrop D. Jordan, "Familial Politics: Thomas Paine and the Killing of the King, 1776," *Journal of American History* LX (1973), 294-308.

10. Swift's *Tale of a Tub* (1704) is a likely source for Burke's imagery of dissenter enthusiasm beginning with degenerating body, afflatus, sexual irregularities, and regicide (pp. 7, 10-12, 25, 78-79, 80), leading to the connection of Richard Price, Hugh Peters, and regicides with enthusiasm, false religion, false analogy, and sexual orgies surrounding the attack on Marie Antoinette (pp. 86-87).

11. *A Letter from Mr. Burke to a Member of the National Assembly in Answer to some Objections to his Book on French Affairs* (1791), in *Works* (Boston, 1867), IV, 29-31.

12. Jean Jacques Rousseau, *Confessions*, trans. J. M. Cohen, Pelican Classics (1953), p. 132. For our knowledge of Burke's reading of the *Confessions* and other works by Rousseau, see Peter J. Stanlis, "Burke and the Sensibility of Rousseau," *Thought* XXXVI (1961), 246-276.

13. For a confirmatory interpretation of *La Nouvelle Héloïse*, see Tony Tanner, "Julie and 'La Maison Paternelle': Another Look at Rousseau's *La Nouvelle Héloïse*," *Daedalus* CV (1976), 23-46.

14. As Burke puts it, "Men are qualified for civil liberty in proportion to their disposition to put moral chains upon their own appetites.... Society cannot exist unless a controlling power upon will and appetite be placed somewhere, and the less of it there is within, the more there must be without" (*Letter to a Member, Works*, IV, 51-52).

15. He sums up the effect of the Revolution as "the effects of unremitted labour, when men exhaust their attention, burn out their candles, and are left in the dark" (*Works*, IV, 54-55).

16. My reference, when I wrote this essay for the Clark Library series (Spring 1976), was to a lecture delivered by Kramnick at Yale University, December 1975. In his book, *The Rage of Edmund Burke: Portrait of an Ambivalent Conservative* (New York, 1977), Kramnick argues that there is a deep ambivalence in Burke's rhetoric, for he is himself in a sense the one "throwing the filth" on the Jacobins; and there are times when we may sense that he admires and even identifies with the Jacobins who are possessing those wives and daughters. "The confrontation was always," he writes, "between bold and adventurous newcomers, who sought power or status, and those in power who were naturally entitled to such privileges.... The very terms of its formulation here—upstart newcomers replacing the naturally privileged—evoke oedipal themes" (p. 109). In other words, in Kramnick's sense, the Jacobins are merely fitted into the formulation Burke had employed often before, deriving from childhood trauma, which long predates the writing of the *Philosophical Enquiry*.

Another important study that has appeared since I wrote this essay is Peter Hughes's "Originality and Allusion in the Writings of Edmund

Burke," *Centrum* IV (1976), 38-39. Hughes's is a serious attempt to get at the peculiar literary quality of Burke's writings.

17. *Speeches of the Right Honourable Edmund Burke* (London, 1816), IV, 164-165.

18. *A Philosophical Enquiry into the Origin of our Ideas of the Sublime and Beautiful,* ed. James T. Boulton (London, 1958), p. 111. Neal Wood's essay, "The Aesthetic Dimension of Burke's Political Thought," *Journal of British Studies* IV (1964), connects this passage, and Burke's categories of sublime and beautiful, with Burke's general theory of government. My reading of Burke's pamphlets of the 1790s is at a deeper level of consciousness, revealed by his excesses of rhetoric, his metaphors, and his half-articulated examples (like the Medea reference in the *Reflections* and the Miltonic ones in the *Philosophical Enquiry*).

19. There is no portrayal of Satan in the passage describing his confrontation with Death. For the equivalent view of Satan, Burke naturally went back to the passage in Book I. Satan addresses Death as a rebel son (11. 681-687), and Death replies in kind to Satan: "Traitor Angel, art thou hee, / Who first broke peace in Heav'n and Faith, till then / Unbrok'n, and in proud rebellious Arms / Drew after him . . ."; and he refers to himself as king (the one unobscure part of him is his "Kingly Crown") and to this realm "Where I reign King, and to enrage thee more, [am] / Thy King and Lord." Among many other examples of Burke's references to the French revolutionaries and their Foxite followers in England as an "infernal faction . . . sprung from night and hell," etc., I would single out Burke's Commons speech of 11 May 1791 where he quotes the Satan-Sin-Death passage to characterize the "anarchy in government" of France; i.e., describing Death the challenger as he appears to Satan (*Speeches,* IV, 31-32).

20. On the next page the example changes to God versus Job, another sort of father-son relationship, and we may recall that his earlier examples were of Priam versus Achilles (p. 34; see n. 24 below), the execution of the traitor Lord Lovat, and God's earthquake sent to chasten the wicked citizens of London (pp. 47-48). Much later (p. 171) he uses the example of Helen-Priam-Menelaus as seen by Priam.

21. I am, in one sense, accepting Paine's view of Burke's *Reflections,* that Burke is writing not history but "a composition of art . . . a theatrical representation, where facts are manufactured for the sake of show, and accommodated to produce, through the weakness of sympathy, a weeping effect" (*Rights of Man,* pp. 71-72).

22. *Works,* V, 393.

23. *Reflections,* p. 34; Thomas Weiskel, *The Romantic Sublime* (Baltimore, 1976), pp. 87-92.

24. Weiskel, *Romantic Sublime,* p. 92. The passage Burke quotes from Homer stops with the simile; he omits: "Thus Achilles gaz'd [i.e., on Priam]: / Thus stood th' Attendants stupid with surprize." Priam's response is to make Achilles "think of thy Father's Age, and pity mine! / In me, that Father's rev'rend Image trace, / Those silver Hairs, that venerable Face. . . ."

25. To Lord Charlemont, 9 August 1789, in *Correspondence,* ed. Alfred Cobban and Robert A. Smith (Cambridge, 1967), VI, 9-12. All the elements of Burke's revolutionary response are already in this letter: (1) "astonishment at the wonderful Spectacle which is exhibited" in France: "what Spectators and what actors. England gazing with astonishment at a French struggle for Liberty and (2) not knowing whether to blame or to applaud!"—i.e., ambivalence: "something in it paradoxical and Mysterious." (3) "the Old Parisian ferocity . . . a sudden explosion." See Conor Cruise O'Brien's interesting introduction to the Penguin edition of the *Reflections* (1968), where he argues that Burke, "in his counter-revolutionary writings, is partially liberating—in a permissible way—a suppressed revolutionary part of his own personality"—i.e., the Irish Burke (pp. 34-35).

26. *Reflections,* p. 9.

27. For Paine's treatment of the theatrical metaphor, see James T. Boulton, in *The Language of Politics in the Age of Wilkes and Burke* (London, 1963), and for a general essay on Burke's metaphors, see Philip E. Ray, "The Metaphors of Edmund Burke: Figurative Patterns and Meanings in his Political Prose" (Ph.D., Yale University, 1973).

28. *Rights of Man,* pp. 69, 80. Cf. the passage in *Common Sense,* climaxing the series of allusions to the false paternal metaphor used by the Tories (see above, n. 9, and Jordan, "Familial Politics," p. 298), in which the primal horde figuratively breaks up and ingests the royal symbol of the father. In *Rights of Man* Paine treats the father as Saturn cannibalizing his sons (all except the first-born): "Aristocracy has never more than *one* child. The rest are begotten to be devoured. They are thrown to the cannibal for prey, and the natural parent prepares the unnatural repast" (p. 104).

29. In later works, the sublime does take on supernatural associations for Burke: "out of the tomb of the murdered monarchy in France has arisen a vast, tremendous, unformed spectre, in a far more terrifick guise than any which ever yet have overpowered the imagination, and subdued the fortitude of man" (*First Letter of a Regicide Peace* [1796], in *Works,* V, 237).

30. Note, for example, the "thrill" Caleb feels in his "very vitals" and even Falkland's insistence that Caleb "shall not watch my privacies with impunity" and his threatening him with a pistol. Compare Caleb's realization in the garden that Falkland is guilty, "My blood boiled within me," with Ambrosio's response (in M. G. Lewis's, *The Monk*) to seeing Matilda's bared breast, "the blood boiled in his veins."

31. For a discussion of the development of this revolutionary paradigm in anthropological terms, see Eleanor Wilner, *Gathering the Winds: Visionary Imagination and Radical Transformation of Self and Society* (Baltimore, 1976), p. 20, and especially the introduction and the chapter on Blake.

32. "Reflections on the Novel" (1800), in *The 120 Days of Sodom and Other Writings,* ed. Austryn Wainhouse and Richard Seaver (New York, 1966), p. 109.

33. *Reflections,* p. 9.

34. See *The Poetry and Prose of William Blake,* ed. David V. Erdman (New York, 1965), pp. 50-51, and Erdman, *The Illuminated Blake*
(New York, 1974), pp. 139-140.

35. Erdman, *Blake: Prophet against Empire,* rev. ed. (New York,
1969), pp. 647, 650. Blake lumps together Burke's *Enquiry,* Bacon's
Advancement of Learning, and Locke's *On Human Understanding* as
empirical treatises and says he wrote comments on them similar to the
ones he is writing on Reynolds.

36. I am referring to the version in the Huntington Library and Art
Gallery, San Marino, California. It is the only version I know of in
which Death, ordinarily a skeleton, is bearded. Blake follows the pattern but alters the dramatic personae: Satan is the young rebel and
Death the old Urizenic figure. Blake's was, of course, one of a great
many representations of Satan-Sin-Death, beginning with Hogarth's,
but picking up impetus after Burke's famous passage prompted Barry,
Fuseli, and others to follow suit.

37. Stedman was also a close friend of Blake's. See Erdman, *Blake:
Prophet against Empire,* pp. 230-242.

38. The only reliably dated works are the prints, and they often add
dates after the fact or change them in later states. But to judge by the
dated prints, it appears that the young man is pretty consistently
thwarted by the old man during the 1780s. There are a few exceptions:
a young man is getting the girl while the old man drowses over the fire
(dated 1785, signed Wigstaed), and another hides under a bed waiting
for the old man to leave his wife, called away on a false alarm (1786,
The Doctor called up or the False Alarm). In the 1790s this sort of scene
becomes more frequent (see, e.g., John Hayes, *Rowlandson, Watercolors and Drawings* [London, 1972], pls. 92, 100). By 1800 the subject
of the triangle is an obsessive subject for Rowlandson.

39. We should see Rowlandson in the contexts of both Paine's opposition to the idea of hereditary succession and primogeniture as an
"imposition on posterity" and the French philosophes' (in particular
Diderot and Helvetius) advocacy of collateral and even broken blood
lines. The arguments centered around the advantage of introducing
energy and fluidity into the aristocracy, introducing new blood into the
pure but stagnant blood lines of the nobility. The bastard as ideal was
rootless but at the same time in the very vortex of society. He was
"nature's nobleman," a product of love not of a contract, of a happy as
opposed to a forced union charged with the duty of begetting an heir,
and in general of nature instead of the sanctimonious legalism that produced attenuated heirs and which despised and feared bastards. One
recalls Goethe's dream of having been conceived by the nobleman who
stopped over with his mother while his father was away from home. (I
am indebted for these remarks to a paper read by Otis Fellows at the
Columbia University Eighteenth-Century Seminar, December 1975.)

For a psychohistorical view, see Fred Weinstein and Gerald M. Platt,

The Wish to be Free: Society, Psyche, and Value Change (Berkeley and Los Angeles, 1969), where it is argued that in the prerevolutionary phase "the revolutionary desire was expressed to the limit only on a metaphoric level, as literature or in a life of sexual transgression . . . [for] when traditional authority has lost the power to persuade, there is no better way for its subjects to declare their freedom than through violations of the sexual codes of the society" (p. 57). This involved "the destruction of patriarchal values" but such ideas "should be viewed as idiosyncratic expressions, reflecting the escape of a repressed wish on the personal level. Moreover, these ideas were unmediated by ego — they represented a barely disguised demand for an unrealizable gratification and were therefore unacceptable to the culture; the oedipal content was too startlingly direct" (p. 59). And so in practice the family part was dropped and only the attack on political authority carried through. "Nevertheless, these ideas on the family reflect accurately the content of the political rebellion, the extent of that rebellion, and the kind of anxiety that was precipitated by action and thought directed against the traditional values of the society" (p. 60).

40. There is no direct documentation to connect Fox with Rowlandson. The latter made political caricatures on both sides of issues, but there is an unmistakable bias toward Fox and his friends.

41. The king was wont to respond (as to the lord mayor on 23 May 1770): "I should ill deserve to be considered as the Father of my People if I made such use of the Prerogative as I think dangerous to the Constitution" (followed, in this case, by Beckford's spirited rejoinder). The prince of Wales's patronage of Rowlandson can be inferred from the fact that he bought the *English* and *French Reviews* prior to showing in the Royal Academy of 1786, as well as others (Hayes, *Rowlandson, Watercolors and Drawings,* p. 11; A. P. Oppe, *English Drawings . . . at Windsor Castle,* [London, 1950], under cat. nos. 517, 510, 511, 530, 541). There are surviving drawings by Rowlandson of the prince (reproduced, Bernard Falk, *Thomas Rowlandson: His Life and Art* [London, 1949], opp. p. 21; according to Hayes, *Rowlandson, Watercolors and Drawings,* p. 80, the prince also appears in *Vauxhall Gardens*). Rowlandson's *Excursion to Brighthelmestone* of 1790 was dedicated to the prince of Wales — perhaps evidence of patronage; perhaps only an acknowledgment of the association between the prince and Brighton (Falk, *Thomas Rowlandson,* p. 100). The most notorious evidence of patronage, however, is the tradition of the erotic drawings executed for (or acquired by) the prince, which were supposed to have been part of the collection at Windsor Castle, but seem to have been destroyed by one of George IV's successors.

As to the prince of Wales and the king his father, when the prince heard the news of the execution of Louis XVI, he was filled with "a species of sentiment towards my father which surpasses all description"; he requested an audience "to express my gratitude to my good and gracious father," and broke with Fox, declaring his support for the king's ministers (John Brooke, *George III* [London, 1970], p. 345, referring to 24 January 1793). But a short while after this he was again ridiculing his father.

42. British Library, Add. MS 47570, f. 191; quoted, John W. Derry, *Charles James Fox* (New York, 1972), p. 322.

43. Derry, *Charles James Fox,* p. 324. Fox liked to draw parallels between the American and French revolutions, and link both to the Glorious Revolution of 1688. The French Revolution was a phenomenon "he constantly sought to confine within the limits of the American example," Derry writes (p. 321). In fact, he was, like the French revolutionaries themselves, caught within an immediate practical political situation, and thus claimed to see himself as a conservative force, defending traditional English liberties and established constitutional values against Pitt and Burke.

44. British Library, Add. MS 47571, f. 144; quoted, Derry, *Charles James Fox,* p. 326.

45. Both can be seen in *America,* plate 3.

46. *An Essay on the Picturesque* (1794), pp. 17-18. The passages referred to run from pages 73 through 87. The present essay is complemented by one more particularly on Rowlandson and the Picturesque, which though written later was published earlier: "The Artist, the Beautiful Girl, and the Crowd: the Case of Thomas Rowlandson," *Georgia Review* XXXI (1977), 121-159.

47. The schoolboy paradigm is really implicit in Paine's opening of *Common Sense,* fifteen years before the fall of the Bastille, where he contrasts society, which promotes happiness, with government, which restrains and punishes our vices. He sets up a convivial gathering (to build a house) against a repressive schoolmaster figure, the monarch whose evil force leads to "a degradation and lessening of ourselves" (p. 66) — precisely the enemy shared by Rowlandson and Blake. For a light-hearted comparison of Rowlandson and Blake (some of which I still believe), see my "The Spectres of Blake and Rowlandson," *The Listener* (2 August 1973), pp. 140-142.

48. Erdman, *Illuminated Blake,* p. 106; *Marriage of Heaven and Hell,* in Erdman, *Poetical Works,* p. 109.

49. Condorcet, *Sur le sens du mot révolutionnaire* (1793), in *Oeuvres* (Paris, 1847-1849), XII, 615.

50. Arendt, *On Revolution,* p. 22.

51. See Paul Zweig, *The Adventurer* (New York, 1975), pp. 142-145, and Jean Starobinski, *The Invention of Liberty, 1700-1789* (Cleveland, 1964), passim.

52. Arendt, *On Revolution,* p. 28.

53. For Smollett and Fragonard, see my *Rowlandson: A New Interpretation* (New York, 1972), pp. 77-78; ibid., pp. 22-23. The dramatic sources for Rowlandson's scenes are obvious, but to reach them we have to leap back (with Rowlandson) to the Restoration, to Molière, and to popular traditions that survived on the continent. In Rowlandson's own

time the London theater softened and omitted such scenes. The old husband or *senex amans* is hardly recognizable in Garrick's mild version of *The Country Wife* called *The Country Girl* (1766), in Frances Sheridan's *The Discovery* (1763), Hugh Kelly's *The School for Wives* (1773), and even in R. B. Sheridan's own comedies. He drops the suggestions of impotence and evokes partial sympathy for Sir Peter Teazle in his *School for Scandal;* indeed, there is evidence that he had originally — before the similar revisions in *The Rivals* brought about by its initial unfavorable reception — conceived the Teazles in the spirit of the Pinchwifes; then he toned the characterization down, and seems to have wished Sir Peter to be played sympathetically. (See Sheridan, *Plays,* ed. Cecil Price [Oxford, 1975], p. 304.)

There is every indication that the theater audience of the 1780s and 1790s was uneasy with explicit sexuality, as it was with explicit politics. The closest thing to "revolutionary" theater was, of course, Beaumarchais's *Marriage of Figaro* (1784), which appeared only in a mutilated form in London. Here the common factor in the conflict between servant and master — Figaro and Count Almaviva — is again sexual prowess, ending in total defeat of the aristocrat.

54. *Journals,* ed. Walter Johnson (London, 1931), p. 422.

Preludium

The shadowy daughter of Urthona stood before red Orc
When fourteen suns had faintly journey'd o'er his dark abode;
His food she brought in iron baskets, his drink in cups of iron;
Crown'd with a helmet & dark hair the nameless female stood;
A quiver with its burning stores, a bow like that of night,
When pestilence is shot from heaven; no other arms she need:
Invulnerable tho' naked, save where clouds roll round her loins,
Their awful folds in the dark air; silent she stood as night;
For never from her iron tongue could voice or sound arise;
But dumb till that dread day when Orc assay'd his fierce embrace.

Dark virgin; said the hairy youth, thy father stern abhorr'd;
Rivets my tenfold chains while still on high my spirit soars;
Sometimes an eagle screaming in the sky, sometimes a lion,
Stalking upon the mountains, & sometimes a whale I lash
The raging fathomless abyss, anon a serpent folding
Around the pillars of Urthona, and round thy dark limbs,
On the Canadian wilds I fold, feeble my spirit folds.
For chaind beneath I rend these caverns; when thou bringest food
I howl my joy and my red eyes seek to behold thy face
In vain! these clouds roll to & fro, & hide thee from my sight.

Pl. 1. William Blake, *America* (1793), Pl. 1.

Silent as despairing love. and strong as jealousy.
The hairy shoulders rend the links. free are the wrists of fire;
Round the terrific loins he siezd the panting struggling womb;
It joyd: she put aside her clouds & smiled her first-born smile;
As when a black cloud shews its lightnings to the silent deep.

Soon as she saw the terrible boy then burst the virgin cry.

I know thee, I have found thee, & I will not let thee go;
Thou art the image of God who dwells in darkness of Africa
And thou art fall'n to give me life in regions of dark death.
On my American plains I feel the struggling afflictions
Endur'd by roots that writhe their arms into the nether deep:
I see a serpent in Canada. who courts me to his love;
In Mexico an Eagle, and a Lion in Peru;
I see a Whale in the South-sea. drinking my soul away.
O what limb rending pains I feel. thy fire & my frost
Mingle in howling pains. in furrows by thy lightnings rent.
This is eternal death: and this the torment long foretold.

Pl. 2. William Blake, *America*, Pl. 2.

The terror answerd: I am Orc, wreath'd round the accursed tree:
The times are ended; shadows pass the morning gins to break;
The fiery joy, that Urizen perverted to ten commands,
What night he led the starry hosts thro' the wide wilderness:
That stony law I stamp to dust: and scatter religion abroad
To the four winds as a torn book, & none shall gather the leaves;
But they shall rot on desart sands, & consume in bottomless deeps,
To make the desarts blossom, & the deeps shrink to their fountains,
And to renew the fiery joy, and burst the stony roof.
That pale religious letchery, seeking Virginity,
May find it in a harlot, and in coarse-clad honesty
The undefil'd tho' ravish'd in her cradle night and morn;
For every thing that lives is holy, life delights in life;
Because the soul of sweet delight can never be defil'd.
Fires inwrap the earthly globe, yet man is not consumd;
Amidst the lustful fires he walks; his feet become like brass,
His knees and thighs like silver, & his breast and head like gold.

Pl. 3. William Blake, *America*, Pl. 8.

Thus wept the Angel voice & as he wept the terrible blasts
Of trumpets, blew a loud alarm across the Atlantic deep.
No trumpets answer; no reply of clarions or of fifes,
Silent the Colonies remain and refuse the loud alarm.

On those vast shady hills between America & Albions shore;
Now barrd out by the Atlantic sea: call'd Atlantean hills:
Because from their bright summits you may pass to the Golden world
An ancient palace, archetype of mighty Emperies,
Rears its immortal pinnacles, built in the forest of God
By Ariston the king of beauty for his stolen bride,

Here on their magic seats the thirteen Angels sat perturb'd
For clouds from the Atlantic hover o'er the solemn roof.

Pl. 4. William Blake, *America*, Pl. 10.

Pl. 5. Thomas Rowlandson, A Domestic Scene (drawing, late 1790s; from the collection of Augustus P. Loring).

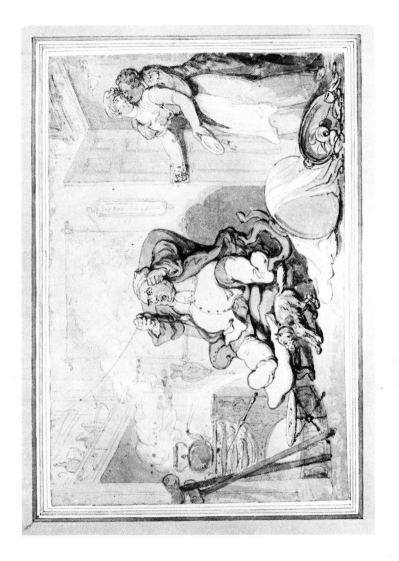

Pl. 6. Thomas Rowlandson, The Disaster (drawing, c. 1800; Boston Public Library).

Pl. 7. Thomas Rowlandson, The Milk Sop (drawing, 1811; London, Victoria and Albert Museum). Rowlandson published the etching (in Thomas Tegg's *Caricature Magazine*) 15 December 1811.

INDEX

Gaunt, John of, duke of Lancaster, 1, 3, 5-7, 10, 11, 19, 20
Gay, Peter, 92, 103, 104, 107
Geneva, Switzerland, 106
George II, 109
George III, 257
George, the, in Acton, 173
Germans, 108
Germany, 169
Gibbon, Edward, 92, 93, 106-108
Gibson, Edmund, 175
Giorgione, 178
Glasgow, Scotland, 107
Globe Theatre, 12, 16, 17
Glorious Revolution, 152, 153
Gloucester, duchess of, 10
Gloucester, duke of, 3, 6
God, 67, 69, 70, 76, 79, 85, 97, 98, 101, 107, 180, 219, 249, 252, 254, 255
Godolphin, Sidney, 129
Godwin, William, 208, 227, 253, 254
  Caleb Williams, 253, 256
  Dramas for Children, 227
  Things as They Are, 253
Gonsalvo, 114-116, 125
Goody Two-Shoes, 217-219, 231, 235. *See also* Margery Two-Shoes; Meanwell, Margery
Gordon Riots, 242, 243
Grande Encyclopédie, 176
Grandison, Sir Charles, 185
Gray, Charles, x
Gray, John Chipman, 47n
Great Tew, 129
Green, 10, 11, 17, 18
Gresham College, 177
Grotius, Hugo, 72
Grub Street, 249
Guildhall, 181

Haberdashers Company, 14
Hale, Sir Matthew, 27, 49n, 52n, 53n
Halifax, Earl of, 173
Halley, Edmund, 153

Hammond, Henry, 95
Harrington, James, 94-102, 105-107
  Oceana, 94, 95, 97
Harry, 223-227
Hartley, David, 83, 97
Harvey, Stephen, 174
Hasidism, 83
Hebrew, 69, 71, 73, 80
Hector, 252
Henry IV, 1, 7. *See also* Bolingbroke, Henry of
Henry VIII, 95, 167
Henry Hotspur, 4
Hertfordshire, 177, 180
Herzl, Theodore, 87n
Hewitt, Margaret, 210, 211
Hexter, J. H., x
High Church, 104
High Courts at Westminster, 13
Hill, Christopher, 123
histoire universelle, 92
Hitler, Adolf, 72
Hobbes, Thomas, 38, 51n, 53n, 57n, 94-102, 105, 114, 128-131
  De Cive, 128
  Leviathan, 95, 128, 129
Hogarth, William, 178
Holcroft, Thomas, 227
Holinshed, Raphael, 2-5, 8, 9
  Chronicles of England, Scotland, and Ireland, 2
Holland, 70, 71, 77, 81, 102, 169, 176, 260
Holmes, Nathaniel, 75, 76
Holt, Sir John, 27
Holy Land, 67
Holy Trinity, 189, 190
Homer, 12, 252
Honoria, 115
Hooker, Richard, 54n, 57n
Hôtel de Ville, 242
Houdetot, Mme. d', 248
House of Commons, 23, 123, 181, 249. *See also* Lower House
House of David, 73, 76

DATE DUE

GAYLORD			PRINTED IN U.S.A.